PROPOSED AIRBORNE ASSAULTS DURING OPERATION OVERLORD

PROPOSED AIRBORNE ASSAULTS DURING OPERATION OVERLORD

CANCELLED ALLIED PLANS IN NORMANDY AND BRITTANY

JAMES DALY

FRONTLINE
BOOKS

First published in Great Britain in 2024 by
Frontline Books
An imprint of
Pen & Sword Books Ltd
Yorkshire – Philadelphia

A CIP catalogue record for this book is
available from the British Library.

Typeset by Lapiz Digital
Printed and bound by CPI UK

Pen & Sword Books Limited incorporates the imprints of Atlas,
Archaeology, Aviation, Discovery, Family History, Fiction, History,
Maritime, Military, Military Classics, Politics, Select, Transport,
True Crime, Air World, Frontline Books, Leo Cooper, Remember
When, Seaforth Publishing, The Praetorian Press, Wharncliffe Local History,
Wharncliffe Transport, Wharncliffe True Crime, White Owl
and After the Battle.

For a complete list of Pen & Sword titles please contact:

PEN & SWORD BOOKS LIMITED
47 Church Street, Barnsley, South Yorkshire, S70 2AS, England
E-mail: enquiries@pen-and-sword.co.uk
Website: www.pen-and-sword.co.uk

or

PEN AND SWORD BOOKS
1950 Lawrence Rd, Havertown, PA 19083, USA
E-mail: Uspen-and-sword@casematepublishers.com
Website: www.penandswordbooks.com

CONTENTS

Dedication

For my wife, Becci.

ACKNOWLEDGEMENTS

This book owes its genesis to an illuminating talk in 2014 by Simon Trew of the Royal Military Academy Sandhurst at The D-Day Story's annual conference. My grandfather was an Arnhem veteran and I have spent a sizeable part of my career working on displays, projects and events about D-Day and the Battle of Normandy. I have long wanted to write something that might add to the historiography of both, but felt that there was not really anything new to say or to add. Simon's talk on 'Is there anything new to say about the 1944 Normandy campaign?' prompted me to look for new angles and sources that had not previously been interrogated. I am very grateful to Simon for this moment of inspiration that has taken the best part of 10 years to realise.

I would like to thank the staff at The National Archives and the Imperial War Museum for their assistance in producing documents for research. When I started work on this book in 2014 few of us could have had any idea how the Covid-19 pandemic would affect our lives. Having hundreds of documents to research and write about was a welcome distraction during lockdown, but social distancing also reminded us how rewarding it is to visit an archive, museum or library, for whatever reason. Access to collections is something that we should never take for granted.

I would like to thank my family, friends and colleagues who have commented on and informed the research for this book and have helped to shape my thinking, often without realising. I gave a talk based on the early research for this book at The D-Day Story conference in 2015 and an early version of this work was presented in 2020 to the Portsmouth Branch of the Historical Association, whose members' comments and questions were also most useful. I am grateful to Al Murray and James Holland for allowing me to talk about my research on their 'We Have Ways of Making You Talk' podcast and Paul Woodage for allowing me to present on WW2TV. Their comments, and those of their listeners and viewers, helped to shape this book.

I would also like to thank Andrew Whitmarsh and Simon Trew for their suggestions around sources. The maps were produced by Paul Hewitt of Battlefield Designs. Any mistakes are entirely my own.

Finally, and most importantly, I would like to thank my wife Becci for her understanding, patience and support during the not insignificant time that it took to research and write this book.

May 2023
Portsmouth

LIST OF MAPS

LIST OF PHOTOGRAPHS

INTRODUCTION

In the early hours of 6 June 1944 a gliderborne party of the 2nd Ox and Bucks Light Infantry seized the bridge across the River Orne in a daring coup-de-main operation. The capture of what became known as Pegasus Bridge was seen as a textbook airborne operation, and was regarded by Air Chief Marshal Sir Trafford Leigh-Mallory as one of the most outstanding flying feats of the war. Elsewhere the British 6th Airborne Division took all of its objectives and played a vital role in securing the eastern flank of the Normandy landings.

Yet just over three months later, in an operation riddled with errors and mistakes, the British 1st Airborne Division virtually ceased to exist as a formation after an epic struggle at Arnhem. Out of over 10,000 men who landed in Arnhem less than 2,000 withdrew across the River Rhine at the end of the battle. How did Allied airborne planning go from such a successful operation as those that took place in Normandy, to the debacle at Arnhem?

Although three months may appear to be a short space of time, the Allies had fought an extremely hard and complex series of battles between D-Day and Arnhem. Of course many people are familiar with the events of Operation Market Garden, thanks to the film *A Bridge Too Far*, a term which has passed into common currency. In the film the commander of the British 1st Airborne Corps, Lieutenant General Sir Frederick Browning, refers to a string of cancelled operations that the Division had been slated to take part in since D-Day.

It is intriguing that these cancelled operations, which form something of a lineage between the successful Normandy operations and the errors of Market Garden, have received such little attention from historians. Not only do they explain how airborne planners lost sight of fundamental principles of warfare, but they represent a central spine amongst – and are irrevocably woven into – the historiography of one of the most controversial campaigns in military history. To what extent did this string of cancelled operations shape the way Operation

Market Garden was planned and subsequently fought? And what can they tell us about the wider campaign?

I must confess to having more than a cursory interest in studying the airborne operations of 1944. My grandfather, Private Henry Miller, was serving in the 11th Parachute Battalion in the 1st Airborne Division. It is all too easy to relegate military history to dates, places and names, but it is also important to remember the human element. On the decisions of generals rested the fate of many thousands of men. Every cancelled operation had an impact – albeit widely varying – on thousands of men. For some operations units and formations were placed at readiness, and in some cases briefed and even assembling at their take-off airfields before the operations had been cancelled. Even before taking off for Arnhem in September 1944, the lives of the men of the 1st Airborne Division were dominated for over three months by a constant process of preparing for and then standing down from operations.

Planning for airborne operations in North West Europe did not take place in isolation. Although airborne warfare was relatively new to both Britain and the United States, both armies had developed their airborne capabilities rapidly. Airborne operations were increasingly key elements of campaigns in North Africa, Sicily and Italy, and of course in Normandy on D-Day. General Sir Bernard Montgomery, the commander of the British 21st Army Group and the commander of Allied land forces for the assault phase of Operation Overlord, was also a convert to the use of airborne troops. There is evidence that Montgomery's planning staff and that of the commander of the British Second Army Sir Miles Dempsey had considered how to use airborne forces not only in the initial assault on D-Day, but also to reinforce the beachhead after the invasion, and then aiding the breakout.

Writing about things that did not happen is aways going to be difficult, especially if we wish to avoid 'whataboutery' and to remain relevant to what transpired in 1944. But I hope that it is clear that things that were thought about, and planned, can tell us much about not only the Allied approach to airborne warfare, but also Allied strategy more generally.

Many of the individuals featured in this book held higher rank after the end of the war. For simplicity personnel are referred to by the rank that they held at the time in question.

Such a complex chain of events is not always easy to explain neatly. As many of these operations overlap in time, I have decided to follow the planning of each operation in isolation to its cancellation. Therefore some of the events may at times appear to take place out of sequence.

If anything, this should be an indication of how complex the situation was for the planners in the summer of 1944. We have the luxury of time to pore over records: they were working on multiple operations at once in what was a relatively short period of time. I am minded to quote the Duke of Wellington's comments on the history of a battle being like the history of a ball.

I hope, as well, that this book shows that whilst D-Day and Arnhem have been very well covered by historians, there are almost always new sources that we can interrogate. The campaign from 6 June until 25 September 1944 lasted for over three months, but the vast majority of writing has focused on a handful of days. There are still thousands of sources in archives and museums that are yet to be interrogated, or would benefit from re-assessment.

I had hoped to write about the full gamut of operations that were planned. However, the amount of sources were so vast that the period from the end of the Battle of Normandy until before Operation Market Garden will be considered in a future publication. Equally it is not proposed to write about D-Day here, only in so much as it relates to the relevant planning of the operations under consideration.

ABBREVIATIONS
AND GLOSSARY

AEAF	Allied Expeditionary Air Forces
AFDAG	Airborne Forward Delivery Airfield Group
AIR	Records of the Air Ministry
Airborne Cigar	Electronic countermeasures system
ANXF	Allied Naval Expeditionary Forces
BGS	Brigadier General Staff
Border	Border Regiment
BUCO	Build Up Control Organisation
CATOR	Combined Airborne Transport Operations Room
COMZ	Communications Zone
COSSAC	Chief of Staff to the Supreme Allied Commander
CSO	Chief Signals Officer
DD Tank	Duplex Drive 'swimming' tank
DEFE	Records of the Ministry of Defence
DUKW	Six-wheeled drive amphibious truck
ETOUSA	European Theatre of Operations United States Army
FAAA	First Allied Airborne Army
FUSAG	First US Army Group
G	General Staff (British designation)
G2	Intelligence Staff (US designation)
G3	Operations Staff (US designation)
G4	Supply Staff (US designation)

GSO1	General Staff Officer (Grade 1)
GSO2	General Staff Officer (Grade 2)
GSO3	General Staff Officer (Grade 3)
HS	Records of the Special Operations Executive
IWM	Imperial War Museum
IX USTCC	IX US Troop Carrier Command
KOSB	King's Own Scottish Borderers
LCA	Landing Craft Assault
LCF	Landing Craft Flak
LCG(L)	Landing Craft Gun (Large)
LCI(L)	Landing Craft Infantry (Large)
LCM	Landing Craft Mechanised
LCP(L)	Landing Craft Personnel (Large)
LCS(L)	Landing Craft Support (Large)
LCS(S)	Landing Craft Support (Small)
LCT	Landing Craft Tank
LCT(A)	Landing Craft Tank (Armoured)
LCT(R)	Landing Craft Tank (Rocket)
LSG	Landing Ship Gantry
LSI	Landing Ship Infantry
LSI(H)	Landing Ship Infantry (Hand-hoisted)
LSI(M)	Landing Ship Infantry (Medium)
LST	Landing Ship Tank
Mandrel	Electronic countermeasures system
MT	Motor Transport Ship
PIAT	Projectile Infantry Anti-Tank
POL	Petrol Oil and Lubricants
Q	Quartermaster Staff (British designation)
RASC	Royal Army Service Corps
RCT	Regimental Combat Team
RE	Royal Engineers

REME	Royal Electrical and Mechanical Engineers
SAS	Special Air Service
SHAEF	Supreme Headquarters Allied Expeditionary Force
SOE	Special Operations Executive
S Staffs	South Staffordshire Regiment
TCCP	Troop Carrier Combined Command Post
TNA	The National Archives
WO	Records of the War Office

Map 1: Overview of planned airborne operations in Normandy and Brittany.
(Source: IWM Urquhart Papers)

Part I – Planning before D-Day

'PENNY PACKETS': EARLY AIRBORNE PLANNING FOR OVERLORD

Although the entry of the United States into the Second World War in December 1941 had prompted serious thought about cross-Channel operations – principally with Operations Roundup and Sledgehammer in 1942 – planning for the Second Front began in earnest in mid-1943 with the appointment of Lieutenant General Sir Frederick Morgan as Chief of Staff to the Supreme Allied Commander, or COSSAC for short.[1]

The Rattle Conference held by Combined Operations Headquarters on 23 June 1943 considered the use of airborne troops in the initial cross-Channel assault.[2] A memo prepared by Combined Operations before the conference suggested that airborne forces possessed great strategic mobility but relatively limited tactical mobility once they had landed. It was thought that they could be used on the front, flanks, rear or lines of communications. The memo also suggested that airborne forces could be used in three ways. They could be used in close co-operation with land forces as part of an all-arms attack. This could involve attacking the enemy from the rear, delaying enemy reserves, seizing and holding small areas of tactical importance to the ground troops, or creating diversions. They could also act independently, or in a harassing role operating in small numbers and potentially at distance from the area of major operations. The memo also suggested that airborne forces could be used during the preliminary bombardment phase, landing in the rear of the enemy's defences to capture divisional artillery areas 2,000–3,000 yards inland from the beaches, which could not be dealt with by naval fire or aerial bombing. It was stressed that they should not be used to capture flak batteries.

Finally, it was also proposed that airborne troops could be used during the initial phases of the landings to create diversions and confuse the enemy as to where the main assault was taking place. The obvious

3

flaw in this suggestion is that it would have been difficult to evacuate them. Capturing a covering position prior the landing of the seaborne divisions would, it was hoped, prevent any enemy reinforcements from interfering with the landings. It was stressed that if used in this role airborne troops should be relieved as soon as possible. The memo argued that airborne troops should not be given the task of capturing airfields as they were likely to be very heavily defended. It was suggested, however, that they could capture disused airfields. The memo saw the operational capabilities of airborne troops as similar to commando troops once they had landed, and that they were similarly uneconomical to use for roles which seaborne commandos could carry out. The memo concluded that the implications of using airborne troops in an assault should be considered from the start of planning, as they would affect the timing of the assault and the weather conditions that could be tolerated. The optimum use of airborne troops would be to capture divisional artillery areas, but other roles could include capturing a covering position to disrupt enemy reinforcements. They could also be used to create diversions.

At the Rattle conference itself the then Commander-in-Chief of Fighter Command, Air Chief Marshal Sir Trafford Leigh-Mallory, argued for a firm policy for the use of airborne forces. He was concerned that there was no clarity around how many aircraft would be available nor the role that airborne forces would be asked to carry out. Although Brigadier Oxborrow[3] agreed with Leigh-Mallory that a firm policy was needed as soon as possible and suggested that the lack of airborne experience – the conference took place before the Sicily landings – made it difficult to develop an operational doctrine. In the absence of any information regarding how many aircraft would be available it would be necessary to consider the matter from a purely military angle. Oxborrow's comment summed up succinctly the Allied dilemma – there was plenty of optimism and thinking but little experience. He informed the conference that the Airborne Division had been given five tasks to study. These covered the neutralisation of enemy artillery covering the beaches, the capture of tactical features in the rear of the beaches with the object of dislocating enemy plans for counter-attack by local reserves, seizing key positions on the final objectives of the assault divisions, seizing ground which dominates the bridgehead and denying it to the enemy until the follow-up formations arrived and delaying the movement of enemy reserves.

Oxborrow suggested that the neutralisation of enemy artillery could be carried out by day or at night but that it could be costly and hazardous. He also suggested that tasks should be allotted to recognised formations with the smallest at battalion level rather than forming ad-hoc groups. He suggested that this task could be carried out more economically by other means.

The capture of tactical features in the rear of the beaches was seen as an appropriate task for airborne forces, as part of the tactical plan of the seaborne assault division. The airborne forces would need to be relieved within a matter of hours and then rely on the seaborne division for logistics until they were withdrawn. Seizing dominating ground inland from the bridgehead was seen as a riskier venture as the airborne forces would have to fight unsupported for up to 36 hours. Brigadier Oxborrow argued that unless they could be employed in enough strength to fight a delaying action with a reasonable chance of success and could be supplied from the air, the task would be too hazardous. Delaying enemy reserves was also seen as a risky prospect, depending on the relative dispositions of enemy and friendly forces. If the task was too far ahead the airborne troops might be faced with overwhelming odds or simply bypassed. The possibility of using a large number of smaller parties over a wide area was considered.

Major General Richard Gale, who had recently been appointed to command 6th Airborne Division and had previously been Director of Air at the War Office and before that commander of 1st Parachute Brigade, was also at the Rattle conference. He suggested that an airborne division should be regarded as a small formation of light infantry and that far from only being useful for one operation prior to relief, airborne forces could be employed in many stages of a wider operation. He argued that the number of troops to be employed need not be limited by the number of aircraft available and that airborne forces could be carried in successive waves and disagreed with Oxborrow's suggestion about splitting airborne forces into what he called 'penny packets', which he viewed as technically unsound.

Lord Louis Mountbatten, who was present as Chief of Combined Operations, asked General Jacob Devers, the commander of the US European Theatre of Operations, what the Americans were planning regarding airborne forces. Devers replied that there were already three US airborne divisions and that he held out great hopes for their use in Overlord. He was also discussing the provision of troop-carrier aircraft for Overlord with the War Department in Washington.

The conference agreed that the role of airborne forces in Overlord could only be decided in direct relation to the COSSAC Outline Plan, and that therefore the sooner that it could be produced the better. It was also agreed that the major limiting factor in the scope of airborne operations for Overlord would be the number of aircraft available.

The widely varying perspectives shown at the Rattle conference show just what a difficult situation the Allied planners faced when it came to finding appropriate roles for airborne forces. The COSSAC plan itself was developed against a background of relatively little airborne experience and any experience that did exist was on a small scale as no Allied airborne operation had yet taken place at a divisional level.[4] As a result an accepted airborne doctrine did not exist. Prior to Operation Overlord airborne operations had only taken place on a brigade level, most recently in Sicily. Planners were therefore not only attempting to integrate a relatively new form of warfare into a combined operation, but they were also contemplating employing it on a scale that had not previously been attempted.

Morgan's ability to plan was hampered by the limited resources that he was allocated and the fact that his relatively junior rank gave him little leverage to request more. This is particularly clear in the way that he chose to employ airborne forces. The air forces suggested that only 643 troop-carrier aircraft would be available, which would be enough to carry only two-thirds of a division at a time. Unsurprisingly Morgan's airborne planning was relatively limited in scope. At first he and his team of planners were inclined to deploy the available airborne troops on the western flank of the landings near Carentan rather than risk them in the Caen area. This later evolved to using two-thirds of a British airborne division to capture Caen and the equivalent of seven US airborne battalions to attack coastal batteries and river crossings.[5]

Morgan's COSSAC plan was presented to the Combined Chiefs of Staff on 30 July 1943. The airborne part of the COSSAC air plan was modest:

> Airborne forces equivalent to two airborne divisions and some five or six parachute regiments will be available, but largely owing to shortage of transport aircraft, it is only possible to lift two-thirds of one airborne division simultaneously, on the basis of present forecasts.
>
> At the same time [as the seaborne landings] airborne forces will be used to seize the town of Caen, and subsidiary operations by commandos and possibly by airborne forces will be undertaken to neutralise certain coast defences and seize certain important river crossings.

For planning purposes Morgan assumed that Overlord would be able to call on one US and one British airborne division, five US parachute battalions and one US airborne tank battalion, totalling some 25,540 men and 54 Locust tanks. The size of this notional force level was not dissimilar to that which would land on 6 June 1944. The biggest dilemma for Morgan was the lack of transport aircraft. It was estimated that on 1 May 1944 there would only be enough aircraft to carry the equivalent of two-thirds of one airborne division, or approximately one-third of the total airborne force in any one lift. This limitation was mainly down to a shortage of glider tugs, and therefore six separate lifts would be necessary to lift the whole force. Morgan had little choice but to plan to deliver the airborne forces for Overlord in three successive lifts over a period of 40 hours, a plan that had strong parallels with what would be seen in Market Garden.

The COSSAC plan was based on a seaborne landing on the east coast of the Cotentin Peninsula, in combination with an airborne assault to capture and hold the neck of the peninsula, which would enable the Allies to capture both it and Cherbourg. Morgan also considered the possibility of capturing the Le Havre peninsula by seaborne and airborne landings in a subsidiary operation. This would later be explored in more detail in the planning for Operation Axehead.

The COSSAC plan stressed that the weather placed greater limitations on airborne formations than it did for seaborne forces. It also suggested that landing gliders at night would be difficult, and that at least a quarter moon would be required for visibility. Daylight operations were thought to be extremely difficult, and heavy casualties were predicted. The COSSAC plan therefore stated that it would be necessary to land airborne forces at night to maintain the element of surprise.

Morgan had to compromise in his allocation of airborne forces, and had identified what he thought were suitable tasks for them given the paucity of transport aircraft:

> It is most desirable to capture early Carentan, the crossing of the River Vire and the crossings of the Aure Inferieure, to prevent their destruction; and to seize the town of Caen. The early capture and neutralisation of the coast defence batteries at Grandcamp and Ouistreham is essential.
>
> All these tasks could be undertaken by airborne forces – if sufficient lift were available. We are, however, limited to the employment of the equivalent of two-thirds of an airborne division in one lift; while the seizure of Caen requires a force of one airborne division, and the seizure of Carentan and the bridge at Isigny an airborne force of the order of two brigades. With our available resources it is not possible to carry out all these tasks.
>
> An attempt to seize Carentan and the bridge at Isigny would be more or less of a gamble. It is probable that preparations for demolition have been made and that in fact we should not be able to prevent them from

being carried out. On the other hand, Caen is an important bottleneck in communications and it is essential for us to seize it if we are to avoid defeat in the early stages. It also provides a valuable pivot for operations to develop the bridgehead.

The seizure of the crossings of the Aure Inferieure is of importance in facilitating the southward advance of the force landing on the western beaches.

We can conclude therefore that the available airborne forces should be used primarily for the capture of Caen and of the two coastal batteries. These tasks cannot be carried out within the time required by the transport aircraft available. As a secondary task, the seizure of the crossings of the River Aure by parachutists is important. Finally, at a later stage airborne troops might be landed to seize and hold the crossings of the River Vire.

Thinking further ahead, Morgan identified several possibilities to employ airborne forces in exploitation tasks after the main landings:

Rapid capture of the Southern bank of the Loire and consequent opening of Nantes might be facilitated by the employment of airborne forces . . . Alternatively this corps might be retained in the United Kingdom with a view to carrying out an amphibious operation with the aid of airborne troops to capture Havre in conjunction with the advance of the main Allied Armies.

In the COSSAC plan the main airborne assault on D-Day would be undertaken by a British airborne division in the Caen area with the objective of seizing Caen and blocking crossings of the River Orne from Caen to the sea. The division would then consolidate and await relief by seaborne forces. However the whole division could not be lifted simultaneously without additional lift.

As a subsidiary assault on D-Day six US parachute battalions would be dropped inland of what would become the American beaches around the Vire and the Aure. One US parachute battalion would attack the Maisy battery, and another would capture the coastal batteries at Ouistreham. The COSSAC report also identified that airborne forces could be used effectively in the US sector to capture Carentan, a key transport town that would need to be secured as quickly as possible to delay the German rate of reinforcement. Morgan also considered the possibility of using airborne forces to capture Alderney. As enemy defences on the Channel Islands were very strong, this would take place only after a heavy preliminary bombardment.

Morgan predicted that the British airborne division used at Caen would be swiftly withdrawn to refit and reorganise in England. It was thought unlikely that an airborne formation could capture Le Havre on its own and that the only suitable drop zones were to the north and east of the town. Once landed the airborne forces would have to assault the defences of Le Havre and would need assistance from seaborne forces. Airborne forces could also capture beach defences from the rear or attack landward defences. The Allies would later consider using airborne forces around Le Havre in August 1944.

The COSSAC plan rejected the possibility of using airborne forces to destroy the Luftwaffe on the ground at airfields in the Caen area. This was not considered feasible due to the large number of airfields and the difficulty of providing air cover for the airborne force. This would, in Morgan's opinion, have meant the complete loss of the airborne force. As it would also be required for other operations after the initial assault this idea was not followed up. At this early stage it is already clear that the Allies were counting on airborne formations being able to execute more than one operation during the campaign.

The process for deciding how to employ airborne forces formed an Appendix in the COSSAC plan. Decisions were to be based on the composition of the airborne task force, the ability of the air forces to lift and deliver, the nature of terrain in the objective area and the ability of the main force to reinforce or relieve airborne forces. Morgan also stipulated that airborne forces should be reinforced or relieved within three days and not to exceed six days. However, Morgan also stated that it was not mandatory that airborne formations be withdrawn from action straight away. This ambiguity suggests how fluid airborne planning was.

It is important to remember that the COSSAC 'plan' was a concept, and was never intended to be enacted in the form that Morgan delivered it.[6] Morgan was also hampered by the resources at his disposal. While he identified Cherbourg and the Brittany ports as the primary objectives for Overlord, he allocated two-thirds of an airborne division to a coup-de-main landing on Caen as he felt that the city was an unrealistic target from the beaches on D-Day.[7] This assessment would turn out to be accurate.

While the COSSAC plan awaited the appointment of commanders to implement it, airborne theorising continued. In October 1943 Morgan visited Washington and while there he was presented with the outline of a plan developed by General Henry H. Arnold, the commander of the United States Army Air Forces, supported by General George C.

Marshall, the Chief of Staff of the United States Army, to make Overlord a primarily airborne operation and to drop three divisions well inland to sever enemy communications and strike out. Morgan asked Leigh-Mallory to come to Washington to comment on the plan. Leigh-Mallory was dead against it. For one, there was nowhere near enough troop lift capacity to deliver such a force. There was a fear of German air attack and flak defences, and it was believed – rightly, as events in 1944 would show – that airborne units should not have to operate against a strong enemy for more than a day or two before relief.[8] That two members of the Combined Chiefs of Staff could propose such a dangerous and unrealistic scheme shortly before D-Day illustrates not only the doctrinal vacuum in which airborne planning was being developed, but also that the close interest taken by so many senior officers overreached their awareness and experience of this new form of warfare.

About the same time that Marshall and Arnold's plan arose the US War Department published its Training Circular 223 'Employment of airborne and troop carrier forces' on 9 October 1943.[9] The circular was endorsed by Marshall and the Secretary of War, Henry Stimson, and included several principles that were thought to be vital to the success of any airborne operation. Even at this early stage US doctrine identified airborne forces and troop carrier units as 'theatre of operations' units which would need to be controlled at a combined command level, which in most cases would be the theatre commander. The US policy was to not delegate command of airborne forces to lower headquarters to ensure coordination at a high level. Airborne units would remain under the direct control of the theatre commander until the moment that they landed in the combat area, when control would be passed to the commander in that area.

The US Circular defined troop carrier forces as: 'Army Air Forces units which are specially organized, trained and equipped to transport airborne troops and supplies into combat. Troop Carrier units should not be confused with elements of the Air Transport Command which have the primary mission of transporting personnel, supplies, and mail between theaters.' This definition is important given the pressure that the troop carrier units would come under in August 1944 to act as de-facto transport units, particularly from US commanders. As will be seen, this proved to be a different matter in practice.

The Circular recommended that airborne troops should be used as part of a combined operation, usually in close coordination with other forces. It highlighted that airborne operations would be difficult to coordinate and therefore should not be undertaken unless vital to the accomplishment of the overarching mission or the objective was out of reach of conventional ground forces. It also suggested that airborne forces should not be used unless they could be supported by other forces within around three days or they could be withdrawn after their mission had been completed.

A fundamental principle of the US policy for airborne forces was employment in mass. The bulk of the force should be landed rapidly in as small an area as possible. Air superiority was a prerequisite for whether airborne operations would be launched in daylight or darkness, and training plans should include rehearsals for specific operations.

The US Circular suggested that routes should avoid naval convoys, or that an air lane should be created that naval forces should not enter. Routes should also avoid anti-aircraft defences. Airborne units should have a reasonable chance of being brought under 'effective command' before starting to fight and drop zones should be sufficiently close to the objective to ensure surprise. Enemy strongpoints between the landing area and the objective should be bypassable and the terrain should be favourable for defence against armoured attack.

The Circular suggested no less than eleven types of missions that airborne units might be used for. These included the capture of 'important tactical localities', attacking the enemy rear or assisting a breakthrough by the main landing force, or to block or delay enemy reserves by capturing critical terrain features. Other options included the capture of enemy airfields, 'vital enemy establishments', to create diversions, to assist the tactical air forces by delaying a retreating enemy and to reinforce threatened or surrounded units. It was also suggested that airborne forces could capture islands and create confusion and disorder among military and civil personnel. The final suggestion was that by their 'mere presence' airborne forces would be a constant threat and cause the enemy to disperse their forces to protect vital installations.

The favourable characteristics of airborne forces were seen as a wide latitude in terms of suitable objectives, a capability to strike deep into enemy territory, speed and surprise, effect on enemy morale, an ability to operate day and night, and the opportunity to prepare and rehearse for a specific operation. Their disadvantages were seen as a dependency on weather conditions, lack of mobility after landing, vulnerability to armoured counter-attacks during landing and assembly, complicated staff planning and coordination and the time required, potentially limited information about enemy territory, the difficulty of assembling after landing and establishing control, and their lack of equipment for fighting a prolonged action.

The Circular suggested that a night take-off followed by a daylight or dawn landing, or a daylight take-off followed by a dusk or night landing might be a 'proper compromise'. This suggests that even at this early stage there may have been differences of opinion within US Army circles.

In many respects the US Army Circular was prophetic. It stressed that the airborne operation should be an integral part of the basic plan and should not be superimposed on an existing major plan. It also suggested that during planning phases of operations the contacts between commanders and staffs should be 'intimate and continuous'. It also stressed the importance of simplicity and the importance of avoiding any plans that were completely dependent on the arrival of any one ground unit.

Meanwhile the British were also attempting to distil their experiences. After the operations in Sicily the War Office and Air Ministry produced a joint report drawing lessons on the employment of airborne forces. Unfortunately the direct authorship is not clear and the document is not dated.[10] The document suggested that once the Army Commander-in-Chief had indicated the role that airborne forces should play, 'preparation, planning and sanctioning of the launching of the operation' should be the responsibility of the Air Commander-in-Chief who would remain responsible until the airborne forces landed. He would therefore require army and naval advisors appointed to his staff. This air primacy reflected how British airborne forces had developed from their early days, when the co-operation of air forces required the ceding of a high level of control.

The report stressed that airborne operations must be planned as an integral part of air operations and needed to be controlled by the same formation controlling all other air operations. Airborne operations should be planned far enough in advance to allow time for training and rehearsals. Any airborne operations crossing the sea should have lanes and beaches kept clear of shipping and made clear to air forces. In terms of when airborne operations could take place at night, the document suggested the equivalent of a three-quarter moon with no haze in Western European conditions but that this could be relaxed if navigational aids were available.

Airborne operations were described as 'air operations of considerable complexity' that would usually have to be carried out against opposition. Aircrews would need to be trained to an operational standard and have had extensive training in low flying, over sea and by moonlight. They would need to be able to drop paratroops as accurately as bombers drop bombs and an analogy was drawn with Bomber Command's Pathfinder Force. The airborne formations should fly concentrated to land the airborne forces concentrated in the shortest time and RAF crews and glider crews should train and live together as teams. In terms of gliders the Horsa was preferred as operations in Sicily had shown that it was more robust than the Waco and was much larger in size and capacity.

It was stressed that airborne forces should be employed concentrated with the aim of landing as many men in the shortest time possible. In this respect gliders offered an advantage due to their ability to carry ammunition, transport and heavy weapons, and to land a body of troops together. Gliders could also be released above flak, minimising risk to their tug aircraft. However, gliders were also limited in their landing zone requirements and potential problems unloading in difficult terrain. Glider landings would also need to be preceded by parachute pathfinders.

It was stressed that airborne forces should not be landed in an area where active operations were in progress nor routed over either enemy or friendly heavily-defended areas unless the importance of the objective justified heavy losses. Dropping zones should be an easily recognisable area rather than a 'pin point' chosen for tactical reasons. Airborne operations were also seen as very vulnerable to enemy fighters and anti-aircraft defences. Unless these were negligible it was thought that airborne operations would have to be carried out at night.

The document also highlighted the potential effect of airborne operations on the enemy. It was thought that 'energetic and determined' action by airborne troops could cause alarm and confusion among the enemy, even by relatively small parties of troops dropped many miles from the main objective.

The conclusion of the document is perhaps most telling:

Many mistakes were made in these airborne operations, the first ever undertaken on a large scale by the Allied forces. In particular, the failure to land the airborne troops in concentrated strength at the selected points might have been fatal against stronger opposition.

It is plain that small bodies of airborne troops accurately dropped can achieve results which would normally require very much larger forces. This is one of the characteristics of airborne troops: the deduction to make from these operations is that even greater results could have been achieved by the same airborne force, or similar results by a smaller force, if a more highly trained air force had been available to drop it and the planning of the air operation had been wiser.

Nevertheless, the airborne forces successfully carried out their tasks and contributed greatly to the success of the operation. It must be remembered, however, that the air opposition was slight, and the ground opposition was less determined than it is likely to be in other theatres of war. It is considered, however, that the value of airborne troops, particularly gliderborne troops, has been proved and that there is every prospect that they will exert an important influence on future operations, provided the lessons learnt are applied, and that suitable crews and aircraft are available.

The document made a lengthy set of recommendations for the future employment of airborne forces. It was recommended that airborne operation should either have a strategic or major tactical effect on the wider operation and that airborne forces should be employed concentrated. Where there was any material air opposition or flak, airborne operations should be carried out at night as this would assist in achieving surprise. It was also suggested that a portion of available airborne forces should be kept in reserve to exploit success and should be fully briefed and prepared to undertake any alternative landing task.

The document identified six potential roles for airborne forces. The first was direct co-operation with the seaborne assault divisions, including neutralisation of enemy artillery covering beaches, the capture of tactical features in the rear of beaches or holding off enemy reserves, and seizing and holding key points on final objectives of assault divisions. The second would be to attack the enemy's flanks or rear in conjunction with a frontal attack by land forces. The third would be to seize and hold bridgeheads at major river crossings or other defiles that were essential for the advance, with Primasole Bridge in Sicily being offered as an example. The fourth role would be delaying actions against the enemy's reserves to prevent them reaching the battlefield, the fifth denying the enemy the use of forward fighter airfields and the sixth to intercept a retreating enemy.

The Airborne Division was seen as being flexible and economical in its organisation and allowed for flexibility in forming what were described as 'mixed groups' according to tasks. One area that was viewed with concern however was the requirement for gliders, which was placing heavy demands on the RAF. Although it was hoped that any divisional operations launched from Britain would require 400 Horsas and 30 Hamilcars it was not thought that it would be possible to land this number in one lift.

Looking towards operations in North West Europe it was proposed to concentrate two British airborne divisions in Britain. Airborne forces were identified as 'the most promising military solution to the continental invasion problem across water' and even at this stage the British planners intended that the initial landings would be backed up by reserve airborne formations.

It was predicated that airborne operations would inevitably be a combination of gliders and parachutists. It was suggested that airborne troops should be briefed with alternative tasks in case they were not landed in the correct place, that they could have secondary guerrilla role and that they could co-operate with sabotage and guerrilla forces such as the Special Operations Executive (SOE) and the Special Air Service (SAS). In the event co-operation with special forces and resistance groups was not as extensive as it might have been.

It was suggested that it was essential that airborne operations should be planned by 'appropriate technical experts of all three services' and that it should be stated early on whether an airborne operation would be a vital part of the wider plan. If this was the case weather considerations would dictate when the whole operation could be launched. It was predicted that weather conditions in North West Europe, even in summer, might mean postponements of up to a week.

It was recommended that the existing 38 Wing should be upgraded to a Group of 180 aircraft and dedicated solely for airborne operations, an expansion would also allow for increased glider pilot training, giving a predicted 625 trained crews by 1 March 1944 if additional crews were recalled from North Africa. Thereafter the training output would be 50 crews per month. In terms of gliders themselves, it was thought that there would be enough gliders for three operations and a reconstitution.

The document also suggested that airborne forces would be 'very valuable' in establishing the initial bridgehead in conjunction with the seaborne assault divisions, and that there were also likely to be opportunities to use them to good effect during the subsequent advance.

These lessons were also digested by some in the airborne community. In his post-war memoirs Brigadier Gordon Walch, Browning's Chief of Staff, referred to lessons learnt in Sicily.[11] He argued that aircrews needed to be experienced in dropping parachutists and towing gliders in daylight and darkness, and preferably exercise with flak to get accustomed. Walch also thought that Sicily confirmed that glider pilots needed to be trained as fighting soldiers as it was unlikely that they would be withdrawn from battle immediately.

Although 6th Airborne Division nominally came under the command of the HQ Airborne Troops, for planning and operational purposes the division worked under Lieutenant General John Crocker's I Corps and Browning had much less involvement than he did with 1st Airborne Division prior to Market Garden. This may also be because Gale was an experienced airborne commander and proactive in his approach to training his division. It had been training in England since early

1943 with the cross-channel operations in mind. At the same time Browning was in the Mediterranean. As their task was a set-piece attack and closely defined planning could be thorough and detailed. The airborne troops were also able to develop a close relationship with their RAF crews.

Walch highlighted several lessons from the airborne operations in Normandy which supported the British doctrine developed prior to D-Day. He felt that when correctly employed airborne forces could be an 'unqualified success' and that their objectives were captured at lower cost than could have been achieved by any other method. However, he also suggested that no airborne unit or task should be vital to the whole operation. He felt that aircrews should navigate individually rather than by 'follow my leader' but that with adequate training glider crews could achieve 'remarkable accuracy'. Other points that occurred to Walch focused on the need for firepower support – that airborne forces needed artillery support 'at the earliest moment', that they needed a counter-mortar organisation and an Air Support Unit. Walch also felt that airborne staff should be brought into planning during the early stages, which is interesting given that HQ Airborne Troops played a relatively minor role in planning for Overlord compared to Market Garden. Walch is often seen as a relatively passive figure in the airborne historiography, but his memoirs – although having the benefit of hindsight – suggest more of a thinker than has often been thought.

In December 1943 planning syndicates at 21st Army Group examined aspects of the invasion plans. One syndicate suggested dropping an airborne brigade east of Caen, and further landings south-east and south-west of Bayeux. This proposal had the drawback of there being few suitable dropping zones, and those that existed were too open and difficult to defend.[12]

Until November 1943 British airborne forces were organised in a rather fragmentary way.[13] This was partly because the scale of airborne operations had never been planned for. Airborne formations in the UK and overseas came directly under the command of the senior formation in the respective theatre and Army Groups or General Headquarters had a small airborne staff to advise. There was a Major General Airborne Forces in the UK, who came directly under the War Office. He was responsible to the Director of Air for the command of airborne depots and for technical development, acted as a technical advisor to the War Office and was also available for consultation with commanders-in-chief. He was also authorised to carry out inspections of airborne units.

However, when as expected 1st Airborne Division returned to Britain prior to Overlord there would be two airborne divisions in 21st Army Group. General Sir Bernard Paget, who at the time commanded 21st Army Group, asked the War Office to authorise a Commander Airborne Troops to command all airborne units and the SAS and to act as an airborne advisor. Paget wanted that this post to be entirely under his command without any dual responsibilities. Paget also specifically requested Browning for this post. Paget's proposals were similar to other specialist advisers at 21st Army Group, such as the Royal Armoured Corps, who were often of the rank of Major General but had no command over units or formations.

Independently Browning, who has been described a 'Whitehall Warrior', had also submitted his own proposals to the War Office.[14] He proposed the formation of an airborne corps to command both airborne divisions, that the corps should be commanded by a lieutenant general and that the Airborne Corps should be a War Office formation temporarily under the command of 21st Army Group. He also suggested that the commander should have direct access to the War Office and that the Major General Airborne Forces role should be disbanded. It is hard to overlook that Browning's proposals were aimed at securing himself an active corps command, a promotion in rank and direct access to the War Office. The War Office declined Browning's suggestions for an airborne corps as it was felt unlikely that all the airborne formations would ever operate together in the field as a corps. It was considered that a corps was 'not necessary and would be wrong in principle'. The War Office was undecided on the matter of rank, assessing that on the one hand the post would have two major generals under command, but would not be an operational role and would not command or control troops in battle. The War Office also decided that the airborne commander would have access through the Director of Air. Many of the aspects of this decision would be quietly overturned soon after D-Day.

However, Browning did achieve his promotion in rank. On 15 November 1943 the Director of Staff Duties at the War Office, Major General Steele, wrote to the Director of Air relaying the decision of the Deputy Chief of the Imperial General Staff to provide a Commander, Airborne Troops for 21st Army Group. The post would hold the rank of Lieutenant General and the existing appointment of Major General Airborne Forces would be abolished. The title of the new commander was suggested as 'Commander Airborne Troops (21 Army Group)'. The argument in favour of this designation was that the post would be specifically dealing with airborne forces in the European theatre. The designation of a corps was not considered justified and was rejected. The commander would be provided with a small staff of around twenty officers, and that they could be of a rank of Major General or Lieutenant General. Such a small staff could clearly never be intended to plan or command corps level operations in the field.

On 22 November 1943 Steele wrote to 21st Army Group and Browning to inform them that the proposal for an airborne commander at 21st Army Group had been approved and would be titled 'HQ Airborne Troops (21 Army Group)'. Even though the War Office had approved the appointment of a Lieutenant General a week earlier Steele stated that the rank of the commander was still under review. The commander would be allowed to correspond with the Director of Air at the War Office, in a similar fashion to the Major General Royal Artillery corresponding with the Royal Artillery at the War Office. Browning was not so much chosen for the new role as slotted in automatically, as the letter stated 'Pending consideration of the War Establishment and promulgation of the details, Major General Browning will be at your disposal'.

As 1943 became 1944 planning for airborne operations was reflecting changing Allied doctrine more widely and was also becoming a battleground for the Allies concerning command, assets, forces and missions. It is also clear, even months before D-Day, that the series of headquarters required to plan airborne operations, and the personalities involved both in Washington and London, would severely hinder planning. Even six months before the start of Operation Overlord, an untidy picture was starting to emerge.

'HIGH HOPES': AIRBORNE PLANNING FROM JANUARY TO JUNE 1944

The first alterations to the airborne element of the COSSAC plan were made soon after Eisenhower and Montgomery were appointed as Supreme Commander and Commander-in-Chief of 21st Army Group in late 1943 and early 1944 respectively. More senior than Morgan, they were able to make substantial changes immediately. A US airborne division was added to land in the Cotentin to support the US landings on Utah Beach after Montgomery had argued that the landings were on too narrow a front. Montgomery also rejected the proposal to drop a British airborne division on Caen – the US Air Force Historical Study describes him as having 'never cared' for it – and switched the British airborne landings to east of Caen around the Orne.[1]

Work also started to integrate the British and American airborne forces. On 10 January 1944 a joint conference was held between 38 Group and IX Troop Carrier Command to discuss equipment and common techniques.[2] It was also attended by representatives from HQ Airborne Forces and the senior staff officers of both 1st and 6th Airborne Divisions. The conference was particularly important as it was increasingly likely that British or American aircraft would be used to land either country's airborne forces and there would be a need for standardised procedures. Much of the details concerned technical aspects such as roller conveyors for dropping supplies and static cables for parachuting. It also recommended the establishment of a conference room with direct telephone lines to 38 Group, IX Troop Carrier Command, US Airborne HQ – which did not exist until much later in August – and British HQ Airborne Troops to enable representatives to hold detailed planning conferences, and to function as a command post during operations. This later became CATOR (Combined Airborne Transport Operations Room), or TCCP (Troop

Carrier Command Post), and was the first tentative step towards centralised coordination of Allied airborne forces.

On 25 January 1944 Browning set down his thoughts regarding the employment of airborne forces during Operation Overlord in HQ Airborne Troops Directive No. 2. The directive, distributed to Montgomery's Chief of Staff Major General De Guingand, Leigh-Mallory's Senior Staff Officer Air Vice Marshal Wigglesworth and Air Vice Marshal Leslie Hollinghurst, the Air Officer Commanding 38 Group, was an attempt to establish a firm policy as to how airborne forces should be used in combination with amphibious landings. Browning estimated that a division could be prepared for an unforeseen operation in 48 hours if photographs and briefing material were available. This timeframe would be shown to be wildly optimistic – Market Garden took seven days from inception to take-off and Browning himself would threaten to resign over a shortage of maps when an operation was planned at only several days' notice.

An initial two airborne divisions would be used in the first wave on D-Day and one division would be held in readiness to be flown in if the advance from the beaches had slowed down or in the event of an emergency. The 'emergency division' would only be able to take on simple tasks due to the lack of time that would be available for planning and the quick turnaround of aircraft returning from the first landings. Another division would be available for longer-term tasks, pre-briefed and with reconnaissance photographs available. Once the fourth division became available the third division would stand down. Thus Browning recognised as early as January 1944 that divisions could not be held at high readiness indefinitely. Despite this, 1st Airborne Division did not get to stand down between early June and mid-September and was stood to more times than it should have been because 6th Airborne Division was not withdrawn in time. In effect it fulfilled the roles of the notional 'third' and 'fourth' airborne divisions, those of both the reinforcement and long-term strategic roles. The dual role that it was allocated complicated planning for its employment.

Whilst planning was continuing in Europe doctrine was also being developed at a considerable distance in Washington. Independently of Supreme Headquarters Allied Expeditionary Force (SHAEF) the US Army Air Force Headquarters developed a plan that expanded on Arnold's previous idea for a large-scale airborne operation deep in France. The plan, written by Brigadier-General Frederick Evans, the commander of I Troop Carrier Command, and Colonel Bruce Bidwell of the Operations Plans Division, was approved by Marshall on 7 February. It proposed a combined drop of two divisions between

Evreux and Dreux on the night of D-Day. These divisions would capture four large airfields to enable two additional divisions to be airlifted in by D+1.[3] Evans and Bidwell flew to Britain carrying a letter from Marshall stating – somewhat paradoxically – that although he did not wish to exert 'undue pressure', he expressed strong 'personal support' for the plan, and criticised previous airborne planning as 'piecemeal', 'indecisive' and 'narrowly conceived'. Expressing 'strong personal support' could hardly be described as not exerting 'undue pressure', and this suggests the pressure that Eisenhower was under from his mentor.

In March the Air Staff at SHAEF were asked to study 'the employment of Airborne Forces in relation to a given plan', which was almost certainly Marshall and Arnold's proposal.[4] The plan envisaged a 'Force A' of six parachute brigades being dropped in the rear of the assault beaches as late as possible before dark on D-1, a 'Force B' of thirteen parachute 'detachments' to be landed further inland and a 'Force C' of an additional airborne division to be landed on D-Day as early as turnaround permitted. The Air Staff were asked to also consider the possibility of all three forces being dropped at the same time. They assessed that this would require minimum troop carrier airfields to launch and the production of 5,300 briefing models and there would be significant issues with briefing such a large force and designating routes. Take-off would also cause considerable problems. It did not take the Air Staff long to conclude that the proposed plan was completely impractical.

The plan from Washington was unsurprisingly rejected by Eisenhower on the grounds that the airborne forces would not be mobile enough once on the ground and that plans to supply them by air would not be feasible. Eisenhower saw airborne forces as aiding a breakthrough rather than being the breakthrough themselves. These fears were certainly well founded, demonstrated by the rate of progress made by ground forces during the Battle of Normandy and the vulnerability of airborne forces far behind enemy lines in Market Garden.

Meanwhile manpower was becoming a problem that would affect airborne planning. As early as 11 March – just under three months before D-Day – it was found that it would be difficult to provide airborne-trained reinforcements once operations began. Steele at the War Office wrote to 21st Army Group, Home Forces and overseas commands suggesting that the situation was made worse by the use of airborne-trained reinforcements once airborne units were in action on the ground, as airborne divisions were designed for short operations and were not suited for a prolonged ground role. Steele therefore suggested that once airborne units had landed they could be made up with reinforcements from the normal infantry pool and could be reorganised once out of the line. Whether this would have been feasible given the airborne formations' esprit de corps is questionable, but that it was being discussed even before D-Day suggests that manpower shortages would have a limiting effect on airborne operations.

Meanwhile the troop-carrier forces were making progress in standardising procedures and equipment. On 28 March 38 Group published a Standard Operating Procedure for Paratroop and Glider Operations, to take effect from 7 April.[5] It covered staff and airfield procedures, loading, marshalling and despatching and aircraft and pathfinder procedures. It also laid out the various responsibilities of air and airborne commanders and headquarters and a standard agenda for co-ordinating conferences and standard forms. 38 Group would organise the commanders conference jointly with airborne forces, organise the co-ordinating conference and select drop zones and landing zones jointly. The Airborne Commander would jointly organise the commanders conference, be represented at the co-ordinating conference and jointly select drop zones and landing zones. An Appendix to the Procedures outlining the structure of Allied Air and Airborne Organisation showed a 'British and US Combined Op. HQ', a headquarters that did not exist in March 1944, and a 'HQ US Airborne Troops', another non-existent organisation.

HQ Airborne Troops Operation Instruction No. 1 was issued on 22 April by Browning's Brigadier General Staff Gordon Walch and outlined the procedures for launching airborne operations during Operation Overlord. 21st Army Group would ultimately decide on the operation to be carried out by airborne troops and would allocate aircraft in conjunction with Allied Expeditionary Air Forces (AEAF). HQ Airborne Troops would retain control of airborne formations until they took off and after landing they would come under the command of formations already in theatre. At this stage there was clearly no intention for a corps-level airborne command to take the field and the role of HQ Airborne Troops role was still limited to an administrative function in mounting operations.

As there was limited accommodation and briefing facilities in camps attached to RAF airfields it would not be possible to move troops taking part in follow-up operations to airfields until the preceding troops had taken off. This affected the ability to launch airborne operations in quick succession. This was also dependent on the availability of transport aircraft and the level of losses experienced in the initial assault.

22

Maps would be a critical factor in launching airborne forces. These would only be drawn from the map depot at Newbury in time for them to be issued immediately before an operation. Although this is perhaps understandable given the broad geographical area in which airborne formations could be expected to operate, it inevitably hampered the ability of planners to prepare adequately for operations. Later in the campaign Browning would make a stand over the issue of map supply.

One of the more unlikely sections of the Instruction warned of the possibility of German parachutists taking part in 'suicide raids' on airfields containing airborne troops preparing for operations. Commandants of transit camps were ordered to prepare a defensive scheme, including digging slit trenches. This warning does seem rather fanciful given the state of the Luftwaffe and the German airborne forces by 1944 and may have been more about getting the airborne troops into the habit of digging in.

A HQ Airborne Troops movement order issued by Walch on 4 May dealt with the movement of airborne troops to airfields prior to operations. 1st Airborne Division could not move to the transport airfields until after 6th Airborne Division had taken off for D-Day, meaning that a follow-up operation could not be mounted until several days afterwards due to the lack of accommodation and the turnaround time required for the transport aircraft. Therefore the division was to be prepared to take part in an operation at 72 hours' notice to remain in action for 14 days afterwards. This timescale would seemingly change for every operation.

The next day, on 5 May, Browning issued a memo to 21st Army Group G (Ops) concerning the weather conditions required to mount airborne operations. These included the visibility, wind speed, cloud base and moon conditions under which pilots – of powered aircraft and gliders – could operate. These also covered the conditions at airfields, en route and around the drop zones. This clearly reinforces that at this stage in the planning for Overlord airborne operations would be commanded through the usual command structures rather than by a dedicated airborne corps-level headquarters.

Although Montgomery is often cited in the historiography of the Normandy campaign and the commander of the British Second Army Lieutenant General Sir Miles Dempsey is often viewed as a relatively passive figure, records suggest that Dempsey played a much hands-on role in formulating airborne theory and developing operations than this reputation might suggest. He also demonstrated more clarity of thought regarding airborne operations than his superiors or his peers.

An undated memo produced by Dempsey several months before D-Day and circulated to his corps commanders Crocker, O'Connor, Ritchie and Bucknall, as well as Browning, suggested that British airborne forces could be used to assist the advance of XXX Corps and I Corps from their D-Day objectives, and that they could well be used in conjunction with VIII and XII Corps who were to land shortly after D-Day and had been given exploitation roles.[6] In another memo dated 21 March 1944 Dempsey cited the lack of momentum after the Anzio landings as a scenario in which airborne forces could be used in place of further seaborne landings to prevent the Allied advance becoming bogged down:

> The objective of the airborne forces must be strictly related in time and space to the main body, and the commander must be ready to employ his maximum force in conjunction with his air-flank operation. Properly employed, such an operation will be of the greatest assistance to the main body in breaking out . . . the available airborne reserve should be of the utmost help in keeping the operation fluid.

Dempsey's planning notes prepared prior to D-Day also suggest that he discussed airborne operations with his corps commanders on several occasions. He also mentioned airborne forces in depth during his briefing at Montgomery's Exercise Thunderclap on 15 May 1944:

> I have already told you how valuable I think 1 Airborne Div may be in assisting the advance of Second Army – being landed behind the German lines in conjunction with a full-scale attack by the main force . . . It is important, therefore, that you should know exactly how it should be used, and the machinery necessary to plan and organise the operation.

The machinery which Dempsey referred to had arisen largely from lessons learnt during a pre-invasion planning exercise. The corps commander and several of his staff officers would be at Second Army Headquarters and as soon as a decision was made to employ 1st Airborne Division, Browning, his staff officers and those from 1st Airborne Division would join the relevant Corps HQ to plan the operation. 1st Airborne Division would be given warning orders so that it would have 48 hours' notice of the operation. The airborne officers would then return to England to issue orders to the division. This was a much more streamlined command structure than would eventually be used in Market Garden and employed Browning as an advisor rather than as an ad-hoc corps commander.

Perhaps one of the most insightful planning exercises before D-Day, and one of the least known, was Exercise Wake. Prior to D-Day Dempsey ordered the commander of VIII Corps, Lieutenant General Sir Richard O'Connor, to hold a staff exercise to study the employment of airborne forces in assisting with a breakout from the bridgehead. VIII Corps was not part of the initial assault forces on D-Day and its units were due to land in the days after the initial landings. Therefore O'Connor's corps had a role to firstly reinforce the assault formations and secondly to attack and expand the bridgehead.

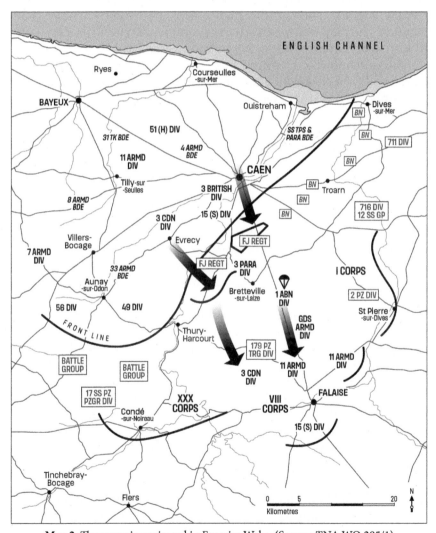

Map 2: The scenario envisaged in Exercise Wake. (Source: TNA WO 285/1)

Exercise Wake took place on 8 May 1944 and was attended by the Commander, Chief of Staff, Commander Royal Artillery, Assistant Quartermaster General and Officer Commanding Royal Signals from 1st Airborne Division; Lieutenant-Colonel Wright and Major Beasely-Thompson from HQ Airborne Troops; and the Brigadier General Staff, Commander Corps Royal Artillery, Deputy Assistant Adjutant and Quartermaster General, Chief Signals Officer and Commander Army Group Royal Engineers of VIII Corps.

On 13 May 1944 O'Connor – who was not present at the exercise – submitted an outline plan to Dempsey based on the results. The objective of Wake was to dominate the Falaise area, particularly its key road junctions. The plan was for an advance commanded by VIII Corps with 3rd Canadian Division under command, using 1st Airborne Division to break out from the Overlord bridgehead through the positions of I Corps and then strike out along the road from Caen to Falaise.

O'Connor felt that this would be a feasible but slow operation and would take between a week and 10 days to complete. The advance by VIII Corps was to be led by three infantry divisions. It would start with an assault crossing across the River Orne south of Caen on the night of D+13/14. As darkness fell on D+13 the 15th Scottish Division was to move forward to the western banks of the River Orne, bringing up enough bridging materials to build two bridges. At last light the next evening on D+14 the assault troops of 3rd Canadian Division were to assault across the Orne and capture a bridgehead big enough to facilitate a bridging operation at Amaye. The Canadians would be supported by over 150 guns, including Royal Artillery units from Corps and Army Group Royal Artillery. At the same time 15th Scottish Division was to capture enemy positions around Bourguébus supported by over 200 guns. Meanwhile I Corps would carry out a diversionary attack from its positions from east of the Orne.

After last light on D+15 1st Airborne Division was to land and take up a defensive position around Cauvicourt, Bretteville-le-Rabet and Urville with the intention of disrupting the enemy's communications. It was predicted that the airborne troops would be swiftly attacked by 2nd Panzer Division and would therefore need to make all possible use of natural anti-tank defences. Given the Airborne Division's relatively light organic artillery, four batteries of 155mm guns were to be on call to provide support from the beachhead. The plan for the airborne landings is interesting in several respects, firstly that they were being dropped only after the advance had already started and relatively close to the front line, and secondly a strong German armoured counter-attack was assumed but not deemed to be serious enough to prejudice the operation.

Also on the night of D+15 the 11th Armoured Division was to be ready to pass through or around 15th Scottish Division as soon as circumstances permitted the next day on D+16. They would reconnoitre on both flanks of 15th Scottish to establish the most suitable side on which to advance. At first light 3rd Canadian Division would advance to and dominate the area of Bretteville-sur-Laize, Fresney le Vieux and Point 183. 15th Scottish Division were to advance to the area Cramesnil-la-Bruyere, Cintheaux and Cuilly. The plan allowed flexibility for 11th Armoured Division to use the most suitable axis of advance, an option that would not be available to their counterparts from the Guards Armoured Division in September.

By the afternoon of D+16 the 11th Armoured Division would have passed through the positions of 15th Scottish Division and after linking up with the Airborne Division would continue exploiting south towards Falaise. 15th Scottish and 3rd Canadian Divisions would follow up and contact 1st British Airborne Division around Cintheaux, Cauvicourt and Bretteville sur Laize. The Airborne Division would then be evacuated from the battle area. It was hoped that I and XXX Corps would advance along with VIII Corps. The airborne landings were therefore clearly not seen as the tip of the spear but as a means of assisting the 'break in' by landing close behind the German lines. The armoured advance was therefore not a do-or-die dash to relieve the airborne forces but instead would use them as a springboard.

In his outline report arising from Exercise Wake O'Connor suggested that airborne forces could be employed in either a tactical role, assisting the ground forces in overcoming the defences in front of them in the initial stages of a battle, or strategically. O'Connor described this more strategic possibility as '. . . dropped much further into enemy country to tie up with, and to facilitate, the rapid advance of armour'. This choice between tactical and strategic use of airborne forces would dog airborne planning for months to come.

All of the British and Canadian corps commanders were sent the results of Exercise Wake and were also provided with a map trace showing the available landing zones in the Second Army area. The results of Exercise Wake also summarised, somewhat presciently, some of the key issues facing the employment of airborne forces:

Should the landing be successful, it seems that the Airborne Div may be employed too late, as by then the battle will be half over. These two objections can be avoided by dropping the Airborne Div in conjunction with the initial attack. But it will mean accepting the risk of a longer delay in effecting a junction with the Airborne Div.

The exercise also led to a number of practical recommendations. As soon as a joint operation involving airborne forces was ordered, a planning team from 1st Airborne Division would go to the relevant corps headquarters. This planning team would include the divisional commander, chief of staff and an RAF representative. It was estimated that the airborne planning team would require four days to mount an operation, and that once on the ground the division would come under the orders of the corps that would be linking up with them. Interestingly this plan foresaw no role at all for Browning.

It has been suggested by that the broad thrust of Exercise Wake towards Falaise is an indication that Dempsey intended to break out on the eastern flank of the Caen bridgehead.[7] It is extremely unlikely that any of the commanders involved foresaw that the exact scenario predicted for the start of Wake would in fact transpire almost two weeks after D-Day. Exercise Wake was exactly that – an exercise, and one to develop procedures and policy rather than concrete plans. The lessons learnt could – and should – have been applied to any similar operation launched from anywhere within the bridgehead. But by ordering the exercise it does suggest that Dempsey was thinking very seriously about using the 1st Airborne Division to aid an advance after the initial landings.

Wake also drew out some valuable lessons for planning airborne operations. Finer details discussed included tactical recognition, wireless connections and the exchange of liaison officers. A signals exercise between the Airborne Division and VIII Corps was also planned, and significant attention was also given to how the relevant artillery commanders would co-ordinate efforts to support the Airborne Division. Wake envisaged the Airborne Division to land a relatively short distance behind enemy lines, after the ground attack had already started and within range of corps-level artillery support. These were policies that were increasingly ignored as the campaign wore on.

There is no evidence that the lessons from Exercise Wake were shared with anyone beyond Dempsey and his corps commanders, nor that it was shared with Montgomery or anyone at 21st Army Group. The points arising were of importance to any headquarters that might have been called upon to mount airborne operations. But these lessons were not shared and airborne operations would be planned by headquarters and staffs who did not have the advantage of having exercised similar scenarios, or exercised with the Airborne Division's headquarters.

Dempsey was clearly influenced by the findings of Wake during his Thunderclap briefing on 15 May:

28

We must concentrate all our efforts during the early weeks of the invasion to ensure that we do not get pinned down. We must retain our ability to keep the operation fluid. We must hold 1 Airborne Div in reserve until it is clear that we may be unable to break out of the ring without their assistance. Then we must use them in conjunction with the main attack to make sure that we do break out.

So I say that the correct use of 1 Airborne Div in the Exercise which 8 Corps carried out was to assist in Phase I or Phase II – to be used in conjunction either with the initial or with the second infantry attacks. If they succeed, we will have broken through the ring and the armour can then play its part.

Dempsey also stressed that a junction between the main force and the airborne force should be effected within 24 hours. He suggested that if the proposed operation was a risky one – water crossings were specifically referenced – then the airborne forces should not be dropped straight away, and their use should be held back until the progress of the battle could be assessed. During Exercise Wake VIII Corps did not land 1st Airborne Division until the assaulting infantry division had broken through the German front lines and had allowed the armoured division the best possible chance of relieving them, a decision that Dempsey approved of.

A key lesson from the planning of the airborne operations that took place on D-Day compared to the subsequent campaign is that set-piece operations offered ample opportunities for training, planning and preparing equipment. A report into the British airborne effort in Normandy described numerous combined airborne exercises held during February, March and April 1944, at battalion, brigade and then divisional level.[8] These were held over terrain like that which would be found in Normandy and included day and night landings and detailed rehearsals for operations such as those at Pegasus Bridge and the Merville Battery. Another unique feature of the airborne operations in Normandy was that most troop carrier aircraft were grounded for three weeks prior to Overlord, which ensured almost 100 per cent availability – a level which would never be achieved again in North West Europe. In this and many other respects comparing D-Day with Market Garden is to compare football matches that were played with a different number of players on each team.

It is not proposed to conduct a detailed examination of the airborne landings in Normandy here – a significant historiography exists, and that is not the purpose of this book. However, it is of interest that very few commanders or planners were able to draw detailed conclusions from the airborne landings in Normandy before Market Garden took place. 6th Airborne Division, for example, was still in the field until late August, only weeks before Arnhem. However, an undated and uncredited report found in the papers of Air Vice Marshal Hollinghurst did analyse the 'British Airborne Effort in Operation Neptune by 38 and 46 Groups'.[9] It points out that 6th Airborne Division's planning was overseen by Crocker's I Corps. It concluded that the landings had confirmed 'high hopes' for airborne forces and that there would inevitably be a 'certain proportion' of failure, particularly in night parachute dropping, and that inevitably a margin of error must remain and be allowed for. It suggests that airborne plans should not rely overly on precision in time or space and that no one unit's success should be vital to the whole operation. It also concluded that the air commander could never guarantee complete delivery to the army commander. The report also concluded, however, that the experiences of Operation Neptune would not necessarily produce a set method for the future as the situation at the start of the landings was more or less static, giving time for planning and use of surprise. It was stressed that similar conditions were unlikely to recur, and that future airborne planning would have to be to a different pattern. This would prove to be more accurate than the author perhaps realised at the time.

1st Airborne Division had returned to the UK in late 1943 and early 1944 as something of a loose administrative headquarters whose brigades had fought relatively independently. Its commander, Major General Eric Down, was a very experienced airborne officer whose replacement in early 1944 has been described as 'strange, if not perverse'.[10] Down was sent to India to command a newly-raised airborne division, even though it was not due to become operational until late 1944, and was still in Britain on other duties until after D-Day. It is likely that Down, with his airborne experience, would have used the planning period differently to Urquhart, who although a very experienced commander lacked airborne experience and was also a Montgomery protégé and therefore unlikely to rock the boat. Even Urquhart himself acknowledged that he had been given a divisional command earlier than he had expected.[11] Buckingham has suggested that the assumption that the division was highly trained is misleading, although Urquhart had an unusual challenge in that he had to command a division that was scattered around the East Midlands.[12]

Urquhart reflected long after the war that many of the personnel in his division were not trained: 'These chaps, the parachute battalions, had just come back from North Africa. They were wonderful individual material but they were not trained.'[13] Even when interviewed decades after the end of the war he was reluctant to be quoted as saying this, but equated the situation with 51st Highland Division, which had performed admirably in North Africa but experienced problems in Normandy.

On the eve of D-Day the Allied forces had made valuable strides in integrating their airborne effort, particularly around equipment and troop-carrier aircraft. Much of the groundwork for the campaign had already been put in place, including the mechanisms for launching operations. Dempsey also appears as a much more prominent figure than he has previously. However, the early signs of problems can be seen. Eisenhower had had to fend off unhelpful interest from Washington, and Browning's position was, even before D-Day, unclear and ill-defined. It would only become clear how much of a problem this would be when the Allies attempted to integrate the command of their airborne forces even more closely.

'SUITABLE AGENCY': THE FORMATION OF THE FIRST ALLIED AIRBORNE ARMY

Even before the Allies had formed corps headquarters to oversee their airborne forces, conversations had already gathered pace around forming an even higher level of command.

The formation of the First Allied Airborne Army is normally presented by historians as something that took place well after D-Day and was formalised during the lead-up to Operation Market Garden. However, the roots of a combined Allied airborne headquarters can be found even before D-Day, and the inter-Allied and inter-service agendas that clouded airborne planning closely reflected the wider political and strategic context of Allied relations in 1944.

SHAEF – and COSSAC before it – had been considering the methods of deploying large formations of airborne forces from late 1943 onwards. On a more tangible level the Allies made efforts to harmonise planning and technical details. The document 'Standard Operating Procedure for Airborne and Troop Carrier Units' was circulated on 5 February 1944 to provide a common basis for liaison, staff procedures, planning and to detail responsibilities.[1] Much of the proposed standardisation was on a technical level, taking in the use of common forms, airfield organisation and the use of pathfinders. The same document also proposed a common planning schedule for airborne operations.

Many of the difficulties that surrounded the Allied airborne effort concerned personalities. Lieutenant General Sir Frederick Browning has proved to be perhaps the most controversial airborne general of the Second World War. He had been appointed as the first commander of the British 1st Airborne Division upon its formation and had developed a reputation as Britain's senior airborne advisor, despite having no operational experience during the Second World War. Browning's future chief of staff, Gordon Walch, first met Browning when he was posted to 214th Brigade which Browning was soon posted to command. His impressions were instant, 'He was renowned for his smartness and turnout at all times and in all conditions, his very strict discipline, his good looks and his physical prowess'.[2]

According to Walch, after Browning, then a Lieutenant-Colonel, had been appointed to command the Small Arms School he had 'disappeared' in 1940 to visit the 1st Battalion of the Grenadier Guards and fellow Grenadier Lord Gort in France. He was not at all happy at being called back to Britain to command a half-trained territorial brigade: '. . . after all, the war might be over, before he, a Guardsman got really involved . . . His explanation to the War Office of his temporary absence was vitriolic; I would not have liked to be on the other end of the phone.'

In 1941 Browning was posted to command 24th Guards Brigade Group, which was probably much more to his liking. When he was then appointed as Major General Airborne Forces in 1942 he sent for Walch to be his GSO1. At this point Airborne Forces was a dual headquarters – nominally it included command of the 1st Airborne Division, but it was also an administrative role. Walch felt that even early on the Air Ministry were not supportive of the airborne effort: 'The Air Ministry were not too sure and they always worried that a commitment to Airborne Forces of any size above that requirement for a battalion would be beyond their resources, bearing in mind particularly the requirements of Bomber Command. It was a frustrating doubt which persisted for many months to come and which we never really eliminated.' The legacy of this unresolved inter-service tension would have serious consequences as the war progressed, the size of airborne forces grew and Allied integration became more and more important.

Walch describes two schools of thought during the development of British airborne forces, that they should be either small scale or used in larger forces. The value of the threat that they posed to the enemy turned opinion towards a divisional level, which in turn meant that the headquarters would have to be operational as well as developmental. Walch states that once the division had been established Browning's thoughts then turned to forming an airborne corps.

However, an airborne corps level headquarters would not be established until early 1944. Walch also recorded that as 6th Airborne Division was under Second Army for planning purposes Browning only had a 'watching brief' over it. Browning had gone out to North Africa as Airborne Advisor and Walch also recorded in his memoirs that when the commander of the 1st Airborne Division, Hopkinson, was killed in Italy Browning had asked to be able to take over command of the division, but that he was 'turned down flat' by the War Office.[3] This suggests, along with his trip to France in 1940, that Browning was itching to get into action.

Each time that units under his command had gone into action at Bruneval, Tunisia and Sicily Browning had acted as an airborne advisor to the relevant headquarters.[4] Once back in Britain he did not waste time consolidating his airborne domain. On 12 February 1944 Browning wrote to Montgomery proposing the formation of an Airborne Base Organisation under his Headquarters Airborne Troops.[5] Browning proposed that the new organisation should be able to start functioning on 1 March and would consist of 134 men, including US personnel, who should be fit for service overseas. Although Montgomery concurred with Browning's proposals they were not enacted. At the same time Browning was also making detailed comments on arrangements at US troop-carrier airfields, to the extent of requesting Montgomery's agreement that US Airborne Forces should provide transit camps at their airfields similar to the British units, even though this was strictly speaking not for Browning or Montgomery to order. As early as March 1944 Browning was routinely referred to by his staff as the 'Corps Commander', even though his command was not at this stage a deployable corps and no evidence has to date been found of this being authorised by the War Office.[6]

During the Normandy campaign Browning spent three days at Bucknall's XXX Corps headquarters from 19 to 22 July. The purpose of the visit seems to have been to enable Browning to see the workings of a corps in the field. Browning described his experience in a letter to Bucknall on 22 July in language that made the experience sound like a novelty: '. . . I have absorbed secretly what I set out to absorb – the background and running of an efficient Corps of the Field Army; and to forget for even a few days that such things as Airborne Troops exist!'[7]

It is ironic that Browning was sent out to shadow Bucknall – who himself would be sacked a few weeks later – and it suggests that HQ Airborne Troops was going to become an operational corps-level headquarters. That he was sent to shadow a counterpart over a month after operations in North West Europe had started indicates a recognition that Browning and his headquarters had a serious lack of experience of command at a corps level. Indeed, he had not commanded in action at any level since 1918.

Airborne operations on D-Day were planned as part of the existing command structure, with close co-operation between ground and airborne headquarters and along national lines. Shortly before D-Day it was reported that the US airborne divisions would be responsible for reconstituting themselves after returning from Normandy, and would also be responsible for maintaining their own echelon in the UK to train replacements.[8] On 13 May 1944 an airborne operations planning meeting at Southwick House[9] chaired by Brigadier Belchem of 21st Army Group was attended by representatives from AEAF, First US Army, Second British Army, HQ Airborne Troops and the US 82nd and 101st Divisions. No representative from SHAEF was present, nor from the British airborne divisions who were represented by HQ Airborne Troops.[10]

Airborne operations were therefore planned very much along national lines, albeit with 21st Army Group having oversight as the land forces headquarters for the assault phase, and AEAF having a veto over the air plans. As Browning was Montgomery's airborne adviser, he was de-facto the senior airborne commander at the time of D-Day but in practice had a very passive role.

One of the most consistently challenging aspects of planning airborne operations was the conflicting demands on troop-carrier aircraft. When not tasked for airborne operations or for training transport aircraft were frequently given other tasks. To co-ordinate this a central tasking point for air transport, CATOR – the Combined Airborne Tasking Operations Room – was established at Eastcote on 1 June.[11] The issue of competing demands would continue, however, and the diversion of transport aircraft to carrying supplies by air would continue to frustrate airborne planning and was never really solved during the campaign in North West Europe.

Airborne planning had been carried out in this manner since the formation of COSSAC in early 1943. SHAEF possessed an airborne sub-section as part of its G3 Division and 21st Army Group relied on Browning's HQ Airborne Troops to advise. Both had devised a series of contingencies for Operation Overlord which were still extant during June and July, and while 21st Army Group acted as the overall land command in Normandy Browning's headquarters was what has been described as the 'primary filter' for airborne operations.[12] By default 21st Army Group's plans division and the British Airborne Corps were also SHAEF's airborne planning machinery, in the absence of any other mechanism.

The impending activation of Bradley's 12th Army Group in France and the prospect of Eisenhower assuming command in France prompted plans for a new set-up. Washington had already been encouraging SHAEF to bring airborne assets under theatre-level control for some time. Marshall and Arnold had shown great interest in the potential of airborne forces from 1943 onwards and both viewed airborne warfare as a strategic weapon, and Eisenhower was under pressure from Washington to consider bolder opportunities for using airborne formations. Indeed, it has been suggested that whilst in the Mediterranean Eisenhower was not keen on airborne forces but had been convinced of their potential by his mentor, Marshall.[13] Simpson, Montgomery's confidante at the War Office, felt that there was increasing pressure at SHAEF to get the US Army Group into action.[14] This may well have been so that the US forces would be removed from Montgomery's command.

On 20 May 1944 Colonel Joe Hinton, the American head of SHAEF's Airborne Sub-section, sent a memorandum to Major General Bull, the Assistant Chief of Staff of SHAEF and head of the G3 Division. He proposed that SHAEF should consolidate control of all airborne troops in the hands of the Supreme Commander, keeping the US and British airborne units together as one 'striking force' and to provide one channel of communication with AEAF. Hinton proposed that the new organisation should become operational between D+6 and D+20. He also proposed a command set-up that would expand the existing British Airborne Headquarters into an Anglo-American staff, and that the planning staff should form a sub-section of SHAEF G-3 Division. The headquarters would be large enough to liaise with SHAEF and to provide Army Groups with an airborne staff as necessary for specific operations. Hinton also thought that airborne divisions being controlled along national lines lacked co-ordination in arrangements with AEAF, which meant that Leigh-Mallory, a Commander-in-Chief, had to deal with divisional commanders during planning for D-Day. Hinton overlooked the existence of the British corps-level airborne headquarters under Browning, although the latter was playing a minimal role in planning. It also meant that the initiation and planning of airborne operations would take place below SHAEF level. Bull clearly agreed with Hinton's proposals and on the same day he sent a subsequent paper to Lieutenant General Bedell Smith, Eisenhower's Chief of Staff, summarising Hinton's suggestions. Bull however proposed that the new organisation should be on the same level as the Army Groups and AEAF.[15]

Despite the enmity between Browning and some of the US airborne commanders SHAEF were close to accepting Browning as the Allied airborne commander. On 24 May 1944 Brigadier Arthur Nevins, chief of SHAEF's G-3 plans and operations division, wrote to Bull concurring with the proposals. Nevins also proposed that General Browning should be confirmed as Commanding General, Airborne Forces. He did not however agree with the formation of an airborne planning section within SHAEF and felt that airborne planning should take place within the Army Groups.[16]

Planning for a combined airborne headquarters became well advanced before D-Day. On 27 May a General Order was drafted announcing the establishment of a Combined Headquarters Airborne Troops, effective the same day.[17] It would supervise training and allot facilities, study and recommend improvements in equipment, techniques and testing, and would co-ordinate supply. It would co-ordinate with the air forces, assemble troops and equipment at airfields and prepare detailed plans in conjunction with the ground and air commanders. It would also establish supply requirements and arrange for the return of airborne units to base after operations. Most importantly, the new headquarters would 'direct and control the execution of plans, except when under the control of the air commander, until the ground force commander takes command'. The communique also concentrated heavily on administrative functions, suggesting that at the end of May the combined Allied airborne command was intended to concentrate on co-ordination, but would also have an operational role commanding airborne operations.

All US and British airborne formations in the North-West Europe theatre would have come under the command of the new headquarters immediately. The General Order was also to announce that Lieutenant General Browning would be appointed as the Commanding General, Airborne Forces. This proposal, if enacted, would have put the combined airborne headquarters directly under Eisenhower and would have put a British General, Browning, in command of all US airborne units in North West Europe. Given Browning's somewhat difficult relations with US airborne commanders, and not to mention his lack of airborne experience, this would have been a volatile appointment indeed and it is hard to see how it could have worked.[18]

On 2 June 1944 Major General Bull wrote to the Chiefs of Staff of the First US Army Group,[19] British 21st Army Group and the Allied Expeditionary Forces, to outline the proposal for an Allied airborne headquarters and attached the proposed General Order.[20] Montgomery's response was swift. On 4 June Brigadier David Belchem, one of Montgomery's senior staff officers, replied to Bull.[21] Whilst agreeing with the rationale for the proposals Belchem said that '. . . it is felt that present operational implications will not permit such an organisation being implemented effectively at this stage'. 21st Army Group argued that an Allied airborne headquarters would be more practical once SHAEF had taken direct command of ground forces. Whether this was an attempt to delay its establishment is not clear. On 8 June Major General Leven Allen, the Chief of Staff of the First US Army Group, expressed similar views in the absence of General Bradley, who was commanding the US First Army in Normandy.[22] Allen recognised the importance of co-ordinating training, equipment and administration, but felt that airborne planning should be placed under a US headquarters given the preponderance of US airborne units compared to British and the difficulty of co-ordinating US and British staff work and equipment. Air Vice Marshal Wigglesworth, the Chief of Staff of AEAF, replied on 8 June stating that AEAF concurred with the proposals.[23]

Bradley's reservations were overruled by Eisenhower. On 20 June Bedell Smith wrote to Bull at SHAEF G3 and copied in Montgomery, Bradley and Leigh-Mallory informing them that Eisenhower had authorised the formation of a combined US-British Airborne Troops Headquarters as a modified corps-level headquarters. Browning had clearly been rejected for command of the new formation, as Bedell Smith stated that it would probably be commanded by a US Army Air Force officer of the rank of Lieutenant-General.[24] It is not hard to imagine that the prospect of Browning taking command would have been unpopular with US commanders. The headquarters would be operational from when SHAEF assumed direct control of the ground forces, effectively acceding to Montgomery's proposal to delay its formation until then.

Although discussions were at an advanced stage regarding the formation of a US Corps to command the American Airborne Divisions – to give parity as the British already had a corps-level airborne headquarters – even after D-Day HQ Airborne Troops was not intended to directly command operations on the Continent. On 15 June a memo prepared by Walch, Browning's Chief of Staff, announced plans for a tactical headquarters, comprising forty men of all ranks, to be prepared to go overseas to Normandy. Its role was to enable the 'Corps Commander' to act as an adviser to headquarters in the field. Therefore what had been established as an administrative headquarters was beginning a drift towards an operational role for which it was neither trained nor prepared, and for which no authorisation has been found.[25] Did Browning feel pressured into converting his headquarters into an operational one by the imminent arrival of a US Airborne Corps, commanded by an experienced airborne general? Referring to Browning as both a 'Corps Commander' and an 'adviser' in the same sentence suggests a lack of clarity and a degree of mission creep.

It has been suggested that the British had intimated to SHAEF that their Airborne Corps HQ might provide a cadre and a commander for the new airborne headquarters.[26] This is not surprising given Browning's known ambition, but as the US were providing the lion's share of the airborne formations and the troop-carrier aircraft – and not to mention that Browning had not exactly made himself popular with the American airborne commanders – it was almost certain that the new command would go to an American. There were lengthy discussions between SHAEF and Washington regarding who was to command the new headquarters. Bedell Smith corresponded with Arnold, the Chief of Staff of the US Army Air Force, who had already discussed the matter with Carl Spaatz, the commander of the US Strategic Air Forces in Europe. Lieutenant General John K. Cannon, the commander of the Mediterranean Allied Tactical Air Force, was Washington's first choice, and it was felt that he was 'far ahead' of any other air general.[27] Other names mentioned were Major General Hoyt Vandenberg, the Deputy Commander of AEAF, and Lieutenant General William Kepner, the commander of Eighth Air Force Fighter Command, in that order. Lieutenant General Harold George, the Commander of the US Air Transport Command, was also suggested, but it was conceded that he did not have combat experience. At this early point Lewis Brereton was not even included on the shortlist.

On 26 June Browning sent his comments on the proposed new headquarters to SHAEF.[28] He suggested that for the new headquarters to be worthwhile British transport aircraft – namely 38 and 46 Groups RAF – would have to be placed under it to simplify co-ordination with the air forces. This may well have been an extension of the inter-service rivalries that had dogged the development of British airborne forces. Browning went as far as to suggest that if this was not done the new headquarters would be superfluous, which seems something of an over-reaction and might have had more to do with Browning wanting to stymie the new headquarters. He also insisted that the SAS would need to stay under the command of British airborne HQ.

Browning's comments underline how airborne forces were at a very sensitive junction of British inter-service politics. He asked if the Chief of the Imperial General Staff, Field Marshal Sir Alan Brooke, had been consulted regarding airborne troops being placed under the command of an Air Force general. He suggested that the RAF might take this as a precedent and then insist that an RAF officer could command British airborne troops. The early development of Britain's airborne forces had indeed been riven with inter-service rivalries. Whatever the motivation it would be hard to describe Browning's attitude as constructive.

His protests do not seem to have been heeded, reflecting the declining influence that the British had. By contrast the RAF were adamant that 38 and 46 Groups would remain under the command of AEAF. 38 Group was part of Air Defence of Great Britain while 46 Group came under Transport Command because it also carried out other transport duties beside carrying airborne troops.

Also on 26 June Marshall signalled Eisenhower regarding the choice of commander for the new headquarters.[29] Arnold felt that Cannon was better qualified than any other available Air Force officer. Before making a final decision Marshall and Arnold wanted to clarify whether the new commander would be commanding airborne divisions on the ground, perhaps concerned, sensibly, that an Air Force general might not have adequate experience of ground operations. It is perhaps alarming that at this point in time Marshall and Arnold were clearly not entirely sure of such a basic consideration.

On 29 June Bull wrote to Bedell Smith summarising the British objections to the new headquarters, namely the placing of army personnel under the command of an Air Force general, the difficulty of separating 38 and 46 Groups from AEAF and the wider role of 46 Group.[30] He noted that no objections had been received from US sources. Bull enclosed a General Order almost identical to the one previously drafted, that described the new headquarters as taking command of US and British airborne formations, US IX Troop Carrier Command, but taking command of 38 and 46 Groups RAF for airborne operations only.

The staffing of the new headquarters was also considered. On 3 July SHAEF wrote to the Adjutant-General at the War Department in Washington regarding US personnel.[31] SHAEF suggested that there were very few senior officers with suitable training and experience available in Europe. They also suggested that although some officers might be found from those who had been wounded in action serving with airborne divisions and who would not be fit enough to return to action, other personnel might be found from the Airborne Centre at Camp McCall in North Carolina. On 4 July Bedell Smith approved the establishment of the headquarters as 58 officers, three warrant officers and 265 men.[32] Only a week later on 11 July Bull suggested that the new headquarters and a new US Airborne Corps headquarters would require between them 94 officers, six warrant officers and 363 enlisted men from the US Army and 27 officers, one warrant officer and 133 other ranks from the British Army – a markedly unbalanced establishment which reflects the manpower available to the British Army at the time.[33] Most of the US personnel would have to be found from men already serving in theatre. At the same time Bull wrote a separate letter to Bedell Smith suggesting that Major General Matthew B. Ridgway should be appointed as commander of the US Airborne Corps.

On 8 July Marshall wrote to Eisenhower again. He felt that his thoughts expressed in his letter of 20 June had 'not been clearly explained' and made comments that were similar to those that he had expressed earlier in 1944:

> Experience has proved that in preparing to utilize large airborne forces there is at present no suitable agency available to the high command to assume responsibility for joint planning between the troop carrier command and the airborne forces. This planning includes joint training, development of operational projects and logistical support until this function can be taken over by normal agencies. It includes also coordination with ground and naval forces . . . It is for these vital purposes that need the man requested from General Arnold. He would not command troops actually fighting on the ground but would be responsible for providing them all logistical support until normal lines of communication could be established. Assuming that an airborne attack by 2 or 3 divisions would take place in a single area, a temporary corps commander would be designated to conduct the fighting on the ground. He would operate under directives issued by this headquarters until his forces could join up with the nearest army, whereupon he would be taken over by the army commander both operationally and logistically.[34]

Marshall also told Eisenhower that Cannon would not be available for the command as he would be involved in Operation Anvil, but told him that 'we need an officer of real ability, leadership and experience':

> The job is a tough one and the great reason that I want an American air officer is so I can give him the necessary operational and training control over troop carrier command and assure the closest kind of cooperation with tactical air forces. This whole activity has been too loosely organized and I want to tighten it up under an energetic man who will do the job properly.

The question of overall command of the new headquarters was clearly still occupying minds. On 10 July Marshall wrote to Eisenhower suggesting Vandenberg as the best candidate for the new command. Brereton was still not under consideration: 'Suggest Vandenberg has the necessary qualifications to perform eminently the functions of airborne commander in the capacity you have outlined. Further suggest that his vacancy as deputy AEAF could be filled by Royce.'[35]

On 12 July Bull wrote to Bedell Smith suggesting that alongside the formation of the Combined Airborne Headquarters a US Airborne Corps also needed to be established.[36] Bull proposed that command of the US Airborne Corps should be given to Ridgway as the senior US airborne officer in Europe and proposed an establishment for the headquarters staff. Bedell Smith replied on 15 July to say that Eisenhower had asked him to limit it to twenty-five to thirty officers plus a few men 'to keep house for them'. This suggests that it was not intended to be a field headquarters. Ridgway was asked to report to Eisenhower at SHAEF Forward headquarters at Southwick north of Portsmouth, code-named Shipmate, on 17 July. Ridgway also visited Bull at SHAEF on 19 July, probably to discuss his proposed new command.

On 15 July 21st Army Group's Staff Duties section circulated an internal memo regarding the planning of airborne operations which summarised the results of a conference held at SHAEF on 6 July.[37] 21st Army Group had originally specified a need for an airborne operation every 60 days from D+90 onwards, using four airborne divisions in rotation for around five days each. It was assumed that the two British airborne divisions would be used every 60 days. Since D-Day the requirement had changed to an operation every 60 days using three airborne divisions. This scheme would see the two British divisions being used every 90 days from D+90 until the end of 1944. The biggest limiting factor on airborne operations would be the availability of gliders. 400 to 500 gliders were required for each operation, with 1,500 in hand at the time of writing and production running at 100 per month. The glider situation therefore meant that realistically only three airborne operations could be contemplated between July and December 1944.

When 21st Army Group's memo was written it had been forecast that enough army and air force equipment was available to mount five complete divisional operations in 1944 and four brigade group operations, while in 1945 it was estimated that six divisional and three brigade group operations could be undertaken.

A key limiting factor on airborne operations, and the British Army in general, was manpower. In July 1944 the British Airborne Forces included 700 glider crews with a training output of 40 crews per month. Losses were predicted to be 20 per cent per operation, but it was thought that the number of glider pilots available would be sufficient. The biggest risk however was the lack of parachute-trained reinforcements, and when 6th Airborne Division had been reconstituted after its return from Normandy no more men would be available. It was hoped that men could be obtained from the RAF Regiment and that around

100 volunteers per month might be found from other sources. Gale estimated that it would take two to three months to reconstitute his division, while HQ Airborne Forces estimated six weeks.

It was not until 17 July that a decision was made regarding a commander for the new Allied airborne formation. General Spaatz called Brereton to lunch at his HQ at Park House. Upon his arrival Brereton was told that he had, after the exchange of messages between Eisenhower, Marshall and Arnold, been proposed to command the Allied Airborne Army. Brereton's diary records that he was disappointed with the prospect of this new appointment:

> I 'took a dim view' of this new assignment. We have made outstanding progress in air-ground cooperation and I am eager to continue to work with General Bradley and the ground commanders who are showing increased respect for airpower. My chief interest at this time is to carry on the development and application of tactical airpower.[38]

Later the same day Brereton and Spaatz met with Eisenhower at SHAEF to discuss the proposed Airborne Command. Eisenhower asked Brereton the prepare a plan that would 'have as its purpose a maximum contribution to the destruction of the German armies in Western Europe', and for 'imagination and daring'. Brereton also recorded in his diary that Eisenhower told him that his name had been approved at the highest level, which Brereton guessed meant Roosevelt and Churchill. This is surprising given that Brereton's name was not even included in the initial shortlists discussed with Washington and that he was clearly appointed as a compromise after more suitable candidates were ruled out.

Although Brereton's command of the Allied Airborne Army has received at best mixed reviews from historians, his early diary entries suggest that he understood the complexities and challenges of his new command.[39] He predicted resistance from the ground commanders and supply staffs who would want to use the troop-carrier aircraft for other purposes. Brereton was also aware that the British had exerted much pressure before D-Day to have a unified airborne command, with Browning in the same role that he had just been appointed to. Eisenhower thought that there might be complications in placing Brereton over Browning, who was his senior. He also knew that Marshall had insisted on the creation of an Airborne Army. Before departing Brereton told Eisenhower that 'if he wanted plans with daring and imagination he would get them, but that I did not think his staff or the ground commanders would like it'.

Even while personnel were being allocated to the new headquarters British commanders were still objecting. On 17 July Leigh-Mallory wrote a long letter to Eisenhower arguing that although he had never disputed the need to create a unified airborne command, he felt that putting the troop-carrier assets – RAF 38 and 46 Groups and the US IX Troop Carrier Command – under the Airborne Headquarters would complicate airborne planning.[40] Leigh-Mallory argued that training needed to be carried out on a national basis and that the time for such basic training has passed. He also argued that transferring the two RAF groups would interrupt their lines of command with the Air Ministry and that the existing channel for recommending improvements to equipment were working satisfactorily. He argued that no problems of co-ordination had been experienced by either the British or Americans. Leigh-Mallory also argued that contrary to the argument that the Airborne Command could take responsibility for air transport, that the air plan needed to be a complete package from the outset. He also argued that the Air Commander-in-Chief must hold a power of veto over the launching of airborne operations. One sensible point that Leigh-Mallory raised was the fact that an Air Force general would not be technically qualified to command forces on the ground, and since he would have control over the air forces, the post would be 'invidious'. In this Leigh-Mallory would prove to be right:

> From time of take-off to landing, an airborne operation being a purely air operation – must be the responsibility of the Air C-in-C, who must retain the power of veto. Thus, an Airborne Commander merely interposes another unnecessary unit in the chain of communications, with consequent delay and clogging of machinery. If the Air C-in-C were not the ultimate authority, air support, which is particularly vital to Dakota Troop Carrier sorties, might conflict with other operations already agreed.

Leigh-Mallory's objections shed light on the problems that had plagued the early development of airborne forces. To gain the support of the Royal Air Force it had been necessary for the army to give the air commanders a veto over airborne operations. This veto became a keystone in inter-service politics and Leigh-Mallory was clearly not willing to countenance surrendering it. His comments also reflect that in 1944 some Allied commanders were indulged in campaigns against each other as much as the enemy – Leigh-Mallory did not object to the new headquarters, he only objected to his command being reduced as a result. On a broader level the British Army's relations with the RAF had deteriorated since 1942, particularly due to Air Chief Marshal Sir Arthur Tedder and Air Marshal Sir Arthur Coningham's resentment of Montgomery. Tedder, the Deputy Supreme Commander, and Coningham, the commander of 2nd Tactical Air Force, had both served with Montgomery in North Africa. Tedder resented Montgomery's fame after El Alaimein, while Connigham's relationship with Montgomery had rapidly deteriorated after D-Day. These personality issues were transplanted into the North West Europe campaign where there were significant issues with the air side of the Allied command.[41]

Leigh-Mallory's letter also addressed the administrative support for British air forces that would come under the command of the Allied Airborne Army. He felt that unless the new headquarters had a comprehensive administrative staff it would not be able to match the support that the RAF's existing Command and Group structure provided. If it did not the relevant RAF Commands would still have to provide support anyway and the air units would then be responsible to two authorities for operations and administration. He felt that the separation of administrative and operational control would be unwise. Leigh-Mallory also felt that the airborne commander should not have control over the transport aircraft when they were taking part in normal supply by air, which should be dealt with by his headquarters.

Leigh-Mallory argued that Operation Overlord had confirmed the suitability of the existing arrangements and described the airborne operations on D-Day as 'one of the most successful features of the invasion' – an assessment that seems have been formed primarily through an air lens. He concluded his letter by arguing that 'Any reorganization which involved a sub-division of air forces is, I suggest, illogical and unsound' and proposed that the new airborne command should be limited to controlling airborne forces only, with the air forces remaining under himself as the Air Commander-in-Chief.

Bedell Smith's reply to Leigh-Mallory on behalf of Eisenhower brushed aside his objections and suggested that Eisenhower had personally studied alternative plans of organisation for more than a year and a half.[42] Bedell Smith stated that Eisenhower was determined to 'test' the organisation now set up. Describing the establishment of an Army-level Allied inter-service headquarters during an active campaign as a 'test' is striking, but then almost every aspect of airborne doctrine in 1944 was a test.

Brereton wrote to Eisenhower on 25 July to offer his thoughts his proposed new command.[43] His recommendations were, in his words, 'at considerable variance' with the brief that Eisenhower had given him on 17 July. Brereton stated that his priority would be to plan for airborne operations between the Loire and the Seine and then in the Paris-Orleans Gap. Given his background in tactical air support it is not surprising that he had also thought about how airborne operations would be supported from the air. He argued that the main air effort would be to disrupt the enemy reactions to airborne troops and to supplement their weak artillery firepower and suggested that this support could come from airstrips within the airborne operational area. He was convinced that direct command of both the air and ground forces had to be held by a single commander. This policy seems to have been derived from Brereton's belief that air support had to be integrated and streamlined, with a minimum of links in the chain of command.

Brereton recommended to Eisenhower that planning and executing airborne operations should be placed under the command of the Commanding General, Ninth Air Force, which at that point in time was himself. His argument was that airborne operations were designed to support the ground forces, in the same manner as close air support. Brereton accepted that this might appear unwieldy but that it would be better than a separate airborne headquarters. Brereton thought that the commanders of airborne troops and troop-carrier formations should oversee training directly.

Brereton also argued that once launched, the responsibility for an airborne operation should rest with the airborne commander and that responsibility for all air activity should be with the air commander. As an air commander by background unsurprisingly Brereton saw the air aspect as having priority. He argued that it was 'upon the success of the air battle that the ground battle is won and lost', no different from the principles by which tactical air support was provided to ground forces. Brereton thought that only a unified command able to give adequate air support to airborne formations, which he correctly predicted would need a reinforced air effort. He also thought that the Allies' logistical resources would make it impossible to employ any airborne force larger than a corps, and that therefore the airborne forces should be placed under the operational control of the Ninth Air Force, comparing the situation to Montgomery's dual role as commander of both 21st Army Group and Allied ground forces commander. This would have effectively removed the US and British Airborne Corps as operational formations and made Brereton a ground commander, an unrealistic proposition. Marshall and Arnold had already expressed concerns around the suitability of an air officer to command troops on the ground.

Given the lack of time available Brereton suggested using the existing chain of command rather than creating an additional new organisation, arguing that it was bound to suffer from a lack of co-ordination and shortage of key personnel. Perhaps most controversially Brereton proposed keeping the operational chain of command for all Allied airborne forces within American rather than Allied structures, through SHAEF and the US Air Forces to the Ninth Air Force, with only a 'co-ordination' link with AEAF. This contradicts Brereton's argument that unity of command was essential, by essentially dividing the Allies on national lines, which was only bound to complicate matters and lead to frayed relations. It would also have diminished the role of AEAF.

It is hard to escape the conclusion that Brereton was not pleased about his new assignment. An airman by background, his analysis of the airborne context shows a strong bias towards air matters. Not only did he try to persuade Eisenhower that his new headquarters was not necessary, but having lost that argument he then attempted to have it amalgamated with his existing role at Ninth Air Force, which would have increased the size and scope of his command. On 1 August – when Eisenhower was already discussing Brereton's impending appointment with Leigh-Mallory – Brereton had argued against the establishment being Anglo-American in set-up, something that Eisenhower insisted upon.[44]

Bedell Smith replied to Brereton's comments on 1 August. He gave him short shift, and told him that the new headquarters had to be an integrated US-British headquarters. He also gave Brereton a similar reply to the one that he sent to Leigh-Mallory: 'The Supreme Commander has personally studied alternative plans of organization for more than one and one-half years, and is determined to test thoroughly the one now set up.'[45]

Staffing the new headquarters proved to be difficult. On 27 July Bull wrote to Bedell Smith after re-examining the manpower requirements. The establishment numbered 46 officers and 244 enlisted men, of whom 16 officers and 102 men were British. Bull explained that the additional US personnel would have to be found from existing airborne formations, converting an existing corps headquarters into the US Airborne Corps and using available US Army Air Force personnel. In addition a proposed structure for the new headquarters did not include a British deputy commander, only a brigadier as Assistant Chief of Staff.[46] Whether this was an oversight or a reluctance to appoint a British officer – who would almost certainly have been Browning – as deputy is not clear. At this stage it was thought that the US Airborne Corps would be named I US Airborne Corps and use the existing XVIII or XXII Corps headquarters as a cadre.[47]

Meanwhile the British worked on staffing their complement of the new headquarters. Lieutenant General Frederick Morgan, who was now Deputy Chief of Staff, wrote to the Director of Staff Duties at the War Office requesting 13 officers and 101 men from the Army and three officers and three men from the RAF.[48]

On 27 July Brereton had breakfast with Spaatz at SHAEF headquarters in London – code-named Widewing – where they discussed the formation of the Airborne Army. The two also discussed ideas with Bedell Smith. Brereton recorded in his diary that 'Already, however, the ground forces are shocked by some of my ideas'.[49] This reflects the general trend of army-air relations in 1944.

Bull wrote to Bedell Smith on 30 July summarising the response to the proposals for the new headquarters.[50] Both Bradley and Montgomery agreed to its formation – although in practice they did not have much choice – as did the US Strategic Air Forces. Leigh-Mallory objected, while Brereton was still making alternative recommendations. Bull recommended that the proposed operational command channels should be approved and issued as part of the General Order establishing the headquarters. This was agreed by Bedell Smith and later approved by Eisenhower.

During June and July 1944 the Allied airborne picture became increasingly complex. It was an inter-Allied and inter-service weapon, and was prone to a large number of strong personalities, both in France, in Britain and in Washington. Although it should be remembered that the Allies were developing this new form of warfare 'on the job', it is already clear that things were becoming increasingly muddled, but as the Americans had the lion's share of personnel in theatre, the pressure from Washington was always going to be key in shaping the command structure.

Part II – Normandy

OPERATIONS WASTAGE AND TUXEDO

Although the story of airborne operations in North West Europe might be assumed by many to have started in the early hours of 6 June, of course the 6th Airborne Division had been training for many months. Indeed, their counterparts the 1st Airborne Division had also started preparing for the Second Front months earlier.

Many of the men serving in 1st Airborne Division thought and hoped that they would go into action on D-Day. Instead, the 6th Airborne Division, who had been training for the landings since 1943, took part. The news that D-Day had taken place had an impact on the men of 1st Airborne. Jeffrey Noble was serving with 156th Parachute Battalion: 'We thought that we were being prepared for the D-Day invasion and a number of exercises took place up until the June in England. What happened of course was that 6th Airborne went in on the D-Day invasion.'[1]

Private James Sims of the 2nd Parachute Battalion, whose recollections were published after the war, described the reaction to the news as a riot. His comrades were only pacified when they were told that they were being held back for 'something special'. Sims also recollected that the personnel of 1st Airborne Division felt aggrieved as they regarded the 6th Airborne Division as 'amateurs'.[2] These accounts show just how little the average private soldier was told about what was happening, a need-to-know basis that was quite normal.

What most of the men would not have known was that their first 'something special' was already in motion as the roots of Operations Wastage and Tuxedo can be found several months before D-Day. Their genesis appears to stem from the pre-invasion planning of Lieutenant General Sir Miles Dempsey, the commanding officer of Second Army. As with Exercise Wake, the planning for Wastage and Tuxedo also suggests that Dempsey had a much more pivotal role in airborne planning than has often been thought.

51

An undated memo by Dempsey, circulated before D-Day, states that he had ordered that one parachute brigade should be on call from the night of D+2 and D+3, and that the rest of 1st Airborne Division should be on standby from the night of D+6 and D+7. Dempsey stated that 48 hours' notice would be the most desirable, but the airborne units could be ordered in at about 12 hours' notice.[3] How feasible it would have been to mount an effective operation at only 12 hours' notice is open to conjecture.

A further memo by Dempsey on 24 March 1944 suggests that originally one of the parachute brigades of the 6th Airborne Division was slated to be held back in Britain – 'Of this reserve, the third para bde of 6 Airborne Div will be standing by for emergency defensive use between D-Day and D+3' – and that these scenarios were seen very much as an emergency option only. In the event, both parachute brigades of 6th Airborne were landed on the night of D-Day, and the emergency role fell upon 1st Airborne Division. Dempsey also expressed strong views regarding the relative merits of using airborne forces in this emergency role:

> It is most desirable that neither of these bdes should be used in this way. If they are, the offensive reserve in the hands of the Army Commander will be reduced to one Airborne Div. the two bdes will have been wasted – for it must be borne in mind that once an airborne formation has been landed in France it will not be ready for a further operation for a month – however soon it is returned to England . . . Provided that neither of these two bdes have been squandered before D+3, a reserve of one div and one (or two) bdes will be ready for offensive operations from D+4 onwards.

These views certainly support a view that Dempsey was, even before D-Day, playing a more prominent role in airborne planning and the development of doctrine than has previously been thought. At the Thunderclap briefing at St Paul's School in London on 15 May, during his briefing to the assembled commanders and VIPs, he again expressed strong views as to the merits of using airborne forces in defensive or attacking roles:

> . . . 1 Airborne Div, which will be ready to land from evening D+6 onwards, of which one Para Bde can be flown in evening of D+2 onwards . . . This latter bde must be regarded simply as a stopgap to be flown in in an emergency. I do not regard it as available for offensive operations, that is to say, to be dropped behind the enemy's lines.

At the same briefing Dempsey described the possibility of flying airborne forces in in a reinforcement role as 'very remote', which suggests that Wastage and Tuxedo were planned very much as a contingency.

On 20 May a staff conference was held at HQ Airborne Troops to discuss potential operations for 1st Airborne Division after D-Day, and on 24 May 1st Airborne Troops Operation Instruction No. 4 was issued.[4] One parachute brigade was to be at six hours' readiness for a fly-in reinforcement operation from 1400 on D+2, and the whole division was to be ready to perform the same role at 24 hours' notice from 1400 on D+6. More detailed Operational Instructions for Wastage and Tuxedo were issued on 27 May.

A subsequent conference was held at Eastcote on 29 May to discuss the air implications of potential operations for 1st Airborne Division. Tuxedo and Wastage envisaged either a parachute brigade or the whole division flying into Normandy in a reinforcement role. Planning for these operations was carried out in some detail, and air movement tables for Tuxedo and Wastage had been compiled and issued before D-Day. Plans were also drawn up for resupply missions, navigation aids and the marking of drop zones. Neither operation was planned to take place until several days after D-Day – from D+2 for Tuxedo and up to D+6 for Wastage – due to the time that it would take the transport aircraft to turnaround from their D-Day roles. Notice periods for these operations would be relatively short – 24 hours for Wastage. In addition the troop-carrier airfields would only just have housed troops from the airborne forces that had landed on D-Day and it would take time for 1st Airborne Division's units to assemble at the airfields. Tuxedo or Wastage could have taken place in either the British or US sectors of the beachhead depending on circumstances.

The short notice at which these operations could have been mounted presented problems for commanders in issuing orders, allowing subordinates to formulate their own plans and liaising with ground formations with which they would be operating. Urquhart issued Operation Instruction No. 3 on 5 June to clarify instructions for recce parties and orders groups.[5] The divisional O-Group would be held at HQ Airborne Troops at Moor Park, 'if time permits'. If there was a sudden emergency two O-Groups would take place, one at the airfield at Brize Norton and one at divisional headquarters at Fulbeck. It was hoped that the divisional commander would be able to give his orders 48 hours before H-hour. However, in the event of a fly-in reinforcement role, it was intended that the divisional O-Group would be held on the Continent after advance parties had landed. It was also hoped that if

53

enough notice could be given for operations then a divisional planning team could fly to the Continent to liaise with ground formations. This planning team would consist of the divisional commander, his GSO1 (chief of staff), the GSO2 (intelligence), the Assistant Adjutant and Quartermaster General, the commanders of the divisional artillery, engineers, signals and glider pilots, the officer commanding the 21st Independent Parachute Company – the division's pathfinders – and a representative from 38 Group RAF.

It is hard to envisage how the division could have conducted a satisfactory O-Group for either of these operations, particularly given the fluid state of operations in France after D-Day, the short notice at which they were expected to take off and the location of 1st Airborne Division's constituent units, which were scattered across England. The mounting of airborne operations, particularly after D-Day, would have taken place when hundreds of thousands of men and vehicles were already on the move towards the embarkation points for Normandy.

Moving the airborne troops to the troop-carrier airfields so soon after D-Day would have been challenging. Seaborne tails would also have to move to the Continent to link up with their units, and space would have to be found on landing craft and ships sailing across the Channel. Waterproofing vehicles for the Channel crossing would also have been time-consuming. It was soon discovered that it would take prohibitively long for the airborne units' seaborne tails to reach their parent formations in France, particularly given the intended short notice for operations and the lack of space in shipping. The units with which the airborne units would be co-operating were ordered to provide transport, as only one LST could be found for Tuxedo and two for Wastage.

Also on 29 May, and probably connected to the conference on the same day, HQ Airborne Troops circulated a map trace with a number of areas pre-identified for use as dropping zones. These covered the area from east of the Orne around what would be 6th Airborne Division's bridgehead, in an area mainly north of the Caen-Bayeux road and as far west as Arromanches. HQ Airborne Forces had assigned each area a number, and if required the ground forces would assign any drop zone a letter. Areas seem to have been selected more for their suitability than any estimate of tactical need, and that only a handful are south of the Caen-Bayeux suggests that these were seen as reinforcement drops, as the road was a D-Day objective.[6]

On 1 June units were warned to refer to any fly-in reinforcement operations as Exercise Camphor, to convey the impression to personnel without security clearance that they were taking part in a routine

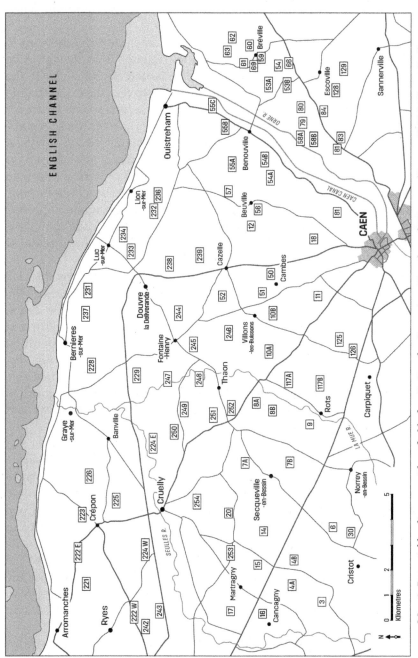

Map 3: Potential landing areas identified before D-Day for Operations Tuxedo and Wastage. (Source: TNA WO 171/368)

training exercise.[7] Indeed, as we have seen, most of the personnel of 1st Airborne Division only found out about the D-Day landings when they were briefed about them on D-Day itself.

On 8 June Brigadier John Hackett's 4th Parachute Brigade went to six hours' readiness to mount Operation Tuxedo. Aircraft would be ready for loading and parachutes would be issued at 1200 on D+1. The interval between D-Day and the brigade going to readiness for Tuxedo was to allow them to recover from the operations on D-Day. However the brigade's troops would be aware of D-Day as soon as it happened – the transport to take them to their take-off airfields would arrive at noon on D-Day. It is unclear with Hackett's 4th Brigade was chosen for Tuxedo, although it may have been because it had previously been an independent brigade in the Mediterranean. The 1st Parachute Brigade was unofficially the senior brigade and the airlanding brigade contained more manpower and heavy weapons, so Hackett's brigade may have been seen as more expendable. This policy would also have retained the other two brigades in case Wastage was called for.

The aircraft for Tuxedo would have been provided by the US 315th and 316th Troop Carrier Groups, with the pathfinders of the 21st Independent Parachute Company taking off from North Witham, 10th Battalion and Brigade Headquarters from Spanhoe and 11th and 156th Battalions from Cottesmore. 4th Parachute Brigade Operation Instruction No. 1 was issued on 26 May 1944. The Brigade Group, less its glider element, would be prepared to drop in a reinforcement role on any part of the Allied forces' front. The brigade would go to 48 hours' notice from 1400 on D+2. At this point the date of D-Day had not been made known to the brigade planners.

The Brigade advance party would fly in with the pathfinders and would drop one hour ahead of the rest of the brigade. It would consist of the Brigade Commander, the Brigade Major, the Staff Captain, the Brigade signals commander, the commander of the Provost Section, the Intelligence Sergeant, a 'G' Clerk, five signallers, four batmen and two provosts. Each Battalion would form an advance party of the battalion commander, the Adjutant or Intelligence Officer, one other officer, three signallers, three batmen and nine other ranks. The relatively senior nature of the advance groups was likely because the brigade would take off with virtually no information – at least with commanders and staff officers arriving early they could be briefed on landing and then brief their units immediately.

The lack of information that the brigade would receive was shown by the subject of maps. The brigade's units were warned that maps would be delivered to their airfields and would be broken down into company bundles. Units would have to be prepared to jump with these bundles and then issue them on landing in France. One wonders what might have happened if the individual carrying a company's issue of maps had been killed or landed away from the drop zone, something that was not an unrealistic prospect.

A revised 4th Parachute Brigade Operation Instruction for Operation Tuxedo was issued on 7 June. The Brigade's troops were to be at two hours' notice to move to airfields from 8 June. The Instruction stated that drop zones were unlikely to be known until the last minute and that commanders had to be prepared to have them pointed out at the airfields prior to take off. The Brigade would drop onto one or two drop zones and would be met by an advance party and liaison officers from the formations with which they would be co-operating.

The advance party would consist of four aircraft carrying a platoon of pathfinders from the 21st Independent Parachute Company, a stick from the Brigade Headquarters and a stick from each of the parachute battalions in the brigade. The Operation Instruction also suggests that Tuxedo would take place with extremely limited prior information. It suggested that drop zones would only be known at the last minute and that unit commanders had to be prepared to have them indicated at their take-off airfields.

The Brigade would drop on one or two drop zones. They would be met by liaison officers from the units that they were reinforcing, either British or American. If the operation took place in the British sector transport would be found from among vehicles held by Second Army and this would consist of twenty-five jeeps and twenty-seven three-ton trucks. If, however, Tuxedo took place in the US sector one LST would be allocated to carry over the Brigade's transport.

4th Parachute Brigade's war diary suggests that two slightly different plans were drawn up for Tuxedo – Tuxedo I would involve the Brigade Group flying in minus its glider element, and could have taken place any time between 8 and 12 June. Tuxedo II, meanwhile, would include gliders and could take place any time from 12 June. Presumably Tuxedo II was planned for slightly later to take into account potential shortages of gliders after D-Day and turnaround of tug aircraft.

On 8 June the Brigade issued an Admin Order for the seaborne element for Tuxedo. Loading of the seaborne element would take place as soon as the parachute troops had taken off – presumably to ensure that the operation was taking place – but information regarding embarkation ports and routes would not be known until shortly before departure. Vehicles were to travel ready for war, and Bren Guns,

PIATs and personal weapons were to be ready for use at all times. Men who were not driving were to be prepared to man weapons and ammunition would be ready to be used immediately.

In the event Operation Tuxedo was not called for, and on 10 June 4th Parachute Brigade reverted to 24 hours' readiness for Operation Wastage. Aircraft for Wastage would be ready for loading from 1000 on D+4. Divisional Headquarters, divisional troops and 1st Airlanding Brigade would take off in gliders from 38 and 46 Group airfields at Broadwell, Blakehill Farm, Down Ampney, Brize Norton, Harwell, Tarrant Rushton, Fairford, Keevil, Membury, Welford, Greenham Common and Ramsbury. 1st and 4th Parachute Brigades, meanwhile, would take off from US troop carrier airfields at North Witham, Folkingham, Cottesmore, Saltby, Spanhoe and Barkston Heath.

As Tuxedo and Wastage were both planned to take place behind friendly lines it was hoped that recce parties would be able to land 12 hours ahead of the main body. Two gliders from divisional headquarters would take off from Brize Norton, two gliders from Greenham Common would carry the advance party from 1st Airlanding Brigade, and four C-47s each for 1st and 4th Parachute Brigades would take-off from North Witham. It was also hoped that a planning team from the division would be able to fly to the Continent to liaise with the formation that they would be operating with and then return to Britain to brief the rest of the division. The planning team would consist of General Urquhart, the GSO1 and other staff officers. Two LSTs would be made available for the division's seaborne tail. This would move to the embarkation port on the same day as the airborne element took off. As with Tuxedo this was presumably to avoid the seaborne tail sailing prematurely and becoming marooned on the Continent.

On 8 June the Division's Tactical Headquarters went to Airborne Troops HQ at Moor Park, presumably to be on hand if Wastage was called for. At 1430 the same day a meeting was held at Eastcote between Major General Urquhart and Hollinghurst to discuss the allocation of tug aircraft once losses from D-Day had been calculated. In the event Wastage was not called for. Indeed, on 9 June De Guingand, at 21st Army Group Main HQ in England, signalled Montgomery in France, 'Have you any ideas use 1 Airborne Div.' Bearing in mind Dempsey's strongly expressed views about not wasting airborne forces on defensive tasks and saving them for offensive action instead, the situation in the Normandy beachhead did not approach anywhere near the critical scenario that might have entailed Tuxedo or Wastage being implemented.

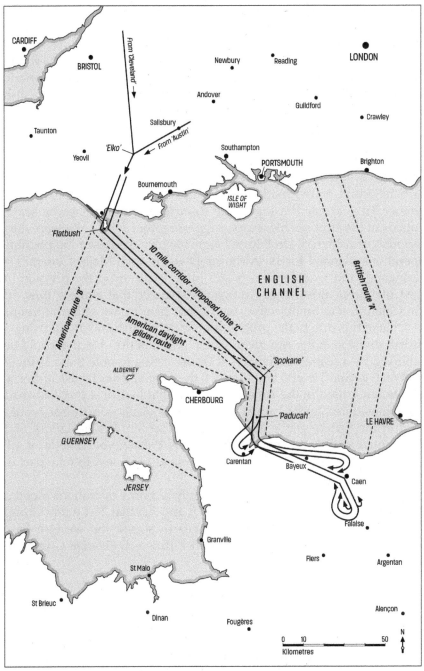

Map 4: Air routes identified before D-Day for Tuxedo, Wastage and Wild Oats.
(Source: TNA WO 205/196)

Wastage and Tuxedo were clearly planned as reinforcement operations not operational jumps, and were designed to fly in either a brigade or division as follow-up formations if, for whatever reason, the flow of follow-up troops from UK was disrupted and the situation in the beachhead was acute. The great storm is an example of a scenario in which air reinforcements might have been called upon. It is also possible that the operations were planned as a way of working up the Airborne Division and the planning staffs and getting them used to their potential role.

Even before the readiness period for Wastage had ended a planning team was called upon to fly to France to discuss another operation with British Second Army. Aside from Dempsey's planning before D-Day, neither Tuxedo nor Wastage were discussed with any headquarters outside of the airborne hierarchy, suggesting that at no point were they seriously considered. On 8 June Leigh-Mallory discussed the possible operations planned for 1st Airborne Division with Major General De Guingand, and whether it was still intended to drop the division in the Cotentin peninsula. De Guingand explained that while cutting off the Cotentin was an objective, he did not plan to use airborne troops to achieve this due to the problems of supply, the difficulty of using a British division in the American sector, and that the objective could be achieved by a seaborne division. It is interesting to note that planning for Wastage and Tuxedo had foreseen the possibility of British airborne troops being used in the American sector, that logistical problems had been considered and planned for, and that American troops would land in the British sector during Market Garden. Leigh-Mallory and De Guingand did not specifically discuss Wastage or Tuxedo at all, even when the 1st Airborne Division was at readiness to take part in either of these operations.[8]

Wastage and Tuxedo were not the only airborne operations mooted for the days immediately after D-Day. It appears that 21st Army Group were considering using airborne forces to secure the western base of the Cotentin peninsula. At 2335 on 7 June – D+1 – De Guingand messaged Montgomery:

> We are examining implications of your plan. Utah beach should be capable maintaining forces required. Area La Haye Du Puits must reply for resupply upon availability of crossings over inundation at 259925 and 309915 and these may be blown. Alternative might be to hold gap to north west about CANVILLE T19 which in view fact greatest threat likely from south would be economical. Airborne tps studying possible use 1 Airborne Div in above area but assume task better undertaken by other tps overland.[9]

On the same day 1st Airborne Division was asked to investigate the area on the west side of the Cherbourg peninsula with a view to a possible airborne operation. The division obtained information from US 82nd Airborne which had previously considered an operation of this nature. The 82nd had originally been due to drop in this area but had been moved to the area inland from Utah Beach shortly before D-Day. There is no evidence that planning for this operation went beyond this initial request. Given the time that it took for US forces to reach the base of the Cherbourg peninsula it is sensible that no airborne forces were dropped there. The operation is referred to as Operation Reinforcement in some histories, probably a reference to its objective as a more formal code name was not allocated.

Major General Urquhart recalled Wastage and Tuxedo clearly: 'My division was to be a strategic reserve. In other words, I was to be prepared to go at short notice to do anything. My first job, if required, was to land a brigade on the beaches, and the second job was to land a division on the beaches.'[10]

By comparison Francis Moore was a junior officer serving with the 1st Airborne Airlanding Battery Royal Artillery. His recollections are rather different:

> On D-Day we were not the Division that landed in France – 6th Airborne did that. We went down to the airfields in Gloucestershire, to Broadwell airfield . . . we were going, I think, the next day virtually, we were ready to go in as the second wave. But I believe the first operation they were going to land us right on top of a German Ack Regiment, which wouldn't have been much good. Possibly that's why it was cancelled.[11]

There is no evidence that Wastage or Tuxedo were considered, which is probably just as well as they would probably have been called on in an emergency in the beachhead. They were also very much aimed at delivering infantry reinforcements, rather than being 'classic' airborne operations in their own right. However, the Allies would immediately pick up the planning for a much more proactive operation, and one that would become much more infamous.

OPERATION WILD OATS

Once the Allied foothold in France became more secure, and Tuxedo and Wastage were not called upon, the thoughts of commanders and planners turned to some of the more offensive and expansive ideas that had been considered before D-Day. The result, Operation Wild Oats, was possibly the most controversial airborne operation planned during the early part of the Normandy campaign. Equally, it has also become one of the most widely misunderstood.

The XXX Corps plan for the Normandy landings was to use 7th Armoured Division to break out of the beachhead on D+4. Despite Dempsey and Montgomery's policy of using 'air hooks' in the breakout from the beachhead, there is no evidence that XXX Corps had given any thought to working with airborne troops after the initial landings. The findings of Exercise Wake suggest that 1st Airborne Division had been allocated to operate with VIII Corps which had been given a follow-up role during the breakout phase. As late as 2 June Wild Oats was being considered by 1st Airborne Division and specifically in the context of operating with O'Connor's VIII Corps. Indeed, as late as 29 May the code name of Exercise Wake was being used interchangeably for Wild Oats.

Considering that HQ Airborne Forces was not an operational headquarters at this point in the campaign Browning was keeping a tight rein on the planning of airborne operations after D-Day. On 24 May he messaged Urquhart:

> No further task has yet been received for your Division, which can be planned in detail on the ground. You are, however, already aware of the other most probable role in which your Division may be used, i.e. to assist in the 'break-out' from the beach-head, and you will continue to give this problem your attention. Should you consider it necessary you may inform Brigade and unit comds and 2nd grade staff officers that this is a possible task, so as to widen the scope of study given to it.

62

You are already in possession of traces giving possible LZ areas, and these are also held by HQ Second Army.[1]

This certainly fits with analyses that Browning was ensuring that he was the chief British airborne advisor, to the extent of keeping Urquhart away from meetings that his counterpart American divisional commanders would attend. This is in contrast with how Gale had planned directly with Crocker prior to D-Day, with Browning playing a minimal role.

Meanwhile, an undated memo that originated from HQ Airborne Troops suggested that 1st Airborne Division could have been landed in a location that was referred to as 'Area J' to facilitate the advance of 11th Armoured Division around D+14. As that division was part of VIII Corps this would again reinforce the conclusion that the division was being held in readiness to work in conjunction with that corps.

On 28 May HQ Airborne Troops signalled 1st Airborne Division and 38 Group RAF outlining four possible operations for the Airborne Division after D-Day. The memo suggests that these operations had been requested from 21st Army Group. The third operation described was effectively what became Operation Wild Oats, albeit without the code name. Its possible circumstances were described as 'About D+7/D+8 the breakout from the bridgehead is being staged against considerable opposition' with the task of 'To drop and seize the high ground 8 miles N of Falaise'. This, again, was almost identical to the scenario envisaged in Exercise Wake.

The air commanders subsequently expressed grave reservations about the launching of airborne operations in daylight. On 30 May Hollinghurst, the Air Officer Commanding 38 Group, wrote a memorandum to Leigh-Mallory at AEAF. He suggested that landing airborne forces at night during a no-moon period would be problematic, and that within six days of D-Day a no-moon period would begin. Morning mists were identified as a problem regarding dawn landings:

The alternative is of course normally to limit the launching of the airborne divisions to moonlight conditions e.g. any 6 days each side of the full moon, confining operations under other conditions to such emergencies as warrant us accepting what may be crippling casualties. The acceptance of this principle (which does not of course rule out small operations in dark conditions) is strongly recommended.

Hollinghurst's proposal, if accepted, would have effectively curtailed airborne operations to only being able to take place on several days out of each month regardless of the tactical situation. This arbitrary policy, which would have been a ridiculous waste of resources by leaving men and aircraft out of action for the majority of the time, suggests that even before D-Day the air commanders were not totally committed to airborne forces as a concept and were not willing to try very hard to help get them into action. As a result of Hollinghurst's memo the air forces expressed concerns over the launching of airborne operations.

On 2 June a conference was held at TCCP at Eastcote to discuss the air plan for a possible operation in conjunction with VIII Corps, which was given the code name of Wild Oats.[2] It was considered that no further planning could take place regarding Wild Oats, pending a decision from AEAF regarding the viability of daylight operations, and that a night operation would therefore be considered. That a policy on whether airborne operations could or could not be launched in daylight had not been agreed so late, only days before D-Day, is both troubling and perhaps indicative of the extent of the power of veto that the air forces had over the launching of airborne operations.[3]

On 3 June a map was issued by HQ Airborne Troops to 21st Army Group, British Second Army and US First Army showing intended air routes for planned airborne operations. The map again clearly shows Wild Oats taking place east of the Orne in an area almost identical to Exercise Wake.[4] This supports the conclusion that prior to D-Day Wild Oats was seen as an implementation of Exercise Wake. The map showed the routes that would be used to transport British and US airborne forces on D-Day, with waypoints code-named Cleveland, Austin, Elko, Flatbush, Spokane and Paducah. Presumably these routes would have been re-used for any follow-up operations. However, the map very clearly shows the air route as turning around just inland from Utah Beach, Sword Beach and the Caen to Falaise road. Whilst these might have been notional, they do indicate the Allied planners' thinking. Several days later on 6 June 1st Airborne Division issued a map trace of the planned divisional layout for Wild Oats, which showed the division as landing around Évrecy.

However, once the Allies landed the situation and rate of progress altered plans. The Allies had not secured as much ground as had been hoped, and as a result the schedule for landing follow-up formations began to slip. This was also exacerbated by weather affecting shipping. VIII Corps would therefore arrive on the Continent later than planned. Wild Oats would be called upon by XXX Corps instead before O'Connor could land in Normandy.

Lieutenant General Bucknall, the commander of XXX Corps, was clear that he had been allocated a task of expanding the beachhead

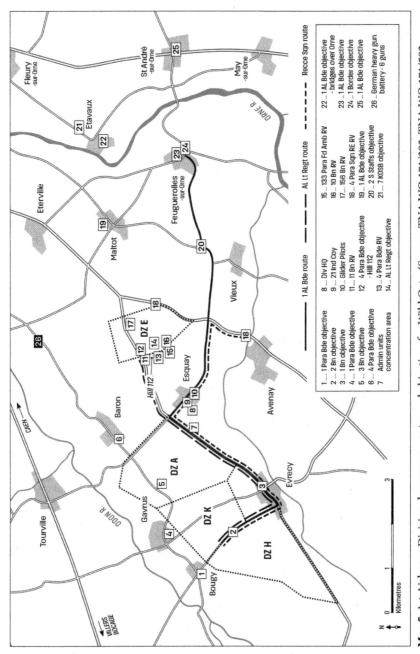

Map 5: 1st Airborne Division drop zones, routes and objectives for Wild Oats. (Source: TNA WO 171/392, TNA WO 171/592 and TNA WO 171/594)

soon after D-Day. The notes from Bucknall's verbal briefing before D-Day suggest that he was planning for a breakout operation in his sector on D+4, code-named Perch, and that 7th Armoured Division were being earmarked to make what Bucknall described as a 'step forward'. Bucknall thought that the Germans would be bound to counter-attack the landings, arguing that 'there is no doubt that his armoured counter-attacks will be serious – more serious than the coastal defences'. Accordingly, on 8 June Bucknall issued his orders for Operation Perch.

Dempsey met with Bucknall at 1730 on 8 June after meeting Montgomery several hours previously. Dempsey told him that he wanted 7th Armoured Division – who had begun landing on the evening of D-Day – kept out of the battle until 10 June, presumably to keep them available for breakout operations. Bucknall was informed by Dempsey that 7th Armoured's objective would likely be Villers-Bocage, and that they would be operating in conjunction with I Corps. Bucknall's diary for 8 June records that he visited 8th Armoured Brigade, an independent armoured brigade, to arrange the attack on Villers-Bocage.[5] They would capture Tilly-sur-Seulles as a start line for Perch.

On 8 June Dempsey met Crocker at 0830 and told him to be prepared to operate east of the Orne in two or three days' time, with a view to capturing Caen from the east. He then saw Montgomery at 1430, before meeting with Bucknall at 1700 at XXX Corps Headquarters. Dempsey's diary records that he told Bucknall to keep 7th Armoured Division out of the battle until the next day, and then to use them to advance to Villers-Bocage and 'swing east on axis Tilly-Noyes so as to come in on the flank and rear of the divisions attacking I Corps'.[6]

The same day Montgomery wrote to his confidante at the War Officer, the Director of Military Operations Major General Frank Simpson, to update him on the progress since D-Day: 'The Germans are doing everything they can to hold on to Caen. I have decided not to have a lot of casualties by butting up against the place; so I have ordered Second Army to keep up a good pressure at Caen, and to make its main effort towards Villers-Bocage and Évrecy and thence SE towards Falaise.'[7]

This suggests that Montgomery had almost certainly told Dempsey to aim for Caen via Villers-Bocage. On 9 June 1944 Montgomery's Chief of Staff, Major General Francis de Guingand, signalled Montgomery 'Have you any ideas use 1 Airborne Div'. This signal suggests that ideas regarding the use of 1st Airborne Division were still relatively fluid, and that Montgomery was also keeping actively involved in decision-making regarding their employment.

It appears that the modification of Wild Oats originated from Dempsey. At 1000 on 9 June Dempsey met Montgomery and informed him that he was planning an operation with 7th Armoured, 51st Highland and – possibly – 1st Airborne Division. Montgomery obviously agreed to Dempsey's plan, as he then met with Crocker at noon and explained the plans for 7th Armoured Division and 51st Highland Division, and his plan to drop 1st Airborne Division south of Caen if both attacks went well. Several hours later at 1200 Dempsey met the commander of I Corps, Crocker, and informed him of his plan. Dempsey stated to Crocker that he was to be prepared to launch his part of the operation on 11 June, and that 'If the attacks of 7 Armd Div and 51 Div went well, the landing of 1 Airborne Div to the SOUTH of CAEN might well be decisive'.[8]

I Corps commanded the British and Canadian divisions that that landed on Juno and Sword Beaches on D-Day. I Corps Instruction Order No.1 issued on 5 May 1944 does not mention potential airborne operations, but does raise the possibility of 3rd Division and 51st Highland Division mounting a converging attack either side of the River Orne if Caen had not been captured by D+5/6.[9]

At 1300 Dempsey discussed the scheme with Browning, explaining that he wanted the operation to take place on the evening of 11 June or later. Dempsey's diary states that Browning then set in motion the machinery for planning the operation and carrying it out.[10]

Meanwhile Bucknall still planned to advance XXX Corps south from the area around Tilly as part of Operation Perch and XXX Corps Operation Instruction No. 2 was issued the same day. The intention was to capture the high ground around Hottot and Juvigny with 7th Armoured Division providing the armoured thrust. However, this advance made slow progress against stiff opposition. Bucknall's diary entry for 9 June states that Montgomery had spent an hour with him and expressed 'delight' at progress and approved his plans.[11]

Plans for Wild Oats were formulated quickly. On 10 June a planning team from 1st Airborne Division flew to Normandy. They attended a conference at Second Army Headquarters on Wild Oats, which was described as an operation in conjunction with 7th Armoured Division and 51st Highland Division in the Évrecy area. A subsequent conference then took place at XXX Corp's headquarters.

On Saturday 10 June Dempsey held a conference with Bucknall, Crocker and Browning, after an earlier meeting with Montgomery and Bradley. Dempsey outlined his plans for Wild Oats and stated that

1st Airborne Division would be dropped to work in conjunction with whichever division made the best progress. Dempsey also ordered Bucknall to switch 7th Armoured Division further west and to make a wide hook through Villers-Bocage. Although XXX Corps' war diary suggests that Bucknall was considering this move before his conference with Dempsey, the latter was vehement that the decision was his:

> Met commander 30 Corps at BAYEUX railway station. He told me that 11H [11th Hussars], in contact with American 5 Corps, were making good progress SOUTH of the road from BAYEUX to CAUMONT. I told him to switch 7 Armd Div from their front immediately, to push them through behind 11H and endeavour to get to VILLERS BOCAGE that way. Provided this is carried out with real drive and speed, there is a chance that we will get through before the front congeals.

Bucknall's diary for 10 June recorded that 7th Armoured Division's attack began at 0700, and Dempsey visited Bucknall shortly after at 0930. There was a conference at Army HQ at 1700 with corps commanders and 'Airborne Comds' – presumably Browning – on what Bucknall described as 'plans for a "Carnival!"'. His diary entry for 10 June also described how 7th Armoured Division had been held up by Panzer Lehr at Raury.[12]

I Corps Operation Instruction No. 2 issued on 10 June outlined a plan for 51st Highland Division, with 4th Armoured Brigade under command, to advance to and capture the high ground south of Caen and control the road exits leading south, south-east and east from the city.[13] The aim was for 4th Armoured Brigade to reach Hubert Folie and occupy the ground between St Andre-sur-Orne and Bourguébus. The operation was to include preparatory naval and air bombardments of areas of Caen. The move of 51st Highland Division towards the start line was a particular problem, as at the time of the Operation Instruction being issued the Division was west of the Orne. At the time that the Operation Instruction was issued on 10 June a junction between the two pincer movements was clearly still envisaged, for 'liaison with 7th Armoured Division' was included. Intriguingly, I Corps Operation Instruction No. 2 mentioned rather vaguely that '1 Airborne Division may take part in the operation. There are alternative plans depending on the situation which may develop on 11 Jun. One provides direct help to 51 (H) Inf Div and the other indirect. Details separately.'

Whilst modifying the plan for 1st Airborne Division based on progress made was no doubt sensible, it also left virtually no time for more detailed planning. There is no mention of this operation, which was codenamed 'Smock', in the 1st Airborne Division war diary, and neither the I Corps or 51st Highland Division Operation Instructions make any further reference to the part that the Airborne Division might have played in the operation.

Dempsey and Bucknall discussed the plans for 7th Armoured Division and 1st Airborne Division – interestingly, 51st Highland Division had already disappeared from his thinking. Bucknall was ordered to advance 7th Armoured Division on the axis Hottot–Noyers while maintaining a strong flank at Villers-Bocage. In the early evening he then met with Crocker, Bucknall and Browning at Second Army Headquarters. They discussed the plan to land 1st Airborne Division on 13 June and Dempsey explained that it would either be with I Corps or XXX Corps, the decision being made the next day depending on progress in the different sectors.[14]

Meanwhile, back in England the air planning for Wild Oats had begun. On 10 June Air Vice Marshal Harry Broadhurst, the commander of 83 Group, flew back to Britain after meeting with Dempsey. Broadhurst, who commanded one of the tactical air formations supporting 21st Army Group, was one of the few airmen that Montgomery trusted. He explained the plan for Wild Oats to De Guingand, and presumably his superiors at AEAF, Coningham and Leigh-Mallory. In his daily signal De Guingand told Montgomery that 'there seemed to be a bit of a problem regarding the flight in'.

Operation Perch was swiftly modified. On 11 June a document that originated from XXX Corps described the concept of what would become Wild Oats as a '30 Corps project for employment of 1 Airborne Division'. The object would be to prevent the enemy from escaping, with Évrecy and Bully being held as pivots. XXX Corps Operation Instruction No. 3 for Operation Wild Oats was issued later the same day. The decision as to whether the operation was to be launched would be taken by Dempsey at Second Army. At this stage the plan still envisaged pincers attacking either side of Caen, with I Corps sending 51st Highland Division south from the Orne bridgehead to capture Démouville, Banneville and Grentheville, and 4th Armoured Brigade to capture Verrières. 1st Airborne Division would land around Évrecy, Hill 112 and St Martin and link up with 7th Armoured Division. The Airborne Division would come under the control of XXX Corps immediately after landing.

Notably the Operation Instruction stated clearly that 7th Armoured Division had to be established around Évrecy before the Airborne Division landed. Bucknall intended that the airborne drop would take place with 7th Armoured Division already holding the drop zones, which would have prevented the risk of an opposed landing or the armoured division having to fight to relieve the airborne troops. However it is unclear whether this was merely an instruction, or whether the drop would *only* have taken place if 7th Armoured Division had reached Évrecy. Post-war, however, the opinion would take hold that Wild Oats would have been similar to Market Garden, namely an airborne division being dropped before an armoured division advanced to link up with it. Bucknall's instructions suggest however that it was intended to be an armoured advance, with an airborne division being dropped to consolidate the objective with infantry once it had been reached.

The intelligence available to XXX Corps identified correctly that Panzer Lehr had been drawn into the Germans' defensive line rather than being held back for an armoured counter-attack. Unidentified tanks had been observed moving behind the German lines, but these were thought to be from 11th Panzer Division coming from Bordeaux or 2nd SS Panzer Division coming from Toulouse. A XXX Corps Intelligence Summary issued on 13 June predicted that the stiff opposition put up the by the Germans on the Corps sector was the prelude to an orderly withdrawal. It was believed that Panzer Lehr might withdraw to defensive positions around Villers-Bocage, and that this could then lead to a stand on Mont Pincon further south. 2nd Panzer Division had not been identified in the battlefront by any intelligence.

Bucknall's diary for 11 June records that he held a conference with Browning and their staffs at 1830 on Operation Wild Oats. Bucknall noted that 'a satisfactory plan evolved but the op is NOT popular!' Unfortunately Bucknall did not record with whom the plan was unpopular or why. Meanwhile 7th Armoured Division's progress had continued to slow – Bucknall put this down to the close county and lack of infantry support. He recorded in his diary 'German build-up becoming hotter! We shall now head for Fillers Bocage [*sic*] sharply!'[15]

At 1800 on 11 June Leigh-Mallory held a conference to discuss what was referred to as Montgomery's proposal for Wild Oats. Urquhart, Hollinghurst and Montgomery's intelligence chief Brigadier Bill Williams were present. At the same time Group Captain McIntyre, AEAF's Airborne Operations Officer, had flown to Normandy to discuss the plan for Wild Oats with 21st Army Group headquarters. Leigh-Mallory opened the conference in a negative manner, as recorded in the minutes: 'He thought this would be a very expensive operation, and that the Army should realise that if it were undertaken it might prejudice the planning of future airborne operations for three months to come.'

70

The troop-carrier commanders, Williams and Hollinghurst, were unwilling to fly the airborne force in during daylight over a heavily defended area. They proposed mounting the operation at night, but Leigh-Mallory cautioned that this would mean flying over the Allied fleet at night and that Allied naval anti-aircraft gunners were 'loose on the trigger'. Urquhart said that he would much rather fly in during daylight given the short notice before the operation, the lack of time to brief his division and that a night drop would leave them badly scattered. Hollinghurst thought that it would be impossible to fly in during daylight. Williams suggested a route crossing the French coast over Utah Beach and flying over mainly Allied-occupied territory.

Leigh-Mallory then spoke to Admiral Ramsay's chief of staff, Rear Admiral George Creasy, by telephone. Creasy told Leigh-Mallory that no guarantees could be given that Allied naval forces would not fire on friendly aircraft if Wild Oats was mounted at night. Leigh-Mallory then telephoned De Guingand to inform him that the operation could not take place at night and that as there was no guarantee that the Allied aircraft would not be faced by friendly fire the operation could not take place.

De Guingand described Leigh-Mallory as 'very much against it', and it seems that De Guingand agreed with him, describing his objections as 'pretty weighty'. The naval forces felt that it would be difficult to prevent anti-aircraft guns from firing at the transport aircraft if the flight in took place in darkness. Leigh-Mallory objected to a daylight operation, as the proposed landing and drop zones were all within range of enemy flak. De Guingand himself described it to Montgomery as a 'risky undertaking', and quite presciently, stated that 'It seems difficult to realise how the Division will be able to pull itself together and become a fighting force under these conditions'.

Even while Wild Oats was being rejected, Dempsey still intended for 51st Highland Division to attack south-east of Caen. At 1915 on 11 June a signal from 1 Corps informed 51st Highland Division that the proposed operation was to be code-named Smock, which is testament to the extent that the Airborne Division played in the initial planning.[16]

Despite the disagreements with the Air Forces, the 1st Airborne Division plan for Wild Oats was issued on 12 June. The initial drop would take place just before dawn at 0425 on 14 June, to take advantage of darkness for the approach flight. 1st Parachute Brigade would land on a drop zone north-east of Évrecy beginning at 0420, secure the landing zones for the division's gliders and then hold the sector north or north-west of Évrecy. 1st Battalion would capture and hold Évrecy and prevent the Germans from using the road network through the village. 2nd Battalion would occupy the high ground north-west of Évrecy, and dominate the approaches to Évrecy from the north, including from Gavrus. 3rd Battalion would hold the landing zone for the glider landings and then occupy high ground south-west of crossroads at Tourmauville. Brigade Headquarters would be established in Évrecy.[17]

4th Parachute Brigade would take off in US aircraft from Cottesmore and Spanhoe. They would land on a single drop zone, capture and occupy the high ground around Hill 112 and be prepared to operate in conjunction with an armoured brigade around Baron. 156th Battalion would occupy the high ground to the north-east and consolidate their positions. 11th Battalion would take up a defensive position covering the approaches to the high ground to the west and north-west and attack and capture an enemy gun battery, and 10th Battalion would be in reserve, covering approaches from the south-east.[18]

Intelligence regarding German positions in the Évrecy area seems to have been sketchy and scant information was passed to the Airborne Division. The airborne troops would literally be jumping into the unknown, and the possibility of having to land in drop zones occupied by the enemy was raised.[19]

1st Parachute Brigade's orders covered Operation Wild Oats and another operation code-named Sampan.[20] Brigadier Lathbury briefed his officers on 12 June, and explained Sampan and Wild Oats as a co-ordinated offensive to cut off the enemy in Caen by moving 7th Armoured Division to Villers-Bocage and then to Évrecy, and by moving 51st Highland Division south through the airborne bridgehead east of the river Orne. The brigade was given two potential roles – to fly in to the area of Ranville, Démouville and Sannerville to co-operate with 51st Division or to land north-east of Évrecy on 13 June.

It is noticeable however that the Wild Oats option contains much more detail in the 1st Brigade war diary. 3rd Battalion would occupy high ground south-west of Tourmauville and deny approaches into Évrecy and Gavrus. 2nd Battalion would occupy high ground north-west of Évrecy and dominate approaches to Gavrus and the main road from Évrecy to Landes. 1st Battalion, meanwhile, would capture and hold Évrecy itself to prevent the enemy using the approaches through the village. If the situation permitted 1st Battalion would also establish a strong cover patrol at Mondeville. It was anticipated that elements of 7th Armoured Division would be in the Évrecy area as early as possible on the morning of the operation and would then head towards Hill 112. An amendment to Lathbury's original orders suggested that 'enemy tanks may anticipate them'. He also anticipated a lack of information prior to take-off and warned officers to be prepared:

> There will be no definite or detailed information regarding enemy dispositions and strength on, and in the vicinity of, the DZ prior to landing. It is therefore the responsibility of sub units on their own initiative to deal with and liquidate immediately any enemy posts interfering with landings. The necessity for getting off the DZ and moving to RVs with all possible speed must, however, be stressed on all ranks who are not immediately concerned with mopping up enemy posts.

As dawn broke on 12 June 7th Armoured Division resumed their attacks on Tilly but were held up. As the front had started to congeal Bucknall ordered 7th Armoured to pull out and redirect its thrust west towards Villers-Bocage, a move which had been first discussed two days previously. Bucknall wrote that the opposition on 7th Armoured Division's front was 'somewhat tough'. He met Dempsey at 1130, and they agreed – in Bucknall's words – on a right hook by 7th Armoured Division to Villers-Bocage. He issued orders for 7th Armoured Division to disengage, and their leading tanks crossed the start line for their new move at 1600. The move went well and by nightfall the Desert Rats were north of Caumont, east of Villers-Bocage. Browning also visited Bucknall for lunch and tea. Meanwhile Wild Oats was postponed for 24 hours. As an illustration of how behind the Allied build up was, Bucknall's third division – 49th Division – had only just started coming ashore.[21]

51st Highland Division's Operation Order No. 2 was issued at 1530 on 12 June. The intention was for the division to capture the line between Verrières, Bourguébus, Cagny and Touffreville with the object of preventing enemy movement south of Caen, forming a pivot in the area of Cagny and dominating the Caen-Falaise road and the bridges over the Orne and Laize at St Andre-sur-Orne and Laize-la-Ville. In the first phase 152nd Brigade would capture St-Honorine la Chardonnerette, Cuverville and Démouville. In the second phase 4th Armoured Brigade would advance and capture the area of Bourguébus, Tilly-la-Campagne and Verrières. Finally, phase three would see 154th Brigade consolidating the area of Le Mesnil, Fremental and Grentheville. Assembly and concentration was again highlighted as a concern. The division was to concentrate around Ranville and Benouville in the airborne bridgehead, in what was already an increasingly congested area.[22] 51st Highland Division's Operation Order makes no mention of an airborne element, nor of operating in conjunction with 7th

Armoured Division. It is possible that the lack of progress made on 11 June had led to the pincer movements effectively being isolated.

However, less than six hours later at 2115 on 12 June I Corps issued an order postponing Operation Smock. The operation was amended to take place on 13 June, and the objectives were modified to St Honorine, Cuverville and Escoville. The order to postpone Smock probably originated from Second Army, as at 1530 on 12 June Dempsey ordered Crocker not to move 4th Armoured Brigade in view of the threat of a German counter-attack north-west of Caen. 51st Highland Division were ordered to 'improve their positions' east of the Orne overnight, which appears to be a tacit acceptance that they would not be able to attack to the south. Although there is no reference to Operation Smock in Airborne documents at either corps or divisional level, 1st Parachute Brigade's Operation Order for Wild Oats includes a reference to Operation Sampan, with the intention to land in the Ranville, Demoville and Sannerville area to co-operate with 51st Highland Division.[23]

7th Armoured Division continued their advance the next day on 13 June and reached Villers-Bocage at 0845. The village was clear of enemy but an attempt to advance on Point 213 had to be abandoned after fierce German counter-attacks led by Michael Wittmann and the Desert Rats withdrew to the west to Tracy Bocage. A XXX Corps report the next day correctly identified that 2nd Panzer Division had arrived in the battlefront. Bucknall described the right hook by 7th Armoured Division as successful and that they were in command of Villers-Bocage. Yet by the afternoon his diary records that a heavy counter-attack by 2nd Panzer Division had beaten 7th Armoured Division out of Villers-Bocage.[24]

On the same day that Michael Wittmann repulsed the Desert Rats the generals were arguing fiercely about Wild Oats. On 13 June Leigh-Mallory discussed Wild Oats with De Guingand. Montgomery had reacted furiously to Leigh-Mallory's refusal to launch the operation:

> Do not repeat not understand refusal of LM to carry out airborne operations. I am working to create such favourable conditions as would make dropping of One Airborne Div in Évrecy area a good operation of war and one which if successful would pay a good dividend. Conditions have not repeat not yet been reached but may well be created by 14 June. LM should come over and see me and ascertain true form before he refuses to carry out an operation. He could get here by air in 30 minutes.

Although Montgomery's reaction – and not to mention his description of Leigh-Mallory as a 'gutless bugger' – was no doubt tactless and not conducive to inter-service relations, his argument that Leigh-Mallory should have flown to France does raise a valid point. The separation of headquarters across the Channel was not liable to encourage swift planning, particularly if the army wanted an operation mounted quickly. And if headquarters were separated, commanders needed to be prepared to communicate and travel back and forth as operations required.

That Leigh-Mallory felt comfortable vetoing the operation without flying to France to discuss it with Montgomery or Dempsey – and that neither of the generals attempted to override him – alludes to the power that the air commanders had over the launching of airborne operations. It is of course possible that if Leigh-Mallory had been more involved in the early planning of Wild Oats he may have been more amenable. Leigh-Mallory had form for being over-pessimistic with his judgement of airborne operations, as shown before D-Day. Richardson, Montgomery's chief planner, felt that Leigh-Mallory's sending of a signal rather than a visit caused a deterioration in personal relations. He described the atmosphere at HQ AEAF as a 'dangerous crisis'.[25]

Despite the air forces' objections Wild Oats was not completely cancelled and seems to have been quietly held in readiness by the army in case conditions changed. It was postponed for 24 hours by 21st Army Group on 12 June, for another 24 hours on 13 June and then suspended on 14 June, but held in readiness at 48 hours' notice, presumably in case conditions became favourable. On 13 June De Guingand wrote to Montgomery and informed him that Browning had met Leigh-Mallory, and that Dempsey had proposed a new date for Wild Oats on 15 June. On 16 June the division was placed at 72 hours' notice, and Wild Oats was only cancelled for good on 17 June.

Despite these postponements preparations for Wild Oats continued on the Continent. A message received by 30 Corps on 13 June indicated that an advance party from 1st Airborne Division would be arriving the next day. On 14 June the re-supply plans for Wild Oats were confirmed, code-named Whiterocks.

1st Airborne Division had not exercised with tanks before D-Day, a deficiency that had been noted by some airborne commanders. Hackett's 4th Parachute Brigade held Exercise Jael, with the object of practicing co-operation with tanks. The exercise was clearly influenced by Wild Oats, and the narrative for Jael gives an insight into how Hackett foresaw the operation developing. The operation had been launched on the night of 15 and 16 June, and 7th Armoured Division had reached Évrecy in time to hold the drop zones. Significant German traffic had been encountered in the area, including the headquarters of 12th SS Panzer Division. Cutting the Villers-Bocage–Caen road was the key objective. It is perhaps insightful that the one airborne commander who had given serious consideration to co-operation with tanks, Brigadier Hackett, was a cavalryman who had fought in tanks in the Desert. Lathbury's 1st Parachute Brigade also gave some thought to co-operation with armoured units. Perhaps also spurred on by Wild Oats, on 17 June Lathbury issued 1 Parachute Brigade Tactical Notes No. 7, 'Co-operation with tanks'.

On 14 June Montgomery wrote to Simpson again. Although he projected his customary confidence that everything was going to plan, he also acknowledged the reverse at Villers-Bocage.

> I had to think again when 2 Pz Div suddenly appeared last night. I think it had been intended for offensive action against 1 Corps. But it had to be used to plug the hole through which we have broken in the area Caumont – Villers-Bocage . . . So long as Rommel uses his strategic reserves to plug holes – this is good.[26]

Wild Oats was the last plan to use airborne forces in the Battle of Normandy. It is not clear exactly why, but a combination of the air planners' objections and the early stalemate followed by rapid progress towards the end of the battle must have played a part. This demonstrates one of the key challenges of airborne planning. In a stalemate it was uncertain if the ground forces would be able to link up in time, yet in mobile operations plans could not be drawn up in time and landing areas could be overrun quickly. Future set-piece operations in Normandy such as Epsom, Goodwood, Cobra and Bluecoat would be drawn up without an airborne component. This is despite several operations bearing strong similarities with Exercise Wake and the concept for airborne operations developed before D-Day.

De Guingand criticised the planning of Wild Oats by Second Army. He felt that the air commanders – in particular Leigh-Mallory – had not been informed about the operation until far too late, and hence had not been involved in its early planning and were therefore able to express their negative opinions too easily. De Guingand was concerned that Dempsey was accepting his proposed operation for 1st Airborne Division as a fact and was basing the rest of his operations on it, when, as has been previously seen, the air forces effectively held a veto over the launching of airborne operations. That they could be planned and proposed, without reference to the air forces who would deliver them, and by staffs who had no prior experience of planning airborne operations, may go some way to suggesting how subsequent operations transpired. There was clearly a disconnect between Montgomery and Dempsey and the air commanders in terms of airborne planning.

Dempsey appears to have been a prime mover in the plan for Wild Oats. In fact, he played a much more prominent and assertive part in the planning and decision-making for Wild Oats than has previously been thought. Dempsey has frequently been characterised as serving as a chief of staff while Montgomery micro-managed Second Army, but the story of Wild Oats suggests a much more complex picture.

Whilst Operation Perch had been planned in concept before D-Day, it is striking that what had been originally proposed in the guise of Wild Oats as a two division pincer-attack either side of Caen, linking up with an airborne division, was gradually reduced to a single attack by a weak armoured division without airborne assistance.

The cancellation of Wild Oats was a low-point in army-air relations during the Normandy campaign. It is hard to escape the conclusion that the air commanders dominated the decision-making. Leigh-Mallory seems to have been hostile to the operation from the start, and while Hollinghurst and Williams attempted to find a way in which the operation could be mounted, Urquhart played a minor role in the air conference on 11 June. The air commanders essentially held a veto over the launching of airborne operations regardless of the effect on the land battle, and which even Montgomery himself – let alone Urquhart – could not challenge. It has been suggested that this veto over the launching of airborne operations was the long-term price of securing the Royal Air Force's co-operation in developing airborne forces earlier in the war.[27] Whether this is the case or not, it is hard not to see parallels with the way in which the air commanders would later dominate key decision making during the planning of Operation Market Garden, particularly the choice of drop zones and limiting the number of lifts that could be taken in one day.

The Wild Oats debacle does seem to have led to something of a 'clear the air' moment between Montgomery and Leigh-Mallory. On 14 June Leigh-Mallory sent a signal to Montgomery regarding proposed roles for 1st Airborne Division, and the two commanders began to discuss airborne operations in a way that would have been useful prior to the conception of Wild Oats.

Frictions between the Army and Air Force commanders dogged the Allied forces throughout the Normandy campaign, particularly in 21st Army Group. On 7 July Montgomery wrote to Brooke stating that he had spoken directly to Tedder about his problems with Coningham, who he felt that the Army had a lack of confidence in. He also felt that the Army was not getting the air support that it needed due to friction between Leigh-Mallory and Coningham. In the same letter, however, Montgomery also conceded that Dempsey and his staff at Second Army 'do not know a very great deal yet about how to wield air power', but that he also felt that Coningham was aware of this and exploited it for his own purpose. Montgomery, in his usual way, explained that he was trying to 'teach' Dempsey about air matters.[28]

It is interesting to reflect on what might have been with Wild Oats. The original concept borrowed much from the lessons of Exercise Wake, carried out by VIII Corps before D-Day. Like Wake, Wild Oats envisaged dropping an airborne division behind the German front lines and relieving it with an armour-led attack. In the event, the advance took place west of Caen rather than to the east as intended during Wake, and the operation was carried out by XXX Corps, as there was not enough space in the bridgehead for VIII Corps to land in time. VIII Corps would later carry out another attack to the west of Caen during Operation Epsom that bore strong similarities to Wake, but without airborne assistance.[29]

How might Operation Perch have fared if 1st Airborne Division had been dropped around Évrecy as hoped? As events at Arnhem would show, airborne troops were extremely vulnerable to armoured counter-attacks if they could not be reinforced swiftly. Even though the arrival of 10,000 airborne troops south of Panzer Lehr's positions, and in a crucial area, would have caused the Germans a great deal of disruption, the swift reaction of the Germans to Allied attacks during the 1944 campaign suggests that any air landing would have been hotly received.

Bucknall's performance throughout the Battle of Normandy was a disappointment to Dempsey, who never seems to have been an admirer, and Montgomery who had specifically requested him to command XXX Corps against Brooke's judgement. Bucknall had previously commanded 5th Division in Italy and letters in Bucknall's papers suggest a very warm relationship between himself and Montgomery, going as far as to virtually beg the latter to take his division back to Britain for Overlord.[30]

After the end of the war Chester Wilmot corresponded with most of the senior commanders in North West Europe, including Bucknall.[31] Even in 1947 Bucknall and Dempsey recalled Perch and Villers-Bocage very differently. Bucknall felt that the plan for Perch was his and that he merely asked Dempsey's permission to carry it out. He did not recall being briefed on the wider objectives of Noyers and Évrecy or the plan for Wild Oats on 12 June and felt that if they had been mentioned he would 'certainly have remarked upon it' as it would have gone beyond his own plan and the resources available to him. He could not recall anything regarding the airborne plans to work in conjunction with XXX Corps and had made no preparations for it. He stated that 'It would have required most careful preparation and co-ordination'. He recalled Perch as being aimed at a 'sharp blow' to extend the beachhead and nothing more, and that it was a Corps objective, not an Army one. He saw Second Army's objective as Caen, and he felt that his operations were not a priority in that regard.

Wilmot replied to Bucknall that Dempsey had told him that he had given orders for 7th Armoured Division's switch to Erskine direct and told Bucknall, and that the plan for an airborne drop at Évrecy was very much in his mind. Bucknall's response was that 'this may be so, but it was not mentioned to me to the extent of requiring extrication, or more troops, and was also very limited, quite rightly, in artillery ammunition allotment'. He went on to say that:

Gen Browning and I had discussed with each other the various possibilities in which we might with advantage employ Airborne cooperation. This was not one of them. Moreover, it is for consideration whether such an op would not have been a dispersion of effort here? The main battle was proceeding for the capture of Caen. Perch was a subsidiary op to fix the front of 30 Corps (and incidentally act as a diversion). 30 Corps was told not to get involved again and to work out the time and space problem.

Wilmot replied that Dempsey had clearly regarded Perch as a more substantial operation, and refers to Dempsey's diary in which he saw XXX Corps as threatening Caen from the west, as well as identifying plans to envelope the city from the east and west. Wilmot suggested that Dempsey had seen Perch as a 'stepping stone to much greater things'. Bucknall responded that he had conceived Perch himself as a local effort to break up opposition on his front, but that it was seized upon by Dempsey as a 'possibly valuable adjunct' to the plan to capture Caen if the battle went well. Bucknall also stated that the success of Perch was not essential to the capture of Caen and that plans to capture Caen were made irrespective of XXX Corps. He also stated that he could not remember the code name Wild Oats, but that his Corps staff and the Airborne staff were not enthusiastic about the operation.

Wild Oats has been subject to some inaccurate descriptions by historians, which reflects the wildly differing accounts from the senior commanders involved. One author has even described the operation as being planned for near Carpiquet in the 12th SS Panzer Division area to block German reinforcements, but was rendered unnecessary by a Canadian ground advance.[32] Whilst Wild Oats was frequently mentioned before D-Day, the concept prior to the landings featured an airborne drop linking up with a single armoured thrust out of the beachhead. The modified plan proposed in the days after D-Day featured two pincer movements east and west of Caen. 7th Armoured Division would advance to the Évrecy area, while 51st Highland Division would attack out of the airborne bridgehead east of the River Orne, to occupy the high ground around Bourguébus.

Veterans recalled Wild Oats very strongly in their memories post-war, and it is the most-cited example of an operation being cancelled at the last minute. The senior commanders seem to have been fairly sceptical about Wild Oats. Urquhart described his relief in his memoirs, and described it as 'aptly named'.[33] John Frost was also not impressed with the plan: '. . . we were very nearly called upon in the early stages and some of the tasks envisaged were hazardous in the extreme. One of the occasions we were to drop virtually on top of one of the panzer divisions attacking the beachhead.'[34]

Panzers do indeed feature strongly in thoughts about Wild Oats. Major John Waddy commanded a company in 156th Parachute Battalion:

It got very frustrating. We actually loaded the aircraft twice if not three times, and another 24 hours cancellation, then another 24 hour stand down. One of them we were very relieved, we got as far as not quite sitting in the aircraft, on the airfield in Normandy, which was going to drop the Division on the ridge South-West of Caen, Carpiquet. Just ahead of an armoured push Op Goodwood. That kept being put back 24 hours and then finally cancelled. And we knew that that it was going to be hard because we were ordered to carry Hawkins Grenades, each man was issued with two of these. And the drill was that as soon as we landed we were going to use these Hawkins mines to blow weapons pits. We knew that we were going to be attacked very quickly. We were lucky that we didn't do it as afterwards we heard that there was a Panzer Division on the ridge. I think it was cancelled because the ground forces weren't ready and hadn't achieved their first objective.[35]

William Carter was serving with 1st Parachute Battalion:

We went to Brize Norton – I think the actual invasion had started then – and we went down there, we were going to be part of an operation, I think they were being held up at the Falaise Gap, and that's where we briefed on dropping to bridge the gap where they were trying to break out. But I think they foresaw that it was going to be a suicidal thing because at the last minute we were cancelled.[36]

Mike Brown was serving as a glider pilot. His recollections show how the glider pilots were supporting both airborne divisions, and that many of the crews who returned from Normandy were at readiness again almost immediately:

> The people hadn't gone on D-Day had already been briefed for another operation. And some gliders had been loaded up ready to go. And some of us, about 10 of us, about 10 crews, were needed to make up the numbers. When we got back to Down Ampney they wanted some of us to go join the other lot and go again. And we were briefed there and then to go. This was, I think it was Wild Oats it was called.[37]

John McGeough was also serving as a glider pilot. His memories included the location of Wild Oats, possibly as glider pilots had been briefed in more detail: 'Another plan which was never put into operation was to land gliderborne troops near the village of Évrecy south of Caen. And our objective was to take out a large house which was the headquarters of the Gestapo. Of course that was cancelled.'[38]

A great deal of hindsight has been applied to understanding of Wild Oats. It is often difficult to discern what are memories and what has been influenced by historiography and popular culture. This is not to suggest that any participants might be inaccurate, but to emphasise that the profile afforded to Arnhem, including legions of books, films and TV series, can have a very formative influence. Indeed, veterans thoughts on Wild Oats often reference the threat of German tanks – a key part of the story of Market Garden.

Some elements of Wild Oats were, on the face of it, more sensible than Market Garden. The distance from the start line of the advance to the landing area was much shorter. The Airborne Division would have landed in a much more compact area, and, critically, the airborne force would only have taken off once the armoured units were on the drop zones.

Might Wild Oats have worked? It might perhaps have been a closer-run thing than many historians have predicted, but as with all airborne operations the margins would have been very fine, and highly dependent on the reaction of German units on the ground.

Part III – Brittany

OPERATION BENEFICIARY

The demise of Wild Oats heralded the end of airborne planning in Normandy itself. However, the Allies had already considered potential airborne operations to support the wider campaign in Northern France. In particular, the Brittany peninsula had been identified as an objective due to its deep-water ports, which would be valuable for securing the logistics of the Allied forces. The US Army had a large number of divisions back across the Atlantic waiting to move to Europe, and securing Brittany would enable them to be shipped directly to France.

Planning for airborne operations in Brittany began soon after the D-Day landings. On 14 June De Guingand wrote to Montgomery regarding airborne operations in the peninsula.[1] He explained that 21st Army Group staff had held several planning meetings and had concluded that it would be improbable that a separate airborne and seaborne operation for the capture of St Malo would be required, and that it would be easier to capture St Malo overland. While De Guingand felt that it should be considered in case the operational situation might change, with the existing enemy garrison and the need to land on either side of the estuary the Allies would not have sufficient airborne troops without 1st Airborne Division. The naval forces were not keen on an assault by sea as it would take away craft which were urgently required for the build-up in Normandy.

On 18 June Browning sent a paper to HQ 21st Army Group and AEAF regarding airborne operations in Brittany, described formally as 'project to increase the speed of build-up of Third US Army without distracting from the Overlord operations'.[2] Browning assumed that '. . . no project is worth consideration by 21 Army Group if it delays the Overlord build-up and operation. The corollary is that no landing craft or ships of the types used for beach landings can be spared from Overlord while the Neptune beaches are used to capacity.' Browning believed that there would be enough spare shipping to land at least one corps as part of a seaborne assault and that a successful operation

85

could make it unnecessary for First US Army to have to bother about Brittany at all.

Browning's paper did not mention St Malo, but described the overall strategy of airborne operations in the Brittany peninsula. Specifically, Browning outlined the requirement for any operations to be the capture of an airfield for landing of airportable formations and sufficient moonlight. There would be a suitable moon period between 28 June and 12 July. It would also be essential to wait until the enemy has no reserves available. A target date of 6 July was suggested for the airborne operation with the seaborne element landing seven days later.

Montgomery's directive M504 of 19 June mentioned that a study was being made

> of the possibility of seizing St Malo by airborne operations from England, and then bringing into that port a Corps of Third US Army . . . If this can be done it would enable the whole tempo of the operations to be speeded up, since Third Army would be in close touch with First Army and everything would thus be more simple.[3]

On 21 and 22 June Leigh-Mallory discussed the St Malo scheme with the AEAF Airborne Operations staff. 'The Army' were described as 'not interested' in Beneficiary due to the strength of German forces believed to be there.[4] There is no evidence to suggest who 'the Army' were, or why they were 'not interested' in Beneficiary. Despite this apparent reluctance, a conference was held in the AEAF war room on 23 June to discuss airborne operations, including Beneficiary. General Whiteley from SHAEF said that 21st Army Group were not in favour of landing troops in the St Malo area as it was too well held for a successful operation. Eisenhower's original suggestion that they should drop the Polish Parachute Brigade and one US Parachute Infantry Regiment in the St Malo area had been made subject to agreement by 21st Army Group, who were now definitely against it and thought that St Malo could be occupied by land operations alone. Leigh-Mallory asked whether it was understood when this decision was taken that the airborne assault was to be followed by further airborne landings or seaborne landings. General Whiteley said that this had been realised and even so the scheme had not been thought practicable. The Army were more in favour of an operation which would help them to seize Quiberon Bay after the occupation of St Malo, since they regarded it as the best port for maintaining their forces. Leigh-Mallory thought that the merits of Brest as a port had been very much underestimated and that the strength of German forces in the Brest peninsula had been overestimated. Already the Allies were debating the merits of three of the Brittany ports.

On 22 June Major General Urquhart visited HQ Airborne Troops at Moor Park where Browning outlined his division's role in Beneficiary.[5] Urquhart then conducted his O-Group on 24 June, but while he was completing his orders information arrived that the operation would not take place before 1 August. A co-ordinating conference took place the next day at Eastcote before 1st Airborne Division's Planning Intelligence Summary was issued on 27 June. The Intelligence Summary focused in detail on the enemy situation in the St Malo area, shows the wealth of intelligence on Brittany that was available to the Allies in 1944, with Appendix A giving an enemy order of battle and Appendix E showing drop and landing zone layouts. The Airborne units certainly seem to have been provided with much more intelligence than during the planning of previous operations, when information ranged from scarce to non-existent, and indeed during future plans later in the campaign.

HQ Airborne Troops Instructions for the planning of Operation Beneficiary were issued on 26 June.[6] The object was the capture of the port of St Malo and to hold it for the disembarkation of Third Army. Two alternative methods were proposed. The first was an assault by the US ground forces from the east near Avranches assisted by one parachute brigade group, probably the 504th Parachute Infantry Regiment, with 1st Airborne Division stood by to reinforce if necessary. The second method was an independent airborne assault followed by seaborne forces from Third Army which would not sail from Britain until St Malo was secured. Naval forces would have to attack coastal defences on several small islands north of St Malo, but apart from that it was hoped that the seaborne troops would be able to sail straight into the port. The second method was favoured by Browning for further planning purposes.

Planning for Beneficiary was to be co-ordinated between Allied Naval Expeditionary Forces, FUSAG (what would later become US 12th Army Group), AEAF and HQ Airborne Troops. HQ Airborne Troops was authorised to plan directly with AEAF, 38 Group and IX USTCC and 504th Parachute Infantry. All airborne forces would be under the command of HQ Airborne Troops, who would provide a Tactical Headquarters to command operations until a corps headquarters arrived from Third Army. HQ Airborne Troops would fly in up to six Horsa gliders. That HQ Airborne Troops – at this time still an administrative headquarters – was planning to take part in an operation for which it had not been established and for which its personnel had not trained, hints at an impetus to get it into battle that would be increasingly evident during the planning for further operations.

1st Airborne Division would be carried in by approximately 300 parachute aircraft and 500 gliders, and 504th Parachute Infantry in about 220 aircraft and approximately 30 Waco gliders. 6th Airlanding Anti-Aircraft Battery was also available to take part if required but its aircraft would have to be provided from the allocation given to 1st Airborne Division. Up to two US Airfield Construction Battalions were shortlisted to take part to repair Dinard airfield. SAS units were also to take part and it was hoped that they would be able to link up with and co-operate with the French Resistance, who were very active in Brittany.

The estimated date for launching Beneficiary would be any time between 6–9 July 1944. The outline plan called for 1st Airborne Division to capture and hold St Malo and a bridgehead east of the River Rance. The division would also be prepared to capture the bridge at La Chambre and after the capture of St Malo be prepared to detach up to one brigade group to assist 504th Parachute Infantry west of the Rance. 504th Parachute Infantry Regiment were to prepare alternative plans for the capture of Dinard airfield and Dinard itself. Browning thought that it was unlikely that the US seaborne troops would arrive for at least 48 hours after the airborne assault and that the airborne troops should be prepared for no relief on the ground earlier than four days after the airborne assault. It is unknown what this advice was based on.

The terrain around St Malo was challenging. The Rance is a steep-sided valley estuary separating Dinard from St Malo, around a mile and a half wide and 10 miles long. The St Malo peninsula itself is high and broken up in the north, but flatter further inland, and there were three road and one rail bridge over river between St Malo and Dinard near mouth. The only bridges over the river were long and high and could have been easily demolished. There were orchards on both sides of the valley and fields in the area were small and bounded by hedges and trees, which would have seriously limited the ability of the airborne forces to manoeuvre after landing. Dinard airfield was heavily defended and intelligence suggested that the runways had been put out of action by the Germans. It was estimated that after capture it might take three or four days to get the airfield operational again.

Unlike earlier plans for airborne operations the planning for Beneficiary included detailed reference to the enemy situation. The 5th Parachute Division were holding the coast between Avranches and St Brieuc. However, if the enemy situation in Normandy deteriorated any further the division would probably be used to reinforce the

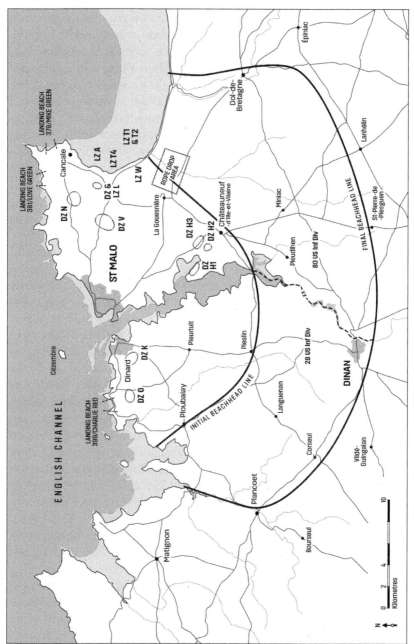

Map 6: Drop zones and objectives for Beneficiary. (Sources: TNA WO 205/845)

front line. The 136th Infantry Division were holding the coast from Dinard westwards and there were possibly up to three battalions in the area including around the airfield. Its personnel were mainly Russian, Tartar and Turkmen and one Russian battalion was thought to have light tanks. It was also assumed that there would be elements of German marines and naval personnel in St Malo along with Luftwaffe anti-aircraft troops at Dinard. Flak was thought to be light except in the vicinity of Dinard airfield and port and coastal defences were believed to be light except around Dinard, St Malo and the islands. St Malo and Dinard had been organised for all-round defence with concrete strongpoints, anti-tank obstacles and gun batteries with linking fields of fire. Like Antwerp later in 1944 the port at St Malo would not have been usable unless the mouth of the river was held on both sides and Dinard and St Malo were captured.

1st Airborne Division Operation Instruction for Beneficiary was issued on 28 June and a Planning Intelligence Summary the next day.[7] 1st Parachute Brigade would land on DZs A and F and would take and hold the town and port of St Malo north of the railway line. After being relieved by 4th Parachute Brigade they would then move eastwards to 'mop up' coastal defences north of the St Malo-Cancale road. 4th Parachute Brigade would land on DZs X and E. They would take and hold the port and town south of the railway lines and then take over the whole of the town while 1st Brigade cleared the coastal defences. 1st Airlanding Brigade would land on LZs L, N and Y and would take up a covering position to the south and east of St Malo. Battalions and companies would be detached for specific tasks including the capture of road junctions and high ground, and clearing the landing zones. Divisional troops would land on LZ Y and Hamilcar gliders on LZ Z. With a Landing Zone on the beach transport routes inland were carefully planned with four routes designated towards concentration areas. Traffic would have to be controlled carefully and beach exits might have required clearing by engineers. The Intelligence Summary gave detailed information of German defences in the St Malo area, many of them identified by the interpretation of aerial photographs. Airborne units would also receive substantial mapping and traces. This is the last mention of Beneficiary in the division's war diary.

SHAEF planning staff held a conference on 29 June and the next day issued a paper considering the logistical implications of airborne operations in Brittany, including Beneficiary.[8] The SHAEF staff were concerned that as Beneficiary would require the capture of both sides of the Rance Estuary the airborne forces would be divided and exposed to defeat in detail. In addition coast defences would have to be captured before seaborne landings could take place. The paper concluded that Beneficiary was likely to succeed only if the present garrison in the St Malo area was substantially reduced.

At the time of planning Beneficiary work was also being done to plan for two other operations, Lucky Strike and Hands Up.[9] 21st Army Group drew up staff studies for Beneficiary and Lucky Strike on 1 and 2 July respectively. A draft outline for Beneficiary was completed on 2 July and shared with First US Army Group on 4 July. A conference on beach reconnaissance for Beneficiary would be held at HQ Airborne Troops on 5 July, with planning teams from 1st Airborne Division and 504th Parachute Infantry Regiment arriving at Moor Park the same day. Details would be tied up with XX US Corps the same day. Planning for Beneficiary was to be completed by the morning of 6 July, while similar processes were taking place concurrently for Hands Up and Lucky Strike.

The airborne planning process sheds light on an aspect of these operations that is often misunderstood. Whilst it is often thought that for every operation thousands of troops boarded aircraft and gliders only to be stood down, this only happened in a small number of cases. A sizeable proportion of the operations did not reach below the divisional level. Perhaps the greatest strain was on the planning staffs, who in early July were planning several tri-service operations concurrently and working with multiple headquarters and formations spread between the UK and the Continent. In early July the planning itself was becoming so congested that the process was scheduled as if it was an operation in itself.

On 6 July Eisenhower sent a memorandum to Bedell Smith.[10] Eisenhower limited airborne operations to the equivalent of a reinforced division until transport aircraft could return from assisting with Anvil in the south of France:

> A basic feature of anticipated operations in northwest France has been the employment of a large, concentrated airborne force. Due to the delay in returning the original three airborne divisions to England, and the fact that 384 of our transport aircraft must go to the Mediterranean by the end of the current month, it would be impossible to do any really large scale operations here before September. However, I do not want to abandon this concept and desire that planning proceed, involving every likely objective for such an operation.

The situation in the Brittany peninsula and the shortage of transport aircraft led Eisenhower to re-consider Beneficiary and order his staff to resurrect the operation with a target date of 4 to 8 August.

The US Army had established Base Sections to organise troops and supplies, and the Base Section No. 1 plan for Beneficiary was issued on 6 July.[11] The Base Section would land across the beaches and restore the port facilities in St Malo, provide service forces and coordinate the phasing-in of supplies. Beneficiary would require the return of an Engineer Shore Brigade from Normandy to Britain with a minimum of 20 days' preparation before the operation. An advance party of 372 Base Section troops would land on D-Day, before the Base Section headquarters would come ashore at St Malo on D+3. It would take 12 days to get the port facilities into operation both there and at Dinard, while XX Corps would support their own troops over the assault beaches assisted by the Engineer Shore Brigade. The Base Section planned to have 20,311 troops ashore by D+22. A 400-bed Field Hospital would be established in St Malo by D+6 followed by a General Hospital at Dol later. Areas had already been identified for fuel, medical and engineer supply dumps.

The Engineer Plan assumed that the port would be captured on D-Day. Engineer reconnaissance elements would land on D+1 followed by the main party of engineers on D+3. It was planned that the port would eventually handle 2,000 tons per day by D+60. The aim was to handle cargo by lighters and small coasters. Fourteen lighter berths would be constructed and a floating berth for coasters, while beach exits would be constructed to allow DUKWs to unload supplies over the beaches. The Base Section would include three Engineer General Service Regiments, three Engineer Dump Truck Companies, a firefighting platoon, the British dredger *Mudeford*, an Engineer Port Repair Ship, an Engineer Construction Battalion, an Engineer Maintenance Company, an Engineer Gasoline General Unit and an Engineer Depot Company.

St Malo was a substantial port. It had four large basins, each accessed via locks. Sites had already been identified for a fuel installation, a tank park, supply dump areas, lighterage pierheads and a floating coaster dock. It was predicted that the port facilities at St Malo would probably be damaged by demolitions, including the locks and gates. It was estimated that 90 per cent of the quays would probably be unusable, and that craft would be sunk alongside and in the channels. This reflected the kind of damage that was found when Cherbourg was liberated.

The period from D+1 to D+10 would be spent on site reconnaissance and the preparation of a detailed construction plan, while engineers would construct beach exits and ramps on the assault beaches. By D+20 it was hoped to have eight lighterage pierheads completed outside of the locked basins and by D+30 a 600ft floating berth for small coasters. The water supply and electrical systems would be repaired by D+30. The lock basins would be cleared by D+40 and six lighterage berths would be completed in the Vauban basin. It was hoped that the port would be operating at full capacity by D+60. A recce party of five officers and 20 men from the 1057th Port Construction Group would land on the beaches on D+1, consisting of two companies from the 378th Regiment and the 373rd Engineer General Service Regiment.

The Base Section also planned a significant road construction programme. In total 96 miles of roads would be built by D+30, at a rate of six miles per day. It was assumed that 75 to 100 per cent of the bridges in the area would be destroyed along with up to 90 per cent of the culverts. Forty miles of railway track would also be laid from St Malo to Pontaubault, south of Avranches. This line would be completed by D+46 and would involve the reconstruction of up to thirty-six bridges.

The Base Section's Quartermaster Plan called for a 250,000ft^2 General Storage area on the eastern outskirts of the town by D+10 and an eight acre fuel storage area to the south east with a capacity of 2,000 tons by D+8. Other quartermaster units in the port area would include a bakery company, five service companies, two gasoline supply companies, two railhead companies, four quartermaster battalions, a sterilisation company, a grave registration company, two laundry platoons and a petrol production laboratory.

The Base Section's Transport Plan would see a detachment from the 12th Major Port (Overseas) take over the running of St Malo and the beaches from D+3. Liberty ships would anchor in the open roadstead and be discharged into lighters and barges or beached at high tide. The 12th Major Port included three Port Battalions, nine Port Companies, a Harbour Craft Company, a Port Maritime Maintenance Company, two firefighting platoons, two Quartermaster Truck Companies and an Amphibian Truck Company. The Base Section's Provost Marshal would have the 79th Military Police Battalion under command. A 150,000ft^2 open-air prisoner of war cage would be set up by D+15 with a capacity for 1,000 prisoners.

From D-Day until D+15 medical casualties would be handled by XX Corps. From D+15 any casualties who would not return to duty within seven days would be evacuated to the UK. From D+5 the 49th Field Hospital would be in St Malo with three surgical teams. The 95th General Hospital would be in the Dol region from D+15, and would have 400 beds by D+22 and 1,000 beds by D+27. There would also be a Medical Ambulance Company, a Medical Depot Company and a Lines of Communications Blood Depot Group. All personnel would be immunised against smallpox, typhoid, typhus and tetanus. The Base Section's medical staff predicted that venereal disease would be prevalent and all medical units were to set up prophylactic stations, with extra stations set up as troop numbers increased. Troops would be briefed to make use of 'mechanical prophylactics' and V-packets.

The HQ Airborne Troops plan for Beneficiary was not issued until 7 July, during the initial window in which it was hoped that Beneficiary might take place.[12] The delay was presumably due to slower than expected progress in breaking out of the Normandy beachhead to the extent that the provisional date for launching Beneficiary was moved to 1 August. The plan envisaged that the 5th Parachute Division was likely to move east towards Avranches to meet the advance of Allied forces from the Normandy area and that it was also possible that the 319th Infantry Division that was garrisoning the Channel Islands could be evacuated via St Malo, and hence strengthen the German forces in Brittany.

Browning would command all airborne troops during the airborne phase of the operation, but the commander of XX US Corps would assume command of all troops once his headquarters had been established ashore. Urquhart would command all troops east of the Rance – airborne and seaborne – until XX Corps arrived, while the commander of 504th Parachute Infantry Regiment would do likewise for all troops west of the Rance until the US 28th Division arrived. In the context of Allied relations with the Polish Parachute Brigade it is interesting that Major General Sosabowski was to be placed under the command of a colonel commanding a US Parachute Infantry Regiment. It is also interesting to contemplate how Browning would have commanded his forces which would be divided by the Rance. It could well be considered that a corps headquarters was not necessary for the carrying out of the airborne operation.

Dinard airfield was not to be captured immediately, but within 24 hours of the seaborne landing to enable reinforcement by air if the seaborne reinforcements were delayed by bad weather. This proscription does seem remarkably similar to Browning's orders to General Gavin during Market Garden to not prioritise the capture of the bridge at Nijmegen, which resulted in it having to be captured several days later in conjunction with the relief forces.

The planned use of SAS troops in Beneficiary showed imagination in the use of special forces that was not always present in other airborne operations. One SAS squadron would drop twenty-five small parties in the general area of Dol, Fontorbon, St Aubin, Montauban, Placort and Dinan to disrupt enemy reserves. The SAS were to be prepared to operate for six to seven days, after which they would withdraw into the bridgehead or contact the 4th French Parachute Battalion in area.

Upon landing the first wave of seaborne forces would come under command of the airborne units. 1st Airborne Division and 504th Parachute Infantry Regiment would each take under command one Infantry Regiment from the US 28th Division, one DD tank battalion, one tank destroyer company, two 105mm field artillery battalions and one of 155mm field artillery.

It was still intended to drop some glider troops on the beaches. The orders stated that the exact times for landings would be dependent on the state of moon and tide as the main landing zone was below the high-water mark. The parachute drops would take place soon after darkness, followed by glider landings. Given the fiasco in Sicily when many gliders were cast off into the sea it is hard not to foresee that dropping gliders on a beach landing zone below the tide line could have been fraught with problems. It appears that Beneficiary declined in priority after HQ Airborne Troops orders were issued, for the war diary does not mention the operation at all after 7 July.

The commander of XX Corps, Major General Walton H. Walker, sent his plan for Beneficiary to Patton on 7 July.[13] He predicted that stormy weather, high tides, offshore obstacles and the rugged coastline would limit the options for landing over the Brittany beaches. Walker argued that the available beaches were widely separated, small and unfavourable for opposed landings. To have a reasonable chance of success, Walker argued, obstacles on the assault beaches would need to be cleared by the airborne troops before the seaborne landings. Even then, Walker thought that delays in landing seaborne troops might subject the airborne forces to defeat in detail. The navy had also estimated that it would take a considerable time to get St Malo into operation after it had been captured.

The XX Corps plan envisaged the Allied forces in the Neptune area having reached Avranches and Argentan before Beneficiary would be launched. The airborne forces would begin landing between 12 and 48 hours before the seaborne forces. They would clear the beach defences and then 'initiate action' to capture St Malo and Dinard as well as the initial beachhead line and begin repairing Dinard airfield. The seaborne forces would land at halfway through a rising tide. Once 28th Division began landing the airborne force would send an airborne element to join the Divisional headquarters.

It was hoped that the airborne forces would be assisted by the French Resistance, who would demolish bridges to isolate the beachhead from

German reinforcements but prevent the destruction of the railway bridge over the Rance at Vicomte and the dam at La Quinardais.

The US Army's Communications Zone – known as COMZ – would land an Engineer Construction Battalion and a reconnaissance force of 200 men to continue clearing the beach defences and to commence work on getting the port at St Malo into service and the 28th Infantry Division would be followed by 80th Infantry Division and 6th Armoured Division. Upon landing 110th Infantry Regiment from 28th Division would come under the command of 1st Airborne Division, but once 80th Infantry Division had landed and passed through, the regiment would revert to their command and assemble around Chateauneuf as a corps reserve.

28th Infantry Division would land with three armoured field artillery battalions equipped with 105mm howitzers, two DD tank battalions, a tank destroyer battalion, one anti-aircraft battalion, a chemical mortar battalion, two engineer construction battalions, a grave registration platoon, six naval shore fire-control parties and two air support parties. The division would land one a two-regiment front with the western regiment over Charlie Red on the Dinard Peninsula and the eastern regiment over Mike Green and Love Green on the Cancale Peninsula. The reserve regiment would land over Dinard but be prepared to switch to the east at short notice. One battalion of the reserve regiment would be prepared to land on Cezembre to neutralise the coastal defence batteries. Divisional headquarters would land on Charlie Red at Dinard and would take command of all troops west of the Rance, whilst 1st Airborne Division would command all troops to the east. Once Dinard had been secured the 504th Regiment and the Polish Brigade would go into corps reserve around Pleslin.

The 80th Infantry Division would have under command a tank battalion, a tank destroyer battalion, an anti-aircraft battalion and two grave registration platoons. It would land with one regiment at Dinard and another at Cancale, with the regiment landing at Dinard coming under the command of 28th Division and divisional headquarters landing at Cancale. The division would concentrate at Limonay and prepare to pass through 1st Airborne Division and occupy the beachhead line east of the Rance. 6th Armoured Division and other corps troops were to be prepared to move to the continent, but their task was not described further. Presumably the armoured division would have had a breakout and exploitation role.

XX Corps directed units on the beachhead line to maintain aggressive patrolling, particularly to the south and south-east. No enemy installations were to be destroyed unless they could not be captured intact. COMZ was to receive priority in St Malo and Dinard after the towns had been captured, to get the port facilities operations.

The Engineer Plan would see three Engineer Combat Battalions landed, with one company on each beach. The assault engineers would deal with the beach obstacles above the tide line at H-Hour, create gaps and mark minefields. They would also breach or bypass obstacles to create two exits from each beach. Each engineer platoon would take along 47 Bangalore torpedoes, 2,470 explosive charges and nine mine detectors. Each assault company would use three 2.5-ton dumper trucks, while the 103rd Engineer Battalion would build roads.

A detailed fire-support plan had been drawn up by XX Corps. It identified the gun batteries on Cezembre and ten emplacements and strongpoints along the coast, including in St Malo itself. Additional targets would be identified as intelligence became available. Naval gunfire would be on call for the seaborne and airborne troops via naval gunfire support parties and air support via air support tentacles.[14] Prior to the seaborne and airborne troops linking up the seaborne troops would only call for fire onto targets firing on the beaches, presumably to avoid friendly fire.

H-Hour would see the 2nd Battalion of 110th Infantry Regiment landing on Beach 379 (Mike Green), the 3rd Battalion of the same regiment on Beach 381 (Love Green) and the 1st Battalion of the 190th Infantry Regiment on Beach 399 (Charlie Red). The rest of both regiments would land within 70 minutes, with the advanced divisional command post arriving several hours later. The rest of the division would land over Beach 399 at high tide on D+1. The Tank Destroyer Battalion would arrive on D+2.

28th Infantry Division's plan for Beneficiary was also issued on 7 July.[15] The division would land and secure a beachhead 'preparatory to further operations'. It was assumed that the 1st Airborne Division would have already cleared the beach obstacles and would have occupied Dinard as well as the initial beachhead line five miles south of St Malo. The division would consist of 13,936 men and 2,227 vehicles along with 7,152 men and 1,770 vehicles attached.

The 109th Infantry Regiment would land on Beach 399 with one battalion in assault formation. After landing they would contact 504th Parachute Infantry Regiment and prepare to advance inland. The 112th Infantry Regiment, minus one battalion, would be in divisional reserve and would land over Beach 399. It would assemble and prepare to advance to either the south or west. The regiment was also to be prepared to land over beaches 379 and 381 if ordered to do so. The regiment's 1st Battalion would land and capture the Ile de Cezembre with a company of tanks under command.

Aerial reconnaissance would take place of the roads and railways between the Fougeres–Vitre area towards Dinan every three hours from daylight until dusk on D-Day. Coverage would also include the three roads leading south from Dinan to Tinteniac, Becherel and Caulnes. On D-10 the Allied air forces would photograph the area bounded by St Cast, Plancoet, Dol de Bretagne and Pointe du Grouin, including Cezembre, to study changes in defence construction. They would also photograph the defences from St Briac to Cancale at low tide on D-10, D-8 and D-3 including oblique photographs like the beach silhouettes produced of the Normandy coastline before D-Day. At H-3 hours the area around the road to Pleslin and La Giolais would be photographed to check for artillery positions and the concentrations of troops. The whole operational area would be systematically photographed to obtain oblique images, with an emphasis on the road network, likely concentrations of reinforcements and beach defences. Once the Allies had landed the west flank would be reconnoitred by the 28th Reconnaissance Regiment from the River Fremur south to Trelat and provide security for the division's right flank between Plancoet and Le Guildo.

The 28th Division Intelligence Summary identified two coastal batteries on Cezembre, the 753rd Wach Battalion in St Malo, a Russian battalion on the coast north-west of Cancale and another on the coast west of Dinard, and a naval battalion on the coast west of Dinard. Two battalions of the 5th Parachute Division were in St Malo and Dinard while the rest of the division was at Dinan. It estimated that the first enemy reinforcements would arrive six hours after H-Hour from the Russian coastal battalions. Within 48 hours the Germans would have brought up four infantry divisions, on training division and three Russian battalions.

First US Army Group's joint plan for Operation Beneficiary was submitted to SHAEF on 8 July 1944.[16] The plan had been drawn up in consultation with representatives from Allied Naval Expeditionary Forces, US Ninth Air Forces, HQ Airborne Troops and the Communications Zone and was intended to provide a framework to allow the forces involved to develop their detailed planning. The operation was to be planned under the co-ordination of FUSAG with US Third Army planning the ground and airborne aspects.

The FUSAG plan gave the objective of Beneficiary as the capture a bridgehead around the port of St Malo to facilitate the bringing-in of supplies and additional troops to assist the breakout from the

Normandy beachhead towards Avranches and Argentan. The joint plan for Beneficiary was divided into four phases. The first phase would be a preliminary bombardment of the coastal defences and anti-aircraft batteries in the St Malo and Dinard area and the island of Cezembre. The second phase would be an airborne landing to neutralise the beach defences and remove beach obstacles, and to capture the landing beaches. The airborne troops would be assisted by SAS units, Special Forces HQ and the local French Resistance. The third phase would be a seaborne follow-up landing, then the landing of specialist troops and equipment to open the port at St Malo.

The topography and tides of the St Malo area were described as formidable, with severely limited options for landing beaches and drop zones. The plan stated that Beneficiary would only stand a reasonable chance of success if the enemy had no reserves available north of the Loire and west of Rennes, except the 'skeleton' forces left to garrison the Brittany coastal defences. The US 28th Division was earmarked for the seaborne assault and was transferred from SHAEF reserve to Third Army. The airborne force would comprise 1st British Airborne Division, the 1st Independent Polish Parachute Brigade, the 504th Parachute Infantry Regiment and the 878th Airborne Aviation Engineer Battalion.

Planning for the airborne aspect of Beneficiary was delegated to HQ Airborne Forces. The airborne units were to land prior to the seaborne landings, clear beach defences and obstacles in the St Malo and Dinard area and seize Dinard airfield. The airborne forces would then link up with the seaborne landings and continue to expand the bridgehead until relieved. Charlie Red beach would be at Saint Lunaire west of Dinard, while Love Green and Mike Green would be north of Cancale. The airborne landing and drop zones would be west of Cancale, around Saint Jouain-des-Guerets, south of La Richardais, south west of Pleurtuit, around Le Grand Tourniole and on the beach north of Pont Benoit.

The air plan stated that airborne forces were to be prepared to carry out the operation from 1 August 1944. Their immediate objective would be to clear the landing beaches for the seaborne troops landing 13 hours later. The next objective would be to capture Dinard, St Malo and Dinard airfield. An emergency airfield would be constructed to enable supplies to be brought in by air. The air plan assumed that the airborne operations could take place in either a moon or no-moon period and provided for night-fighter support for the airborne troops in the event of a moonlight period.

The airborne forces would be landed by IX US Troop Carrier Command assisted by 38 and 46 Groups RAF. 1st Airborne Division would drop on the St Malo peninsula to clear beach defences and then assist in the capture of St Malo itself. The US 504th Parachute Infantry Regiment, along with the Polish Brigade, would drop on the Dinard side of the estuary, capture and clear enemy defences, capture the airfield at Dinard and the town itself. SAS troops would be dropped in the south of the St Malo peninsula to disrupt enemy movements.

The FUSAG Joint Plan for Beneficiary was published on 8 July.[17] This mission was to 'Land, assist the seaborne landing by clearing the beach defences and beach obstacles in the St Malo-Dinard area, and seize the initial bridgehead including the Dinard airfield' and to 'Continue the operation to expand the bridgehead under command of Third Army Seaborne Task Force commander when he becomes established ashore'. Upon landing and establishing his headquarters the commander of the seaborne task force would assume command of all Allied troops in the bridgehead. The initial beachhead line was to be roughly 5 miles inland from St Malo to the south end of the Rance Estuary, while the final beachhead line was to be 10 miles inland. 28th Division would occupy the western side of the Estuary around Dinard and the 80th Division would hold the area from St Malo to Cancale.

The Joint Plan's intelligence annex demonstrates how the Allies were able to build a detailed picture of the movements of German units in North West Europe. It predicted that the Germans would have a fighting power equivalent to five divisions to oppose the Allies on the line Avranches–Domfront and that this would eventually reduce to four. It was thought that another four infantry and one of two Panzer divisions may reach the sector by the time the Allies had turned the Avranches corner. Allied intelligence estimated that Brittany was garrisoned by approximately 100,000 German troops. About half of these were formed into divisions with the rest made up of naval coast artillery, assorted infantry, anti-aircraft personnel, Luftwaffe ground personnel, labour and other miscellaneous units. Most of the garrison was either spread along the coast or in the ports. All divisions had sent battlegroups to Normandy.

The coastal defences in the St Malo sector from St Brieuc to Cancale were manned by four or five Russian battalions under 136th Infantry Division, whose headquarters was believed to be at Tressaint. The battalion around the Cancale areas was believed to have several light tanks manned by Russians and Italians. The coastal batteries were manned by naval personnel from the 260th Naval Coast Artillery Battalion. St Malo itself was garrisoned by the 753rd Wach Battalion.

The most formidable German formation in the area, the 5th Parachute Division, was also nearby. Although a newly formed division its personnel were thought to be first-class.

The terrain was thought to be favourable for defence. The Rance Estuary was the critical feature of the terrain inland from St Malo. It had an 18-foot tidal range, and a tidal stream of up to eight and a half miles per hour. Inland the country was mainly agricultural and bocage-like, similar to Normandy. The Chief Engineer at ETOUSA – the US Army's European Theatre of Operations – had identified nine beaches suitable for amphibious landings but suggested that the beaches east of Point du Grouin were sheltered from the prevailing winds, while the beaches to the west were exposed to the north and north-west. The beaches south of Cancale were thought to be suitable for glider landings.

The St Malo defences were described as an incomplete loop with a radius of six miles, made up of tank ditches, roadblocks and strongpoints in the outer perimeter. There were also concrete emplacements at artillery battery positions. The beaches all had underwater obstacles and had been mined, and likely air-landing areas had been obstructed. Long-range coastal guns on the Channel Islands would also limit the sea approaches. The port at St Malo had several locks which were vulnerable to demolition and the narrow approach channels would be easy for the Germans to mine. However, the St Malo garrison was thought to be short of fuel and ammunition, primarily due to problems transporting supplies from the main dumps to the battle area in Normandy.

The FUSAG intelligence assessment concluded that the Germans would defend St Malo and Dinard with the 5th Parachute Division while manning the coastal sector with four or five Russian battalions, including several French light tanks. It was thought that the Germans would probably reinforce the St Malo area with elements of the 319th Infantry Division from the Channels Islands before Beneficiary started and that once the Allies were approaching Avranches they might reinforce Brittany with two or three divisions from Normandy.

In terms of the likely German rate of reinforcement it was predicted that by D+1 they would have reinforced Brittany with one division or elements from tactical reserves and strengthen the St Malo and Dinard garrisons with the equivalent of three parachute battalions from Eastern France. By D+2 the St Malo area might be reinforced by the equivalent of two brigades from the 266th and 275th Infantry Divisions on the south-east coast of Brittany. The Germans were also likely to harass the Allied sea lines of communication with the coastal batteries on the Channel Islands, the island of Cezembre and from the Brittany coast, as well as with mines, E-boats and U-boats.

FUSAG did not think that it was likely that the 319th Infantry Division would be withdrawn from the Channel Islands as by remaining there it threatened the sea approaches to Brittany. Avranches was identified as a key point, and it was thought that the Germans would realise that once it had been reached they could be outflanked in Brittany. FUSAG thought that they might look to reinforce Brittany with two or three divisions from France or Belgium. It was anticipated that the Germans would react quickly to an airborne assault, with the whole of the 5th Parachute Division and several of the Russian battalions manning the coast. The Allies also had an incredibly detailed picture of the ammunition and fuel dumps in the area as well as the Germans motor transport and logistics.

The administrative planning would be carried out by FUSAG and would be executed by Third Army, while COMZ would be responsible for mounting the US part of the operation. During the operation all Allied forces would use American supplies. All casualties would be evacuated to the UK by LST and other craft over the beaches until medical facilities were established in the port. Once the port of St Malo was in operation the beaches close to the port would still be used to increase capacity. The allocation of shipping would be made by 21st Army Group from the shipping already allocated for Overlord.

The Ninth Air Force Outline Plan was issued on 9 July.[18] The anticipated date of the operation would be dictated by the progress of the land battle in Normandy and by the moon period. Postponements or cancellations would be communicated through AEAF to Ninth Troop Carrier Command and TCCP at Eastcote six hours before H-Hour.

As well as transporting the airborne forces from bases in the UK and the Cotentin Peninsula, Ninth Air Force would also provide close air support and air defence. It would involve eight groups from IX Troop Carrier Command along with 38 and 46 Groups RAF under command, all of XIX Tactical Command reinforced with a wing from IX Air Defence Command, IX Bomber Command, 878th Airborne Aviation Engineer Battalion and detachments from I Air Force Service Command. The air operation would also call on 150 heavy bombers from the Eighth Air Force and RAF units, including night fighters.

The Ninth Air Force plan assumed that the airborne landings would take place at night. Bombers would fly south simultaneously with the airborne convoys and would attack targets in the south of the Cotentin peninsula as a diversion as well as dropping Window to confuse enemy radar. German radar would be jammed with Mandrel and

Airborne Cigar, electronic countermeasures systems, which would be timed to coincide with the airborne convoys. Ninth Air Force would maintain standing patrols of six fighters over the Cotentin peninsula as well as six aircraft to escort the troop carriers. Six sorties would be flown around Rennes to prevent enemy interference from the south and between eight and ten intruder sorties would be flown over German airfields in the area. Four Mosquitos would attack searchlight and flak defences around St Malo shortly after H-Hour. The fire plan would be co-ordinated with Allied Naval Expeditionary Forces (ANXF) and a Fighter Direction Tender would be used.

The airborne pathfinders would be dropped by twelve Stirlings of 38 Group. At the same time SAS Troops would be dropped by eight Stirlings and five Albermarles in the area south of the St Malo peninsula and would operate against enemy lines of communications, with the code name 'Sampan'. Thirty minutes later six Horsas would land on LZ 'L' carrying one company of the 1st Battalion of the Border Regiment who would overcome the enemy defences at the western end of Cancale beach where the main glider force would land. Simultaneously six Stirlings from 38 Group would drop paratroops at Pont Benoit to secure the eastern end of the beach landing area. Fifty minutes after H-Hour 275 C-47s of IX Troop Carrier Command would drop the 1st Parachute Brigade on DZ 'N', and the 4th Parachute Brigade on DZ 'V'. One hour and 30 minutes after H-Hour divisional troops would land on LZ 'H', followed half an hour later by 409 Horsas towed by IX Troop Carrier Command C-47s carrying the 1st Airlanding Brigade to LZs 'A' and 'T'. Six Horsas and 28 Hamilcars would land on LZ 'W'. Once Dinard airfield had been captured 135 Wacos, towed by C-47s of IX Troop Carrier Command, and six Hamilcars towed by 38 Group Halifaxes would land.

XIX Tactical Air Command would provide two flights of fighter aircraft over the beach areas, a squadron of fighters for continuous cover over the naval convoy and four groups of fighter-bombers on ground alert to attack pre-identified targets. It would also provide fighter escort for Ninth Air Force bombers. IX Bomber Command would provide eleven groups of medium and light bombers for attacks on targets identified in the fire plan, at a level of one group per battery. Any attacks requiring fragmentation bombs would be passed on to Eighth Air Force's heavy bombers. If required second sorties could be launched on targets, with a turnaround time of six hours.

Ninth Air Force's Intelligence Summary suggested that weaknesses identified in the enemy during the Battle of Normandy were becoming increasingly acute, and that '. . . all indications point to the decline of the Nazi Military Regime'. The Luftwaffe were thought to have a total of 685 aircraft in North West Europe, including 440 fighters. Air opposition was therefore expected to be negligible.

The Naval Fire Support Plan was issued on 8 July.[19] It would provide naval fire support for the airborne and seaborne forces, neutralise the coast defences on Cezembre and then support the advance inland. The bombarding force would consist of two battleships, two heavy cruisers, two light cruisers and six destroyers. A further support group would consist of six Landing Craft Gun (Large), six Landing Craft Tank (Rocket), six Landing Craft Support (Large), eight Landing Craft Tank (Armoured) and six Landing Craft Flak. LCS(S) would precede the leading assault waves. The LCG(L) would accompany the leading waves on the flanks, while the LCT(R) would fire from 3,000 yards offshore.

Four Forward Observer Groups would be provided to control naval gunfire, each consisting of one officer and two men. Two naval liaison groups of one naval officer and five men would be attached to the 1st Airborne Division. The target list attached to the Naval Plan was exhaustive and included grid references for no less than eighteen gun batteries, forty-three emplacements, pillboxes, infantry positions and six minefields.

Despite this extensive planning Beneficiary seems to have slipped in importance, although Montgomery's directive M510 on 10 July again mentioned St Malo. Montgomery stressed the importance of gaining possession of the Brittany peninsula from an administrative point of view – he described it as 'essential'. However, Montgomery also went on to say that he would prefer capturing Quiberon Bay to St Malo: 'I do not want to have to use these [airborne] troops for an operation against St Malo; I prefer to take St Malo from the land . . . these troops will then be available for the operation of seizing the Vannes area, and subsequently of operating to secure Quiberon Bay, or L'Orient.'[20]

On the same day Richardson at 21st Army Group wrote to Browning and informed him that a reconnaissance could not be carried out of the beaches planned to be used for Beneficiary, as given the relative importance of the operation the risks could not be justified.[21]

On 12 July Major General Bull wrote to Bedell Smith in response to Eisenhower's memorandum of 6 July.[22] Bull explained that the plan for Beneficiary had been drawn up by FUSAG under the direction of 21st Army Group. Bull felt that with the airborne forces available the capture of each shore of the estuary and the elimination of coastal guns, including on islands, would be a difficult task. While conducting this operation a substantial perimeter would have to be held to enable sea and air reinforcement. The landing of seaborne reinforcements would be hazardous owing to tidal conditions, numerous off-lying rocks and the risk of mines. Even after capture of St Malo movement through the port was likely to be unpredictable due to the narrow approaches. Bull concluded: 'For the above reasons, it would seem that this operation would be exceedingly difficult and not one which would justify the use of our limited airborne effort.'

Although it would seem that the tide was turning on Beneficiary, Montgomery was still stressing the importance of the Brittany ports. On 21 July he wrote to Simpson at the War Office: 'But we must get Brittany and the ports in that area. So the next thing must be "the swing" of the western flank, and I shall put everything I can in to getting it going. If we do not get the Brittany ports we cannot develop our full potential.'[23]

After Brittany had been captured the US Army carried out a detailed study of beach defences in the peninsula including at St Malo and Dinard.[24] St Malo beach itself was defended with barbed wire and tetrahedron obstacles, placed in two rows and some with mines fixed to the top. These obstacles had been placed so that they would be 1.5m below water level at high water. Further out was an unidentified new type of steel obstacle, and further still a row of steel hedgehogs. It was thought that further out there would probably be posts with mines. The sea wall at the top of the beach was almost 3ft high and topped with a barbed-wire fence. The Germans had also blocked the entrance to the harbour with a boom.

Across the Rance Estuary at Dinard the obstacles were made mainly of wood and included sawhorse ramps and posts, both with mines attached. They extended out to the low-water mark. Although the beach was small it was enfiladed by cliffs and easily defended. All beach exits were defended by anti-tank walls with elaborate barbed wire obstacles. The entire shoreline was backed by gun emplacements and flamethrowers had been set into the defences with the ability to be fired remotely. Some of them had been placed so that their flames would detonate pre-positioned naval shells.

Both St Malo and Dinard were also well organised for defence from the landward side. Anti-tank roadblocks had been used widely and an anti-tank ditch 15ft wide and 10ft deep ran about two miles inland. Several flooded areas were defended with obstacles, including upright sections of railway track.

It is hard to escape the conclusion that it would have been very challenging for the airborne engineers to clear the beach obstacles sufficiently before the seaborne assault took place. Indeed, the engineer units who landed to clear obstacles on the Normandy beaches on D-Day had been trained and equipped specifically for this task. Whilst the Royal Engineers have always prided themselves on an ability to take on challenges, the lightly-equipped airborne sappers would have been up against it.

Operation Beneficiary was one of the most complex and detailed plans drawn up between D-Day and Operation Market Garden. A tri-service operation aimed at capturing a heavily defended port, it also included a substantial amphibious landing. It demonstrates the numerous factors that came into play in planning airborne operations as part of broader strategy. Urquhart was certainly happy about its cancellation, feeling that St Malo was too strongly defended.[25]

Beneficiary was very much the first in a series of operations planned to capture the defended ports in Brittany. It was also the first truly inter-Allied operation to be proposed, with a mainly British airborne force supplemented with an American parachute infantry regiment, and then coming under the command of an American corps. It was, in many ways, a scaled-down version of D-Day.

Early in 1944 Allied airborne forces tested inter-operability of equipment. Here American troops of the 490th Quartermaster Depot and the 101st Airborne Division test British pannier baskets for dropping supplies for airborne troops inside a C-47 Dakota, January 1944. (USNA, ETO-HQ-44-468)

Here American airborne troops unload a British Horsa glider in early 1944.
(USNA, ETO-HQ-44-249)

(From left to right,) Lieutenant General Lewis Brereton, Lieutenant General Carl Spaatz and General Eisenhower inspecting a US airfield in England while Brereton still commanded the Ninth Air Force. (USNA, 55055AC)

General Sir Bernard Montgomery, commanding 21st Army Group, Lieutenant-General Miles Dempsey (right), commanding Second British Army, and Lieutenant-General Omar Bradley, commanding First US Army, in front of Monty's staff car near Port-en-Bessin on 10 June 1944. During this meeting they discussed plans for Operation *Wild Oats*. (Historic Military Press)

Allied air superiority was a key factor in considering airborne operations. Here USAAF C47s of the 96th Troop Carrier Squadron fly over Utah Beach. The 96th was a part of the 440th Troop Carrier Group, 50th Troop Carrier Wing which was based in the Exeter region around the time of D-Day. (Conseil Régional de Basse-Normandie/USNA)

The Allies had to plan operations around their limited number of gliders. Here cattle graze around an Airspeed Horsa Mk.I in a field in Normandy - the white star on the fuselage indicates that this particular glider was used by an American unit. (Conseil Régional de Basse-Normandie/USNA)

The siege of Brest destroyed or damaged virtually every building in the city. This photograph was taken on 26 September, shortly after the Brest was captured (USNA, A61319AC)

When the Allies captured Brittany heavy bombing was required to neutralise heavily defended ports. This photograph shows US Ninth Air Force fighter-bombers targeting the island of Cézembre off St Malo. (USNA 53866AC)

The US Army captured thousands of German personnel in the Brittany ports. This image shows prisoners of war captured at St Malo, 18 August 1944. (USNA, 61371AC)

OPERATION SWORDHILT

Although much effort was invested in developing plans to capture St Malo, the Allies also considered airborne operations to capture the other ports on the peninsula, including much further to the west. A clear trend emerges – the Allies, motivated by logistics and the need to maintain the increasing armies on the Continent, needed to secure deep-water ports quickly.

Although its original inspiration is unclear, the original idea for Operation Swordhilt appears to have come from AEAF who produced an outline plan for an air landing in the Brittany Peninsula on 20 June.[1] The object of the proposed operation was to capture the port of Brest, occupy the peninsula and accelerate the rate of Allied build-up on the Continent.

Two weeks after the D-Day landings in Normandy the Germans had already been removing their higher-grade and more mobile formations from Brittany. A considerable portion of the forces that were left were non-German. Brest was heavily defended to landward but it was hoped that these could be neutralised by bombing. A map attached to the AEAF plan suggested that there were 76,500 German personnel in Brittany, with at least 7,000 thought to be Russian and 19,000 naval and Luftwaffe personnel. All of the German divisions in Brittany were lower-grade coastal defence formations. The exception was the 3rd Parachute Division around Morlaix and Roscoff, but this had already begun to move to Normandy.

An airborne force would land in the Morlaix-Lannion are in north-west Brittany, capture Morlaix airfield and neutralise the enemy defences covering the sea approaches to St Michel-en-Greve. An armoured division would then land by sea along with its artillery, and two to three infantry divisions would be airlanded into Morlaix airfield, with their vehicles and heavy equipment being landed by sea. To land these divisions would take around 1,000 aircraft sorties per division and each division would take up to 24 hours to assemble. A new landing ground would be constructed, and it was hoped that

Lannion airfield could also be captured as at least two landing grounds were essential to meet the troop carrier lift requirements, and a third was seen as very desirable to allow a fighter wing to operate and provide air cover. Contact would be made with the SAS and Resistance organisations in the Peninsula. Once the force was assembled and in place, the port of Morlaix would be captured, followed by Brest.

The three ports in the immediate beachhead area – Roscoff, Morlaix and Perros-Guirec – were each believed to have a capacity of 500 to 600 tons per day although would be difficult to use due to the presence of rocks and strong tides, although there were believed to be good landing beaches in the bay of St Michel-en-Greve. The AEAF plan intimated that the area had been selected by XX US Corps for its landings, suggesting that the air planners had liaised with them when drawing up their plan.

Air support would include the neutralisation of Vannes and Kerlin-Bastard airfields on night of D-1 and D-Day, the provision of bombers on call to attack centres of resistance, fighter cover for daylight resupply missions, the destruction of radar installations in North Brittany and, if necessary, day fighter defence of the landing beaches once a third air strip became available. The whole force of up to five divisions would have to be maintained by air, requiring an airlift of 2,500 tons every 24 hours. This would require around 850 C-47s. It was suggested that supply dumps be set up in southern England around airfields to ensure rapid turnaround of aircraft.

The AEAF outline plan for Swordhilt seems to have then been shelved for almost a month, until it was examined by the SHAEF planning staff of Commander J.R.A. Seymour, Brigadier K.G. McLean and Group Captain H.P. Broad, who issued their comments on 19 July.[2] The SHAEF planners considered that the airborne operations would be feasible against the level of German forces in Brittany and that the operation could be carried out in daylight. The airfields at Lannion and Morlaix had been disrupted since AEAF's plan and would therefore need to be repaired or temporary strips would have to be constructed to land infantry divisions by air. It was thought unlikely that any infantry could be landed by air until two to three days after the initial assault. As a result a proportion of the follow-up forces would have to be landed from the sea.

The beaches at St Michel-en-Greve and Locquierc were thought to be reasonably sheltered and suitable for staging amphibious landings, although their very flat gradients meant that landing craft and coasters would have to beach and then wait for the return tide in order to float off. They would only be able to beach at or near the high water line. The landings would have to take place in daylight due to the offshore hazards along the Breton coastline, and the weather was predicted to deteriorate after September.

It was estimated that the beaches around St Michel-en-Greve would be capable of receiving 5,000 tons of supplies per day. This was thought to be sufficient for the Swordhilt task force, and the small ports of Morlaix and Roscoff could also be used. Eventually the whole force would be maintained through Brest as the beaches could not be relied upon once the weather deteriorated into the autumn.

The SHAEF planners thought that there was a considerable Maquis presence in Brittany, believed to consist of 7,000 armed men, which might have increased to 30,000. These would have been of considerable assistance in delaying the movement of enemy forces.

The SHAEF planners stressed that the required 45-mile advance from the beaches to Brest, the port's strong landward defences, the need to clear the covering peninsulas and the importance of guarding the rear and flanks of the force meant that it could take more than a month to capture Brest itself. Working backwards, the planners concluded that the latest possible date to launch would be 1 September and that therefore planning had to start by the second week in August.

The Allied airborne forces available were the 1st British Airborne Division and two US Airborne Regimental Combat Teams. The seaborne forces would comprise the US 80th, 94th and 95th Infantry Divisions which would be available in Britain from early September. The infantry divisions were scheduled to go to Normandy but would be diverted for Swordhilt. The armoured division would be either of the 6th or 7th US Armoured Divisions and the British 52nd Division could be released from War Office reserve if necessary. These diversions would have some cost on the build-up in Normandy but the planners rightly suggested that similar forces would need to be found to clear Brittany from Normandy anyway.

The planners felt that Swordhilt would be most feasible if the deception of Operation Fortitude held and the Germans were not able to send reinforcements west from the Pas de Calais area. If Fortitude failed and the Germans were in a position to reinforce Brittany Swordhilt would be much more hazardous, and the planners even used the example of Anzio for how the operation might become roped off by significant opposition. The presence of so many Maquis and the Allies' overwhelming air superiority were also key factors in Swordhilt's favour. On the negative side the advance from the beaches to Brest would be long and forcing the defences of the port and the covering peninsulas would be difficult. The planners therefore increased the number of infantry divisions to four.

The wider strategic context of the North West Europe campaign in 1944 also influenced planning for Swordhilt. The Allies' logistical planning assumed for the capture of the Brittany ports by 1 September and any delay would have serious repercussions on operations. The planners concluded that it would be most effective to be able to capture the Brittany ports by advancing overland from Normandy. Swordhilt was seen very much as a contingency for a subsidiary operation to speed up their capture. The SHAEF planners concluded that Swordhilt could not be launched before 21 August given the time required for planning and movement, and not after 1 September given the weather constraints and that the Allies would depend on beach maintenance for a month afterwards. Swordhilt therefore only had a very narrow window – 12 days – in which it could be launched.

The planners concluded that Swordhilt would be most useful if the Allies found themselves in a situation where Brittany ports could not be captured by 1 September, and if the deception of Operation Fortitude continued to contain German forces away from Brittany. Swordhilt was also seen as opening up the sea routes to Quiberon Bay and allowing the clearing of the Brittany peninsula.

The SHAEF planners, not surprisingly, had a more detailed impression of the likely German opposition. It was thought that approximately 5,000–6,000 men would oppose the airborne landings initially. It was thought unlikely that the Germans would be able to bring up significant reinforcements before D+2 apart from battlegroups sent from 343rd and 246th Infantry Divisions. The Germans could also weaken their garrisons in southern Brittany and send two regiments each from the 265th and 275th Divisions, which could arrive by D+7. There was no evidence of armoured units in Brittany. It was estimated that the Germans might be able to spare one infantry division and possibly a tank battalion from Normandy, which would be unlikely to arrive before D+12. The Brest garrison was unlikely to be reduced below 17,000.

The coastal defences between Morlaix and Brest were light and not continuous, with seven strongpoints defending the beaches at St Michel-en-Greve. The defences were not deep but there were numerous anti-glider obstacles there and at Locquierc. These obstacles needed to be cleared, a task which would slow down the seaborne forces. The towns of Morlaix and Lannion had light perimeter defences and their airfields were protected by six heavy, thirty medium and twenty-four light flak guns.

The terrain was also challenging, with numerous river valleys to be crossed. There were light perimeter defences at three villages between

Morlaix and Brest, at Landivisiau, Lenneven and Landermeau. The landward defences of Brest were strong, in terms of ground defences and anti-aircraft guns. They extended outwards for a two-mile radius from the port, which was also well protected from seaward. There were heavy anti-aircraft defences on key points at the Pointe de l'Armorique and the Crozon Peninsula. Each of these peninsulas would have to be neutralised together with guns on Pointe de St Mathieu before the port could be opened. These peninsulas were separated from each other and from Brest by the Rivers Elorn and Aulne, meaning that clearing them could be a lengthy and costly business. The similarity with the clearing of Antwerp later in 1944 is obvious.

The SHAEF planners' report was forwarded to Richardson at 21st Army Group by Brigadier McLean at SHAEF G-3 on 21 July 1944.[3] McLean stressed that Swordhilt was only worth taking further if the Brittany ports could not be captured by September, and only if Fortitude held. McLean did, however, suggest that Swordhilt might give a better dividend than Hands Up. Already it is clear the window for launching Swordhilt was very narrow.

Despite McLean's lukewarm summary of Swordhilt, 21st Army Group decided to commence planning. A preliminary planning conference was scheduled for 26 July, which was later rescheduled for the next day. The various branches of 21st Army Group, ANXF and AEAF were asked to send representatives.[4]

One issue that was vexing the planners engaged in putting together airborne operations was the availability of airborne units. The 1st British Airborne Division was being held in readiness to reinforce the beachhead shortly after D-Day or for exploitation operations later on. The 6th Airborne Division had landed on D-Day and would not come out of the line until late August while the US 82nd and 101st Divisions did not return to Britain until early July and mid-June respectively. It was estimated that neither of the American divisions would be ready for action again until 15 September while the US 17th Airborne Division was due to arrive in Britain in mid-August and would be ready for action a month later. It was estimated that in an emergency one US division, possibly the 82nd, might be ready for action on 1 September, but as of 22 July neither SHAEF nor ETOUSA would commit to firm dates.

Between the circulation of the SHAEF planners' memo and the meeting at 21st Army Group detailed planning had already in fact begun.[5] On 23 July Colonel J.N.V. Duncan of the Q(Movements) staff at Rear HQ 21st Army Group wrote to Commander G.W. Roswell of ANXF with an estimate of the shipping requirements for Swordhilt.

The total requirement was estimated as five Landing Ships Infantry (Hand-hoisting) or (Medium), eighteen Landing Craft Infantry (Large), fifty-four Landing Ships Tank, sixty Landing Craft Tank, eight Landing Ships Infantry (Large), thirty-two Stores Coasters, thirty-nine Motor Transport Ships, thirteen Stores Ships and one Motor Transport or Stores Ship.

On 25 July Lieutenant Colonel Britten of 21st Army Group G(Plans) circulated a first draft outline plan for Operation Swordhilt for discussion at the planning meeting on 27 July.[6] This plan was similar to that proposed by AEAF. Swordhilt would be controlled by 12th US Army Group and that the command of the airborne operation would depend on whether US or British airborne divisions were used, with HQ Airborne Troops taking command if British. It is not clear how the operation would have been commanded if it was to be based on US airborne forces, as the US Airborne Corps had not been activated yet. The plan stipulated that no information regarding Swordhilt was to be made available to the French, probably due to a fear of leaks. The initial plan also proposed that the advance from the bridgehead would take the form of two axes, with one directly towards the port of Brest and the other crossing the Elorn river and seizing the Morgat peninsula. The seaborne assault would be led by a commando brigade which would land on the beaches at Locquierc and St Michel-en-Grave.

Around the same time a draft was produced by 21st Army Group G(Plans) for Bradley at 12th Army Group.[7] The original document, written in Montgomery's name but not signed, is undated and it is likely that this directive was not issued. The directive included an objective for Swordhilt: 'You are directed to carry out a combined sea and airborne assault in the Morlaix area with the object of securing initial beaches and air strips necessary for the build-up of a major force, and then capturing Brest . . . Operations will then be developed to clear the enemy out of Brittany.'

The directive to Bradley stated that Browning would be given command of the airborne assault, suggesting that 21st Army Group were still striving for British primacy in airborne command. It was also suggested that overall command of Swordhilt would be delegated to Third Army, raising the intriguing prospect of Patton commanding Browning. It is hard to imagine two more different characters. Detailed planning would be led by HQ Airborne Troops working under Third Army, in conjunction with AEAF. The naval force would be commanded by the commander of the Eleventh Amphibious Task Force.

The planning for Swordhilt would need to start at least 37 days before D-Day, given the combined operations aspect of the operation.

Ships and landing craft would need to begin loading stores 16 days before, with personnel embarking four days prior. The first convoy would need to sail on D-2.

A document entitled 'Note on Swordhilt', uncredited but issued by 21st Army Group G(Plans) on 26 July, sheds light on the planners thinking: 'If planning is to be done quickly we must decentralise down to the actual commanders who are concerned with the operation. Airborne corps must plan with the air commander in charge of troop carrier operations.' The document also suggested that 'Forces should be strong in armoured cars and armour. At all costs we must avoid being bottled up in a bridgehead. Armour must be used boldly in conjunction with Maquis and air supply.'

One of the strengths of Allied planning during the latter stages of the Second World War was the ability, through Ultra decrypts and other intelligence sources, to gather information as to the location of German units and the likely actions of German commanders. On 26 July Brigadier Bill Williams, Montgomery's Brigadier General Staff (Intelligence), sent a paper highlighting the likely enemy reactions to Swordhilt. Williams' staff predicted that the initial landings would be opposed by elements of the 266th Infantry Division which was holding the coast between St Brieuc and Morlaix. The division was already depleted, having sent a battlegroup to Normandy, with its remaining strength the equivalent of about one infantry regiment plus divisional troops. The advance on Brest would be opposed by the 343rd Infantry Division, who were at present holding the coast between Morlaix and Brest. The only other field division occupying Normandy at that time was a battlegroup of the 265th Infantry Division on the south coast.

Williams predicted that once Swordhilt was launched the Germans were likely to guess from the substantial airborne force being used and the lateness of the season that further major landings would be unlikely in the rest of 1944. Knowing that a landing in the Pas de Calais was unlikely the Germans would probably release more reinforcements for Normandy, particularly the five to six infantry divisions and one panzer division in reserve. Williams also predicted that the Germans would attempt to bottle-up the Allies in Brittany similar to how they had in Normandy. It was predicted that it would take a minimum of three weeks for reinforcements to arrive from north of the Seine and any forces released from the Biscay coast could arrive in about 10 days. Williams predicted that if the Germans were unable to contain the Allies in the west of the Brittany peninsula they would probably fight a delaying action for as long as possible to prevent an Allied advance turning the flank of their forces in Normandy.

Given the inter-Allied aspect of Swordhilt, a British staff increment would be embedded at the US Army Headquarters responsible for commanding the operation, and on 27 July Britten at 21st Army Group G(Plans) circulated a proposed establishment. The team of twenty-three officers would be led by a Brigadier or Colonel General Staff and would include artillery, engineer, signals and medical advisers and a cipher detachment. The staff would be required at short notice and that the Military Secretary at 21st Army Group would have to produce the officers urgently. Tactfully, it was suggested that the head of the British increment should not outrank their American equivalent.

An undated and unattributed memo found in 21st Army Group files summarises the merits of Swordhilt compared to Beneficiary. If the object was to unlock the Brittany deadlock the author felt that the objective must be St Malo, and that the distance, time and the size of force required for Swordhilt precluded it being an operation to break a deadlock. If, however, the objective was to be Brest then Swordhilt was preferable. Swordhilt was seen as being almost certain to succeed, and that Brest would secure the American build-up over the coming winter. There were also naval advantages in securing Brest early, in terms of control of the seas around Brittany and neutralising the U-boat bases. The disadvantages were that Normandy would lose momentum and that the Allies would be maintaining two separate bridgeheads for several months. Beneficiary was seen as being a relatively short-term operation whereas Brest was a longer-term project.

21st Army Group's Movements and Transport staff also estimated the effect that Swordhilt might have on the ongoing build up in Normandy, particularly as the proposed operation would involve withdrawing shipping and aircraft that would otherwise be used to carry reinforcements across the Channel. On 26 July it was estimated that the withdrawal of LCTs from the Normandy shuttle would delay the build-up of 'awkward vehicles' by 28 days, and the use of LCTs for carrying motor transport and stores was already critical and would become worse. It was planned to withdraw fifty-four LSTs from Overlord for use in Swordhilt, meaning that only nine would be available every day to evacuate casualties from Normandy and only thirty for ferrying rolling stock to the continent. It was estimated that this would mean a delay of 12,000 vehicles over 28 days. The withdrawal of Motor Transport and Stores Ships, on the other hand, would not have any effect on the Overlord build-up.

On 26 July 21st Army Group's Quartermaster Branch estimated the rate of build-up that might be possible during Swordhilt.[8] On D-Day the Allies could land one Infantry Division and elements of an

Engineer Shore Regiment, a total of 20,500 men and 2,660 vehicles. By D+4 the beachhead would hold two Infantry Divisions at light scales and an Armoured Division at war establishment, for a total of 69,900 men and 10,860 vehicles. However ANXF had not approved the size of the convoy necessary to deliver this rate of build-up but were known to be examining the problem.

Montgomery's directive M515 was published on 27 July.[9] It directed 12th Army Group to 'examine the problem of seizing the Morlaix area' and to plan the operation as per discussions between Montgomery and Bradley. Montgomery also stressed again the importance of the Brittany ports to the Allies' logistical situation: 'The present period is a critical and important time. The summer is drawing on and we have not many more months of good campaigning weather; there is still much to be done; we must secure the Brittany ports before winter is on us.'

21st Army Group also requested an assessment of the support that the French Resistance would be able to give to Swordhilt. A report was received from the 3rd Special Forces Detachment on 27 July. Unlike in Normandy the more rugged terrain in Brittany provided ample opportunities for the French Resistance. A large number of SAS units and Jedburgh teams – three main teams of Allied special forces with the objective of aiding the Resistance – had already been dropped to arrange for the reception and distribution of equipment dropped by the Allies. On 11 July it was estimated that there were 5,330 armed resisters in Normandy, a figure that could have increased to 16,800 by 11 August. Many of these were either in Maquis groups in the hilly and woody inland regions or in the inland towns with only a small number located near the coast, particularly close to Brest. This is not surprising given that the German defences were concentrated along the coast. Resistance groups were generally immobile and they would be unable to operate effectively more than 15 miles from their home areas or towns. It was suggested that they would be able to assist the Allies by undertaking static Home Guard-like duties as they lacked the organisation and supporting firepower to withstand enemy attacks, nor would they be able to attack well-prepared enemy positions. Experience in Normandy suggested that resisters, armed and unarmed, would report to any Allied military forces within walking distance and that they would accept orders enthusiastically. They would, however, need to be fed and supplied, which would add to the Allies' already stretched logistics.

It was hoped that the Resistance would be able to contain the German forces along the south coast of Brittany and delay reinforcements from reaching the Swordhilt area. The large number of Resisters in Morbihan would be ideal for helping with this and if SAS or similar special forces were dropped close to natural bottlenecks they would be able to co-ordinate and stiffen the resistance. Closer to the landing area and around Brest resistance groups could delay the movement of reinforcements, prevent demolitions and provide guards for strategic points such as bridges. It was possible, but unlikely, that the Resistance would be able to play much of a role in securing Brest, nor would they be able to prevent the Germans rendering the port installations inoperable. Further east it was hoped that the Resistance could co-operate with the French Armoured Division in its advance eastwards. It is possible that a French Armoured Division was selected for this task to facilitate close co-operation during the advance.

On 27 July 21st Army Group G(Plans) listed points that required urgent action, probably as a result of the planning meeting held the same day. These points included what vehicles needed waterproofing and when, when the planning group would convene, when units would be withdrawn from France, how much the French in exile could be told, whether AEAF would designate the Ninth Air Force to be responsible for the air operations, if the War Office would release 52nd Division from its strategic reserve, what training with tanks would be required and how the armour and infantry would be brought together, and what were the most suitable dates, times, tides and phases of the moon for all of the forces involved.

On 28 July the order of battle for Swordhilt was confirmed. The operation would now be commanded by Simpson's Ninth Army. The airborne force would be commanded by HQ Airborne Troops and would consist of the 1st British Airborne Division, 101st US Airborne Division and the 1st Polish Parachute Brigade with the 52nd Division as an air-landed follow-up. An unspecified US Corps would command the seaborne force – XX Corps had been mentioned previously – and would probably consist of the 94th Infantry Division and one US Armoured Division, provisionally the 7th Armoured Division. There would also be three or four US Tank Battalions or the British equivalent.

An Engineer Appreciation of Operation Swordhilt was circulated by 21st Army Group's Chief Engineer on 28 July. The beach defences were thought to be formidable, consisting of a belt of unidentified obstacles running the whole length of the beaches 400–500 yards below the high-water mark. Both beaches were backed by a sea wall and possibly by mines. The clearance of lanes through the obstacles and the preparation of beach exits was thought to be within the capabilities of airborne engineers. It was thought that the task force could reach Brest from the landing area by road without crossing any major obstacles, but that Bailey bridging materials should be provided to bridge any unforeseen dry gaps in the broken terrain. The engineering appreciation suggested that the roads from the landing area around Morlaix to Brest crossed numerous culverts.

The force's biggest challenge would be in capturing Brest itself, and it would also be essential to capture the Crozon peninsula south of Brest which commanded the Brest roadstead. In turn for land forces to reach this area they would have to cross the River Aulne. The northern landward defences of Brest included barbed wire, anti-tank ditches, Belgian Gates, pillboxes and minefields in a perimeter that was approximately three and a half miles long. The eastern defences consisted of the seventeenth-century city walls and a tidal river.

The force would require specialist support from an Assault Regiment of the Royal Engineers, consisting of three or four squadrons, who would need preliminary training with the division with which they would assault Brest. 42nd Assault Regiment Royal Engineers was highlighted as being available and in the UK, and it was also suggested that Sherman Crab flail tanks might be useful for breaching minefields.

As well as the usual complement of brigade and divisional engineers it was suggested that Swordhilt would require a substantial level of additional engineering support. From the US forces this would consist of five combat engineer battalions, two light pontoon companies carrying a Bailey bridge each, a half treadway company, a light equipment company and a detachment maintenance company. The British forces would contribute 13 Army Group Royal Engineers and the three squadrons of 42nd Assault Regiment Royal Engineers. One US airborne aviation engineer battalion would be landed with the airborne forces to construct temporary airstrips along with another engineer aviation battalion and a maintenance company that would land by sea.

21st Army Group's Quartermaster (Movement) Staff also began detailed planning of shipping.[10] In a memo circulated on 28 July two alternative schemes were proposed. The Allied naval commander refused to allow any deep-draught shipping in the anchorage, which precluded the use of larger transport ships. The build-up would therefore need to be completed by Landing Ships and Landing Craft. The withdrawal of shipping from Operation Neptune would reduce the British and American build-up to a few ships daily and would only allow for three Landing Ships Tank to evacuate casualties from the British and US sectors respectively every day for approximately 30 days. This shortfall would be overcome by loading hospital carriers at the Mulberry Harbour and at Cherbourg. Swordhilt would also mean that no LSTs would be available for the ferrying of rolling stock for a period of 30 days, but this was not thought to be critical. The Build Up Control Organisation would need to continue the function that it had performed during Operation Overlord and some of the southern base sections in the south-west ports would have to be reactivated for Swordhilt.

Once captured Brest would also have to be defended against air attack. On 29 July Lieutenant-Colonel Dunbar Bostwick of the US Ninth Air Force estimated that its air defences and air-warning requirements would be an anti-aircraft brigade of six battalions with a total of 128 guns, along with a searchlight platoon. The air warning would be handled by a signal air-warning battalion and a fighter control squadron. The total personnel would consist of 6,000 men and 1,300 vehicles.

Richardson sent a brief to 21st Army Group's Chief of Staff, de Guingand, on 29 July 1944. He stressed that Swordhilt would be a major operation requiring five to six divisions along with an army headquarters and army troops. Richardson outlined Operation Swordhilt as consisting of air landings by two airborne divisions and one air-transported division. This force would secure airstrips and beaches to allow the build-up by sea of a force of one infantry division, one or two armoured divisions, corps artillery and additional supporting troops. Richardson's brief consisted very much of the plans that had already been drawn up, but also stated that no detailed planning could be done until a planning group was assembled in England, consisting of the US Army Headquarters that would command Swordhilt, the British Increment embedded with that Army, Eleventh Amphibious Naval Task Force, Ninth Air Force, HQ Airborne Troops, the US Corps Headquarters that would command the seaborne landings, and representatives from 21st Army Group, ETOUSA, the War Office and the RAF. Syndicates from the divisions concerned would also be required. A subsequent memo suggested that even bringing together the planning group would not be straightforward. Assembling many officers from many different headquarters required a suitable location with living accommodation and messing. Syndicates were to bring their own clerks, drivers, batmen and transport. It was suggested that the US Army HQ that would be involved could arrange for a US mess and that HQ Airborne Troops could do likewise for the British contingent. Ascot and Wentworth were suggested as suitable locations close to the other airborne and air force headquarters west of London.

Richardson suggested that Swordhilt might be opposed by elements of 266th Division, equivalent to a brigade group, who were between St Brieuc and Morlaix. The advance on Brest would come up against 343rd Division who were between Morlaix and Brest. 265th Division on the south coast of Brittany might also send a battle group. There were also about 50,000 garrison troops of inferior quality, mainly Russians, as well as local defence battalions, flak and coastal defence units. About 12,000 of these were in Brest and the German build-up would increase from half of a division on D-Day to six divisions by D+31 to D+40. It was thought that the Germans would lose the bulk of two divisions and all of the garrison troops in the battle for Brest, leaving four weak infantry divisions by D+40 to oppose the Allied expansion eastwards towards Normandy.

Richardson suggested leaving one airborne division for the local defence of the bridgehead. The armoured division would be used for flank protection and for delaying action far out from the bridgehead by small armoured patrols. This would then leave the two US infantry divisions and 52nd Division to carry out the advance on Brest. It was hoped to capture Brest by D+15 before the Germans could reinforce the garrison. Heavy bombing would be used to neutralise coast defence batteries. Richardson also hoped that Swordhilt could make maximum use of the substantial Maquis presence in Brittany by delaying enemy moves, holding defiles and generally harassing the Germans. Allied Tactical Air Forces would also be called upon for interdiction.

If Brest was captured quickly the sea build-up to be transferred to the port from the beaches at St Michel-en-Greve. After Brest was captured one division would be left for its defence while the remaining four divisions would turn eastwards to clear Brittany and join up with the Allied forces advancing from Normandy.

Richardson assumed that if D-Day took place about 7 September Brest might be captured on 22 September (D+15) and the advance eastward might start on 25 September. Brittany might be cleared by the end of October. However, on the same day a message from Richardson stated that 'It has been decided that no further action will be taken regarding the planning of Swordhilt'. Although there is no evidence as to why Swordhilt was cancelled, as with many planned airborne operations a degree of planning continued even after it had been cancelled. A handwritten note found in the 21st Army Group G(Plans) files, unattributed but dated 31 July, reads 'Swordhilt is revived'. The note suggested that the seaborne assault would be cancelled but the Chief Royal Engineer was asked to give more details of the obstacles that would need to be crossed to get to the Crozon Peninsula. There is no other evidence of how much work went into a revived version of Swordhilt or why it did not take place or why it was revived.

Swordhilt was only planned or discussed in higher headquarters. Born out of AEAF, it was passed to SHAEF and then to 21st Army Group G(Plans) to develop. Although the planning was relatively detailed it does not seem to have been delegated down by Army Group level. If Browning or his staff at HQ Airborne Troops were involved in the discussions around Swordhilt there is no evidence as to their input and there is no reference to Swordhilt in 1st Airborne Division's war diary. It is therefore an example of a planned airborne operation that occupied much staff time in a relatively short period of time but would have been unknown to almost all of the Allied airborne personnel in Britain in 1944. They did not develop plans or give orders, personnel were not briefed and they did not assemble at airfields or board aircraft prior to its cancellation. Its impact on the morale of the 1st Airborne Division, for example, would have been non-existent.

Much less planning was done for Swordhilt than for say Beneficiary, with no drop zones identified, and no operation orders completed. Although planning for Swordhilt was scant, it once again emphasises the increasingly tri-service and Allied nature of not just airborne operations, but any operations in the 1944 campaign. It is also notable that the idea for Swordhilt seems to have come from the air forces, who were not always keen on airborne operations.

By contrast the next proposed operation, although equally little-known as Swordhilt, would generate more extensive planning than most airborne operations that actually took place.

OPERATION HANDS UP

It is perhaps indicative of the varied nature of Allied airborne planning that one of the least known operations that were considered in 1944, also generated by far the most planning and was among the most complex. Although it dwarfed the plans developed for Beneficiary and Swordhilt, it was again aimed at securing a deep-water port, albeit via a sheltered anchorage and artificial harbour rather than a defended port.

We have seen how even before D-Day the Allied planners had been looking at prospective operations, led by a need to secure deep-water ports to bring reinforcements and supplies direct from across the Atlantic without needing to disembark in Britain first. Although their focus was partly on existing ports such as St Malo and Brest, attention was also drawn to the large sheltered anchorage at Quiberon Bay on the south coast of Brittany.

The Allies' overriding concern, apart from establishing a secure lodgement area in Normandy, was to capture and develop ports for the landing of US reinforcements. Cherbourg alone would not be sufficient and the Brittany ports were therefore the initial objective of Patton's Third Army. Operation Hands Up was born from the Allies' need to capture and bring into operation deep-water ports soon after the Normandy landings. These would be particularly important for sustaining the American build-up as they would allow reinforcements to land directly on the Continent.

Hands Up predated D-Day by several months. FUSAG prepared a study on the development of what they referred to as 'the Quiberon Bay project' on 5 April. On 14 April the Chief of the Plans and Operation Section at SHAEF G3, Nevins, wrote on behalf of Bull to Crawford, the Assistant Chief of Staff for G4 at SHAEF.[1] SHAEF G3 considered that the plan was operationally sound and proposed no revision of an original directive that had been issued by SHAEF 10 March. Eisenhower signalled his agreement with this to 21st Army Group on 24 April.[2]

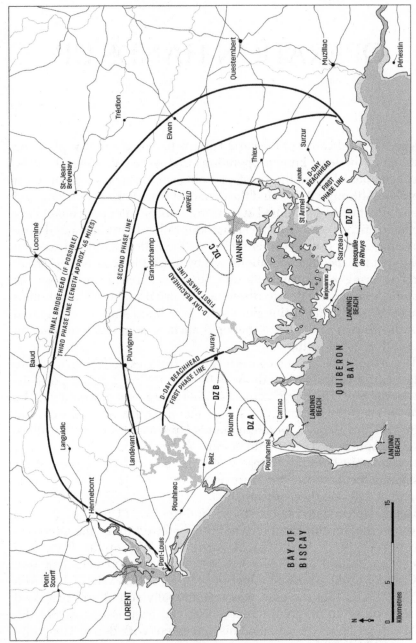

Map 7: Drop zones and objectives for Hands Up. (Source: TNA WO 205/665)

28 April

On 28 April De Guingand wrote to Bradley to ask for his comments on the proposals for Operation Chastity, an operation to establish an artificial port in Quiberon Bay, by 8 May.[3] He explained that the project, which had been drawn up by Com Z and approved by 21st Army Group and SHAEF, was to develop Quiberon Bay and adjacent inlets and estuaries into a large artificial port area. Details of the project and capacities were still being worked out, but it was planned to have a capacity equivalent to Nantes and St Nazaire, which would be useful if the enemy had sabotaged those ports. De Guingand argued that carrying out Chastity did not necessarily require a crossing to be captured over the Loire, which would be needed to capture Nantes or St Nazaire. Bradley was asked to examine the plan, which would give the First Army – reinforced by Third Army – the mission of capturing Cherbourg, driving south towards the Loire to cut off Brittany, then securing the Quiberon Bay area. To enable Quiberon to be used Belle Isle would also have to be captured, along with other small islands. De Guingand suggested that airborne troops or rangers could be used for this – the first mention of airborne troops taking part.

6 May

On 6 May De Guingand wrote on behalf of Montgomery to the Commanding General of FUSAG.[4] The original SHAEF directive had been amended on 29 April so that the primary mission of the US forces would be to secure the Quiberon area so that it could be developed as a major port. Third Army would be expected to clear 'Newington' (likely the code name for Brittany) and open the Brittany ports, especially 'Malvern', thought to be a code name for Brest. De Guingand also questioned whether Swordhilt or Chastity would support Third Army's mission more effectively. Having examined FUSAG's estimate of the situation for Swordhilt, 21st Army Group and the Allied Naval Forces were both critical of the operation. If the Quiberon Bay area was not secured it was thought that it would unlikely that the US forces would be able to drive further into Brittany to link up with troops landing in any case, but if Chastity was secured then it would be possible to maintain the US XX and XXI Corps in Brittany. With these formations it was felt that Third Army would be able to capture Brest from the landward side without the need for Swordhilt. Quiberon Bay had therefore, for the time being, been given priority and FUSAG were ordered not to prepare detailed plans for an airborne operation at Brest.

13 May

A week later on 13 May De Guingand, who it is already clear played a prominent role in the strategies behind airborne planning, wrote to Bradley – although the message was signed by Richardson – regarding Operation Chastity.[5] He informed him that it had been decided that the capture of the area required to implement Chastity was 'a matter of highest importance' and had been assigned to First Army. Bradley was asked to prepare plans to carry out the mission including the destruction of the batteries on Belle Isle and neutralising naval batteries at Lorient. Ramsay had ordered Admiral Alan G. Kirk, the commander of the Western Task Force on D-Day, to carry out the naval planning. De Guingand stressed that the advance towards Quiberon Bay should not 'point too early to the ultimate destination', and that it should be possible to deceive the Germans into thinking that the thrust would be south towards the Loire. Bradley was asked to submit his plans and inform 21st Army Group of the requirements to implement Chastity by 1 June 1944, including airborne troops, air lift, naval forces and naval lift. It was assumed that Third Army would eventually be tasked to carry out the operation. A meeting to discuss the plan took place at Southwick House on 17 May, and two days later De Guingand wrote to FUSAG, Bradley, SHAEF, ANXF, AEAF and the commander of Task Force 122 to confirm that FUSAG would be responsible for the planning of Chastity, but that detailed planning may be delegated to Third Army.[6]

9 June

On 9 June Brigadier-General H.B. Lewis, the Adjutant-General of FUSAG, wrote to Montgomery regarding 'Special Requirements for Operation Chastity'.[7] Third Army had produced a tentative outline plan for the capture of Belle Isle, which had been shared with Task Force 122 and Ninth Air Force. Third Army planned to use an amphibious-trained regiment, an engineer shore brigade, a naval shore fire-control party and naval shore personnel, none of which were immediately available in Britain and would have to be made available from Normandy. The plan also envisaged two parachute regiments making an airborne assault, and it was thought that if the Germans began withdrawing from Belle Isle the parachute regiments should be able to capture it alone.

The Third Army Outline Plan to 'assault and reduce Belle Isle' was issued by Major General Hugh Gaffey, the Chief of Staff, under the authority of Patton. It consisted of a combined seaborne and airborne assault on the island supported by naval and air bombardment to destroy the enemy batteries. Paratroops would land in the south-eastern half of the island to present the movement of enemy reserves to the east of a line between Parlevant and Kervarigeon and they would also capture commanding ground to enable the seaborne troops to land. The enemy batteries at Kerviniec and Cape Locmaria would then be captured and destroyed. The seaborne assault force would consist of one regiment, preferably amphibious trained and from 28th Infantry Division. This would land after daylight in the Port Sables and Port York area.

The Third Army plan obviously assumed that Quiberon Bay had already been captured, after which the Allied naval forces would move the necessary ships and landing craft to a mounting area inside the Bay. Third Army also assumed that the landing craft would be able to turnaround and collect follow-up troops from the 'mainland' to the island if necessary. The seaborne forces would total over 4,000 men in the assault regiment, a 4.2in mortar battalion, a 155mm howitzer field battalion, a tank company and an engineer shore battalion, along with other support troops.

13 June

On 13 June, a week after D-Day, De Guingand wrote to Montgomery regarding the importance of capturing the Brittany ports:

> The forecast of maintenance capabilities is very encouraging. It may well be that the Brittany ports will not be as necessary as we first thought. If this is so, and the enemy's effective formations come out of the Brittany peninsula, it is possible that the whole tempo of our advance towards the Seine and onwards might be accelerated . . . I have ordered the planners to go into the whole problem, and I will let you have the conclusions we reach in a few days time.[8]

The next day De Guingand wrote to Montgomery again regarding Beneficiary and Hands Up. The Rear HQ staff had held several planning meetings and submitted their conclusions to 'master'. Regarding Quiberon Bay De Guingand wrote:

> This may well be worthwhile. Again it will require the use of 1 Airborne Division . . . We will get ahead with the planning, and I will keep you informed . . . It is fairly certain that a seaborne assault in addition to the air landing is off. The best plan would appear to be to land your airborne Brigade, follow it up by a Division or Divisions carried by air, and immediately beaches are secured to sail in further reinforcements.[9]

Despite this evidence the AEAF Official History suggests that Hands Up was proposed on 22 June by the Airborne Operations staff of AEAF as an alternative to Beneficiary:

> At 1830 hours on June 22nd the Air C-in-C saw Colonel Bagby (Airborne Ops AEAF) who had been at Southwick House for a conference with the Army on airborne operations. The Army were not interested in the St Malo plan which they regarded as hazardous in view of the strength of German forces believed to be there, and proposed an alternative plan for using airborne troops to make an early capture of Quiberon Bay . . .[10]

15 June

On 15 June De Guingand spoke to Whiteley, the Deputy Assistant Chief of Staff of SHAEF G3, to ask if the SHAEF planners could examine the possibility of an operation to capture Quiberon Bay.[11] De Guingand told Whiteley that the SAS and French Resistance 'seem to be having a fairly good time in that area', and that the German forces in Brittany appeared to be of secondary quality. He suggested an airborne operation to capture Quiberon Bay for the Chastity project, followed by a seaborne division. It is possible that the great storm had made De Guingand think about speeding up reinforcement of the beachhead.

An uncredited aide memoire in the SHAEF G3 files on Hands Up sheds light on what it described as the 'Quiberon Bay project'.[12] Written on 15 June, it stated that 'Early seizure of sufficient port capacity in Brittany is essential to the rapid build-up of our forces preparatory to advancing eastwards across the Seine'. The original plan for Overlord had envisaged a drive south from the beachhead to capture the ports at St Nazaire and Nantes to bring in maintenance for the US forces. To do this the Allies would need a bridgehead south of the Loire but maintaining forces south of the Loire by about D+40 would be difficult if the US forces were still being supplied from the Normandy ports, due to limited road transport and long lines of communication. The author therefore suggested that it would be dangerous for the US forces to reach the Loire without having secured the Brittany ports, and that a delay in gaining a major port would also lead to delays crossing the Seine. Quiberon Bay had been selected for the Chastity project, it argued, as it would be possible to develop it rapidly. What the Allies really needed was additional deep-water port capacity. The plans developed before Overlord foresaw the Allies using all of their deep-water port capacity including Nantes, St Nazaire and Quiberon Bay. However, even just over a week after the Normandy landings SHAEF predicted that even with Quiberon Boy in operation by D+180 there would not be enough capacity to maintain all of the planned troops in theatre. In short, to maintain the planned rate of build-up the Allies needed additional capacity, and if Quiberon Bay could not be secured they would have to accept a reduction in the rate of build-up equating to eight less divisions by D+150. The aide memoire concluded that the development of Quiberon Bay as a deep-water port was essential to support operations in southern Brittany, and to maintain the planned rate of build-up for the advance across the Seine.

17 June

On 17 June a planning team from ANXF, AEAF and SHAEF were asked to examine the Chastity plan alongside the developing proposals for an airborne operation.[13] SHAEF noted that the SAS and French Resistance had been able to operate in Brittany successfully and that the German divisions in the area were of a secondary quality. It was suggested that an airborne operation could reinforce the resistance movement around Quiberon Bay. A seaborne division would land 'hot on the heels of the airborne assault', and would probably have to land in landing craft prepared for an opposed landing. SHAEF G2 were also asked to investigate the beach conditions required for an assault landing.

21st Army Group's appreciation of an 'Independent operation to secure Quiberon Bay', code-named Hands Up, was published on 17 June.[14] The intention was to use airborne troops and seaborne Rangers or Commandos assisted by SAS Troops and the Maquis to seize the Quiberon Bay area, land follow-up forces by sea, establish a firm bridgehead, and allow the early implementation of the Chastity project. This would be bolstered by the French Resistance. Lorient and St Nazaire would be neutralised, which it was hoped would hasten the collapse of German resistance in Brittany. The Germans were thought to be swiftly transferring their higher-grade and mobile formations from Brittany towards the fighting in Normandy and a considerable number of the static troops that remained were non-German. The Germans were thought to only have horse-drawn artillery left and very few tanks, while the Allied bombing of the bridges over the Loire made it unlikely that reinforcements would arrive from the south.

The SAS had established a base around 15 miles north of Quiberon and had linked up with 3,000 armed Maquis. It was suggested that the Maquis, whose morale was high, might be able to control enough ground to allow airborne forces to land unopposed. The SAS had even contacted Russian troops fighting for the Germans who had offered to switch sides. It was thought that the German reactions to the airborne landings were likely to be slow, which would give the Allies time to secure phase lines. Lorient, a strongly defended fortress, was 15 miles away and there were many coastal and anti-aircraft batteries in the area. The beaches in Quiberon Bay were defended by strongpoints, minefields, emplacements and pillboxes, but the defences overall were thought to be 'not formidable'. Belle Isle, which was slightly offshore, was known to be garrisoned with several medium batteries as well as flak, and there was also a battery on the Quiberon peninsula covering the approach to the bay. Suitable landing areas were thought to exist for airborne landings, and HQ Airborne Troops were making a detailed study of the terrain. The airfield at Vannes was identified as an opportunity to land supplies and reinforcements. The beaches were thought to be suitable for Landing Craft Mechanised, Landing Craft Tank and Landing Ships Tank, and there was sufficient capacity for unloading vehicles and stores. Launching the operation depended on an appreciation that the enemy grip on the area was slackening on D-10 and that they would not be able to bring in reserves.

The 21st Army Group appreciation planned for a minimum of four airborne brigades landing on D-Day on DZs A, B, C and D. They would capture the beaches, mop up enemy resistance and reduce the beach defences. The 21st Army Group planners felt that the plan needed a force of two airborne divisions but that it could also be accomplished by four brigades. SAS Troops and Maquis would assist by delaying enemy movements and organised bodies of Maquis would reinforce the airborne troops and form outposts. In the afternoon of D-Day reinforcements would be landed by air at Vannes airfield, which would have been captured by the first lift. Either on D-Day or D+1 an air and naval bombardment would neutralise the coastal and flak batteries on Belle Isle and amphibious landings would capture the island. Then either on D+1 and 2 or on D+5 and 6 a seaborne division would land – the US 28th Infantry Division was earmarked as it had been trained in assault landings – supported if necessary by DD tanks. It would land on the beaches, move inland and capture the second phase line. At least one US Regiment would be loaded into Landing Ships Infantry, Landing Ships Tank and Landing Ships Gantry. A beach group, admin troops and some motor transport for the airborne troops and Maquis would also be brought in by sea and more airborne reinforcements and supplies would also be landed on Vannes airfield. Between D+7 and D+12 a second division and more support troops would be landed, and the bridgehead line would be pushed out. From D+14 onwards Transportation Corps and engineer troops and equipment would be landed to begin constructing the Chastity project.

The date for D-Day would depend on the speed with which the enemy forces in the area diminished. The naval lift for the first convoy into Quiberon Bay would need to carry a reinforced division at minimum scale plus the appropriate motor transport – the division would require 2,000 vehicles, the beach group 300, the airborne troops 200 and the Maquis 100. At least 1,600 of these vehicles were to be loaded into 30 LSTs. Landing Craft Assault and LCMs would land the troops, while LCTs would help expedite the landings. If DD tanks were used extra LSTs would be required. A stores lift of approximately 2,000 tons per day would be required, rising to 3,000 tons by D+15. The naval implications had not yet been examined but were critical to the plan and would have to be studied before planning could proceed.

Hands Up would be at a long distance from air bases in the UK, although Quiberon was within range of troop-carrier and glider aircraft. In the event of insufficient naval resources being available two alternatives were suggested. The first would see the airborne forces reinforced by a reduced-scale infantry division that would be landed at Vannes airfield by troop-carrier aircraft. This would require the infantry to leave behind their motor transport, which would be brought by sea in any case and was therefore not much different from the original plan. The second option, if the enemy situation deteriorated seriously, was for a small mobile column to advance from the Normandy bridgehead to reinforce the airborne forces. The 21st Army Group appreciation identified landing beaches on the tip of the Quiberon peninsula, Carnac, Kerjouanno, Tumiac and Samzum on Belle Ille. Drop Zone A was south of Ploumel, B was east of Ploumel, C was north-west of Vannes and D was at Sarzeau.

The 21st Army Group appreciation of Hands Up published on 17 June also considered the movement implications.[15] It proposed landings in the Port Maria, Plage de Quiberon, Port Galiguen, Plage de Carnac and Petit Mont areas subject to a more detailed examination including charts and aerial photographs. However, the beach at Petit Mont was considered the most suitable owing to its gradient and good exits. Part of an Engineer Special Brigade would be needed to prepare the beaches and to help land personnel, vehicles and stores and additional troops would also be required to operate the Chastity project.

21st Army Group thought that LCTs could not be used to lift motor transport for the assault divisions due to the distance involved – LCTs had been designed to cross the English Channel, and were poor seaboats. It would therefore be necessary to use LSTs and Motor Transport ships. A lift of forty LSTs and five MT ships was suggested. LSIs would be required for the assault itself and about forty to fifty

LCTs could be sailed to the area empty to assist with ferrying troops and vehicles ashore. The diversion of shipping from Normandy to Quiberon Bay would mean a shortfall of 15,000 vehicles on the planned build-up. A further 1,500 vehicles would be left behind schedule due to the need to remove LSTs 20 days before the operation for loading. It was estimated that 2,000 tons of stores would be required every day, rising to 3,000 tons per day after five days until Quiberon Bay was fully opened. Stores would be discharged from ships by DUKWs and lighters.

21st Army Group suggested that LSTs and LSIs could load at Plymouth and the MT ships could be loaded at either Southampton or the Bristol Channel. Troops would need to be marshalled at least seven days before D-Day. Planning would have to commence on D-40 and the engineer special brigade would have to be withdrawn from Normandy on the same timescale. The LSTs and LSIs would have to be withdrawn on D-21 and loading with stores would commence on D-20, before vehicles would begin loading on D-10. Even at this early stage 21st Army Group highlighted the risk of sailing convoys to Quiberon Bay, where they would be vulnerable to U-boats from Brest and St Nazaire. 21st Army Group concluded that Hands Up 'might be feasible' but noted several complications. Among these were the loss of naval lift from Normandy, the difficulties in getting equipment to the area, the need to withdraw an Engineer Special Brigade, and the naval problem of sailing convoys through waters close to U-boat bases.

On the same day Montgomery wrote to Ramsay, Leigh-Mallory and Browning regarding Hands Up.[16] He attached copies of an 'Army appreciation of an independent operation to secure Quiberon Bay by an airborne assault followed up by the landing of seaborne forces'. He suggested that the operation might take place if the enemy situation in Brittany deteriorated and requested that the naval and air planning staffs carry out further examination of the plan.

18 June

On 18 June members of the SHAEF planning staff – Lieutenant Colonel Curtis of G2, Brigadier-General Maclean and Colonel Hinton of G3, and Colonel Whipple of G4 along with Captain Walter from ANXF and Group Captain Broad from AEAF – were asked to examine the feasibility of 21st Army Group's appreciation of an operation to capture Quiberon Bay. They met the next day on 19 June.[17]

19 June

On 19 June Richardson wrote to Colonel Albrecht, the chief of staff of the US Army's Western Base Section, enclosing copies of the 21st Army Group appreciation for Lucky Strike and Hands Up. Richardson stated that: 'It will be appreciated that neither of these Operations is firm, and that planning is still only in its earliest stages. These papers therefore merely represent a first and tentative appreciation of what might be feasible under a particular set of circumstances.'[18] Richardson's statement reinforces that it is a mistake to think that all airborne plans had the same likelihood of taking place – many were indeed no more than planning exercises.

20 June

On 20 June the Chief Engineer's Office at ETOUSA signalled to Task Force 122 that the beaches on Belle Isle that had been identified for intelligence gathering had been code-named Massachusetts (Samzun), Virginia (Port Yorch) and South Carolina (Bourdardoue).[19] This use of US states for beach code names is consistent with the use of Utah and Omaha on D-Day.

21 June

On 21 June Browning met with Leigh-Mallory to discuss future airborne operations, including Hands Up. Leigh-Mallory reported that the Army were not keen on Beneficiary but had proposed Hands Up at Quiberon Bay. Several days later a conference took place at AEAF headquarters to discuss airborne operations.[20] The meeting was attended by Major General Whiteley from SHAEF who reported that the Army considered Quiberon Bay important as it was the most suitable port for bringing in reinforcements and maintaining the Allied forces in Brittany.

24 June

On 24 June 21st Army Group issued a paper on 'Subsidiary operations to further Overlord', which was sent to FUSAG.[21] The US headquarters was asked to prepare detailed plans for Operation Hands Up. The paper explained that although the objectives would normally be best achieved by 'normal land manoeuvres', it was also believed that detailed plans needed to be prepared so that they would be available if circumstances required the operation to be implemented. Hands Up was described as '. . . an operation with the mission of capturing, by an independent force, a bridgehead covering the Quiberon Bay in order to permit the landing of construction stores and personnel so that the Chastity project might be commenced before the area is linked on the ground with our main forces'.

FUSAG was authorised to consider the use of airborne forces as well as seaborne reinforcements. The paper also explained that it was unlikely that Hands Up would be mounted unless enemy resistance would be slight and the force could be maintained by sea. If the campaign lasted into the autumn, which would make it impossible to land construction materials for the Chastity project over the beaches, it was felt that Hands Up might be justified. This illustrates one of the main dilemmas of airborne planning – the need for weak-enough resistance to make the operation viable, but enough opposition to make the operation worthwhile.

21st Army Group's paper stated that Quiberon Bay would be suitable for the landing of airborne forces and that HQ Airborne Forces were making a detailed study of the terrain. The first day would see a minimum of four airborne brigades – the equivalent of a US airborne division or a reinforced British airborne division – dropped to secure an initial beachhead and neutralise the beach defences. The afternoon would see reinforcements landed by air at Vannes airfield. It was suggested, however, that four brigades would struggle to carry out these tasks and capture Vannes airfield, and that it would be preferable to allocate two divisions.

27 June

On 27 June Captain Maurice Mansergh, Ramsay's Deputy Chief of Staff, wrote to SHAEF, AEAF and 21st Army Group regarding the naval implications for Hands Up in reply to 21st Army Group G(Plans) letter of June.[22] ANXF, he said, would need an Outline Plan to carry out detailed planning, which would need to be prepared by FUSAG along with representatives from ANXF and AEAF. He suggested that due to the short timescale the SHAEF sections of ANXF and AEAF staff should take part. The commander of the 11th Amphibious Force, Rear Admiral Hall, would be given responsibility for planning future amphibious operations in the US sector and would liaise with FUSAG.

Mansergh also forwarded with his letter some notes based on a preliminary study of the naval aspects of Hands Up. He drew attention to the substantial number of escorts that would be needed due to the presence of U-boat bases at Brest and the Loire ports. These, he said, would have to be taken from those off the Normandy beachhead. The ANXF staff thought that the approach to Quiberon would be difficult and a passage through De La Teignouse would be impossible as it was only four cables wide and the tidal stream ran at four knots. The naval forces would therefore need to use the southern passage between les Grands Cardineaux and Plateau du Four, which was deep and six miles wide. Ships would have to pass Croisic Point from 10 miles out due to shore batteries. ANXF felt that the only suitable beaches for landings were between Petit Mont and Grand Mont as they had good gradients at all states of the tide. They were, however, exposed to south-westerly winds and exits for motor transport would be difficult due to sand dunes. Batteries on Belle Isle covered the western approach to Quiberon Bay, meaning that the island would have to be captured or neutralised. The southern approach had several covering batteries, including an 11in battery at Croisic Point which would have to be neutralised, and a 15in battery on the Quiberon Peninsula itself which had an all-round traverse.

Mansergh suggested that a convoy on D+1 could consist of three LSI(L)s or other personnel ships, five MT or stores ships, thirty-three LSTs, three large stores coasters and three flotillas of LCTs. D+3 would see seven stores coasters arrive followed by six Liberty ships on D+5 carrying stores. A convoy on D+7 would bring two personnel ships, ten LST and fifteen MT or stores ships. From D+12 six Liberty ships would bring in stores every seven days. Shipping for the Chastity project would begin to arrive from D+14 onwards once the beachhead was secure. The navy assessed that a minimum of forty-five escorts would be required to protect these convoys. This number would have to be increased if any aircraft carriers or bombarding ships were added. Even so, Mansergh stressed that losses from U-boats 'must be expected'. The operation would involve a long approach through waters that were very suitable for mining and would require a 'very considerable' minesweeping effort. As Quiberon was such a distance from Britain an advanced minesweeping base would have to be established. The RAF had not been consulted on the part they might play in bombarding enemy defences but Mansergh thought that their contribution might be limited to the neutralisation of the battery on Croisic Point. The naval staff were concerned that as the airborne forces would be dropped at least 24 hours before the arrival of the amphibious force it would give the Germans ample time to concentrate U-boats to attack the amphibious convoys and to lay mines. There were U-boat bases at Lorient, St Nazaire, Bordeaux, La Pallice and Brest, but air bombardment would do little good as the U-boat pens were well defended.

The planning for Hands Up shows how it is a mistake to view airborne operations in 1944 in isolation. Hands Up was really a 'mini

D-Day', of which the airborne element was just one part. Indeed, Hands Up would take place at a much greater distance from Britain and close to several enemy-held fortified ports. Indeed, in many respects it was more complex than D-Day.

28 June

The SHAEF G3 planning staff had been asked to examine plans for Lucky Strike, Beneficiary and Hands Up and on 28 June they circulated their report to ANXF, AEAF and SHAEF.[23] Their study focused on the logistical aspects of each operation. They stressed that the early capture of the Seine ports would not make up for a failure to secure the Brittany ports as the latter were vital to the US build-up. Not having the Brittany ports in operation by October would lead to a deficiency of eight divisions. The planners estimated that the Germans would not have any mobile reserves left in Brittany, and that one US corps advancing from Normandy would be able to capture St Malo rapidly. After mid-July an additional corps should be available to advance to Quiberon Bay, after which the 'St Malo Corps' would clear the rest of the peninsula aided by the Maquis. Securing St Malo would allow the US forces to support six divisions in Normandy, which would free up maintenance to support formations advancing to the Seine. The capture of St Nazaire, Lorient and Brest were also of great importance to the Allied naval forces due to the threat of U-boats – until they were captured any operations in southern Brittany would require a heavy naval escort. The planning staff concluded that any operation that was opposed would be hazardous. In the case of Hands Up this would be particularly so as the airborne landings would be divided by an estuary and could be defeated in detail. Quiberon Bay was only 30 miles from the U-boat bases and the naval convoys would therefore be vulnerable. The airborne landings would also alert the Germans to the impending arrival of forces by sea. If, on the other hand, German resistance was light the SHAEF planners argued that the overland advance from Normandy would be so rapid that the advantages of an airborne operation would be minimal and the effort would not be justified.

29 June

Although the British Army possessed two airborne divisions in the North West Europe theatre, thoughts had already turned to expanding this force with troops who could be flown in by aircraft to captured airfields or improvised airstrips. On 29 June HQ Airborne Troops asked 21st Army Group when a British formation would be available in an air-portable role.[24] 21st Army Group's Staff Duties section told HQ Airborne Troops to plan on the basis that 52nd Division would be available to take part in Hands Up. However, it had not yet been allocated to 21st Army Group and was still under War Office control. The target date for it being ready to take part in operations was 24 July. Later the same day HQ Airborne Troops asked 21st Army Group for permission to contact 52nd Division directly regarding the planning for Hands Up and pointed out that the planning for the operation would need representatives from the division to be at Moor Park from 5 July. Browning's command was therefore due to expand even further.

1 July

HQ Airborne Troops published a planning programme for the period 1 to 15 July, during which Beneficiary, Hands Up and Lucky Strike were concurrently in various stages of planning.[25] FUSAG was to 'start considering' Hands Up on 3 July, while HQ Airborne Troops would start studying the operation on 5 July and issue intelligence information on the same day. The Corps Commanders Conference for Hands Up would take place in the afternoon of 6 July and the Air Co-ordinating Conference on 9 July. All plans for Hands Up were to be completed by 15 July. It is hard to escape the conclusion that HQ Airborne Troops was overloaded with planning, especially considering it had not been set up as an operational headquarters and had to liaise with so many other headquarters from all three services, and from different nationalities.

2 July

On 2 July Browning wrote to 21st Army Group regarding his tactical headquarters for Hands Up.[26] He explained that as a result of planning for these operations, 'it is clear that a HQ is required to command and coordinate the Airborne Forces being employed'. Browning selected himself for the role, indicating that his headquarters was the only one available. However, he suggested that although it was not organised as a fully-operational headquarters he would be able to form a Tactical Headquarters from its war establishment. He did however request the formation of a Corps Signals for which he would require additional Royal Signals personnel. He asked the Chief Signals Officer at Airborne

Troops discuss the matter with the Signals Officer-in-Chief at 21st Army Group to develop a Corps Signals establishment. It is difficult not to think that Browning was already over-reaching both himself and the capabilities of his headquarters, not to mention self-selecting himself to command a corps in action.

The Joint Planning Staff's Outline Plan for Hands Up was published on 2 July.[27] The message accompanying the plan stressed, however, that no action was to be taken to implement it. The object was 'To assist and expedite the cutting-off of the Brittany Peninsula and the capture of Quiberon Bay by Third US Army'. The operation would be carried out by the 1st Airborne Division and the 1st Polish Parachute Brigade combined with a seaborne assault by a Commando Brigade, followed by an airlanding by 52nd Division. This force would secure air-landing strips and beaches to allow build-up and maintenance to arrive by sea and air for 14 days, by which time it was thought that Third Army would have linked up overland. British forces would be relieved as soon as possible after link-up.

For the operation to be launched 12th Army Group would have to have reached a line between St Malo, Rennes and Laval and enemy opposition would have to weak enough that Third Army could be confident of reaching Quiberon Bay within a fortnight. Airfields would need to be established in the Rennes area and if possible 84 Group and XIX Tactical Air Command would be operating from the Continent. Hands Up would only be launched if the Germans had no uncommitted mobile reserves left in Brittany. The operation would require a four-day window of weather suitable for operating troop-carrier aircraft and constructing airstrips. At least 30 days would be required to mount Hands Up, but this was dependent on whether units would have to be withdrawn from Normandy. The operation would be commanded by 12th Army Group through Third Army. The airborne operation would be commanded by Browning and the troop-carrier operations by Williams. All Allied troops in the Quiberon Bay area would be commanded by Browning until a link up was made with Third Army, at which point Browning would come under Patton's command. The naval part of the operation would be controlled by ANXF while the command of the convoys and the defence of the anchorage itself would be delegated to Rear Admiral Hall, the commander of the Eleventh Amphibious Force. Even though this arrangement would also have been used for Beneficiary and Swordhilt, it is hard not to come to the conclusion that Browning and Patton working together would have been problematic at best.

3 July

A 'Q' meeting took place at SHAEF on 3 July, chaired by Major General Humfrey Gale.[28] The Q Staff were anxious about the forecasted date for the capture of Quiberon Bay. They had been planning on the original date of D+47 but realised that that was now optimistic. They stressed that it was essential for Quiberon to be secured by D+60 at the latest if it was to be developed before the winter weather set in, and pointed out that this would coincide with a favourable moon period in early August. The naval representative at the meeting refused to say that it was impossible to escort a convoy into Quiberon if it were still in enemy hands but pointed out that it would mean withdrawing escorts from Normandy to do so. This, it appears, the navy were not keen to do. The meeting concluded therefore that even if Quiberon was captured first, Brest, Lorient and St Nazaire would have to be secured soon after. Naval intelligence had identified a 'considerable number' of U-boats in the Brittany ports which would pose a risk to the naval convoys, which would have to sail without shore-based air cover. The capture of Vannes airfield however would negate this. The Q Staff were wary of the risk of failing to secure either the Brittany ports or the Seine ports – they described it as 'falling between two stools' – and thought that the Brittany ports would be more important logistically than those on the Seine. The planning staffs were therefore asked to work backwards from the D+60 deadline to work out the date by which Montgomery as Commander-in-Chief would have to decide if the operation was viable, and if so to allocate forces to carry it out.

A report by SHAEF's planning staff, published on 3 July, examined the relative merits of Hands Up, Beneficiary and Lucky Strike.[29] The SHAEF planners predicted that there would be little opposition in Brittany and that the bulk of the Germans' mobile units in Brittany would be drawn to the Normandy battle, leaving behind only static coastal units. Brittany was identified as an important objective, more important in fact than the capture of the Seine ports. It was estimated that if the Brittany ports were not opened by October the scheduled rate of reinforcement would be reduced by eight divisions, and this would increase from October onwards.

7 July

On 7 July Colonel C.R. Landon, the Acting Adjutant-General of FUSAG, wrote to 21st Army Group regarding the withdrawal of US troops from Normandy for future airborne operations.[30] Planning for Beneficiary and Hands Up had indicated that both operations would require an

Engineer Special Brigade, all of which were currently employed on the beaches of Normandy. If they were to take part in further operations they would need to be withdrawn to Britain 30 days before for refitting and training. For planning purposes Landon suggested a target date of 1 August, which meant that if the planned operations were to take place in the available moon periods they would need to be withdrawn at once. The units already on the Continent included the Engineer Special Brigade Headquarters, three Engineer Construction Battalions, one Joint Assault Signal Company, one Medical Battalion, one Quartermaster Battalion and three Amphibious Truck Companies. The removal of DUKW companies would affect the build-up in Normandy. Landon also drew 21st Army Group's attention to the US 28th Infantry Division's status as a SHAEF reserve formation. It had been released by SHAEF for amphibious operations but would not be able to take part in these without the support of an Engineer Special Brigade. Landon thought that troops from No. 1 Base Section, which was part of Com Z, were scheduled to move to Normandy in the next few days. As the Base Section was due to provide support troops for Beneficiary and Hands Up he suggested that they be returned 'without delay', particularly as No. 1 Base Section was charged with carrying out Chastity. He felt that in the current tactical situation there was no need for the troops to be in Normandy.

8 July

Hands Up was at the limit of the operational range for airborne forces based in the UK. Some informal notes in Hollinghurst's papers suggest that as of 8 July the route considered for Hands Up would either take Route A crossing the south coast at St Albans Head, making landfall at Plurien and then to Vannes, or Route B which would cross the coast at Portland Bill. Route A was 294 miles, whereas Route B was 292 miles. It would take at least 70 miles for the formations to gather. One problem was the operational radius of Albermarle and Horsa combinations, which was only 340 miles. As a result on the return Albermarles might need to land in the West Country or at Hurn or Tarrant Rushton airfields. Hollinghurst suggested that paratroops should land first from 2359 onwards, followed by gliders at 0700 on D-Day and then at 0030 on D+1.[31]

On 8 July Richardson wrote to Browning regarding the availability of aircraft for Hands Up.[32] Four hundred and twelve aircraft had been allocated to Anvil and therefore could not be included in planning for operations from the UK for the near future. It was also understood that IX Troop Carrier Command had fewer aircrews than aircraft. Richardson's notes prepared prior to a meeting at FUSAG on 8 July tell us much about the planning of Hands Up.[33] He stated that the object of Hands Up was ' . . . to secure the Chastity area at an earlier date than would be possible by a land advance pure and simple. This earlier date arises owing to the necessity of getting the port construction started before the bad weather sets in.'

Richardson was also concerned 'at all costs' that the operation must not become a liability as it would be very costly for all three services. It would not be launched unless there was a chance of the US ground forces reaching Quiberon Bay within a short period, which he defined as 'say three weeks at most'. This seems wildly optimistic considering what transpired at Arnhem. At this early stage in the planning Richardson also suggested that US 504th Parachute Infantry Regiment to take part and suggested that 52nd Division could be replaced by a US division in the air-transportable role. Richardson also stated that command would have to be exercised by a small corps headquarters and that if both divisions taking part were British this would be HQ Airborne Troops. Richardson suggested the period five days before and after a full moon were suitable, which limited likely dates to the periods from 31 July to 9 August and 28 August to 7 September. As the Q staff had suggested that the Chastity project had to begin by 15 August at the latest, this left 9 August as the last date that Hands Up could realistically take place unless the Airborne forces were willing to accept a no-moon period. Richardson thought that the administrative issues of the operation, which involved all three services, would be considerable. Personnel and liaison officers would have to be exchanged between headquarters to create planning and operations staffs and a British element would need to be added to the US beach organisation to handle British supplies coming over the beaches. Richardson suggested that problems would inevitably arise and was concerned about medical services and reinforcements. Additional signals units would also be required. He also suggested that some US quartermaster and engineer units would have to be withdrawn from France if the US 28th Infantry Division was used as the amphibious assault formation. Perhaps Richardson's biggest concern was the lack of time. He suggested that a planning group be set up in England with representatives from Airborne Forces, the RAF and IX Troop Carrier Command, along with US Third Army and 52nd Division and the US 28th Division if these were used.

9 July

On 9 July 21st Army Group invited representatives from SHAEF, AEAF, ANXF, FUSAG, Third Army and HQ Airborne Troops to a meeting on 11 July to discuss Hands Up. De Guingand specifically requested the presence of Bull from SHAEF and Browning.[34]

G Plans notes for the meeting suggest that the planners were occupied with Belle Isle.[35] They had identified the island as an 'effective keystone' to the coastal defences of Quiberon Bay as the batteries on the island were interlinked with others at Lorient and St Nazaire. Although the planner's notes suggested that Belle Isle would have to be neutralised before a seaborne assault, this was later marked 'no'. The German garrison on the island was not thought to be strong, consisting mainly of 2,500 coastal artillerymen and naval personnel. 21st Army Group's planners concluded that it would not be possible to mount an operation against Belle Isle on what it called the 'lavish scale' originally planned by Third Army. However, the island was a formidable obstacle and would have to be neutralised before Quiberon Bay could be opened fully as a port. They concluded that a heavy air bombardment followed by an airborne assault and commando landings from the sea would be the best course of action.

On 9 July De Guingand chaired a preliminary meeting on Hands Up at 21st Army Group Main HQ, which at this point was still in England. The meeting concluded that there was a 'distinct possibility' that Hands Up would be mounted as a separate operation, and noted that the last convenient date in a full-moon period would be 9 August. 21st Army Group was planning for 52nd Division to take part. The scope of Hands Up was described as 'to secure a bridgehead round Quiberon Bay. Intended that force should be joined by US Third Army from N as soon as possible. Force must not become involved in mobile operations to the detriment of its main task, though possibility of securing Lorient should be borne in mind should enemy disintegrate completely.'

Two advantages of Hands Up were stressed. Firstly it would secure Quiberon Bay in time to satisfy the requirements of Com Z for the Chastity project, and secondly it would leave a larger proportion of Third Army free to turn west and capture Brest. In terms of responsibility for planning 21st Army would take over from FUSAG – presumably as the latter was not yet operational – and retain command until Third Army had effected a link-up. It was suggested that the commander would be Browning. A number of points were highlighted for further discussion at a later meeting. These included the naval implications of escorting convoys to Quiberon Bay while Brest, Lorient and St Nazaire were still in enemy hands and the size of naval force that this would entail. The size and nature of the force required to capture Belle Isle was also queried. The required air support would also need to be assessed, including the possibility of flying fighters from Vannes airfield. Deception was also considered. The meeting highlighted two main administrative problems with Hands Up. While the maintenance for the force in the bridgehead would be a mainly British commitment as the majority of the airborne forces would be British, the administrative personnel from COMZ involved in developing the Chastity project would be American. The main supply route would be by sea with casualties being evacuated by air and reinforcements and only 'special equipment' arriving by air. It was argued that supporting Resistance groups in Brittany should not be a British commitment, as the peninsula was in the US sector. They should, it was argued, be armed with US weapons for supply purposes.

Also on 9 July a conference was held at HQ Airborne Troops at Moor Park to discuss the airborne element of Hands Up, possibly as a result of the earlier conference at 21st Army Group. The conference was chaired by Browning, and attended by Urquhart, Williams, Hollinghurst, representatives from First US Army Group and the commander of the US 504th Parachute Infantry Regiment.[36]

10 July

Montgomery's directive M510 published on 10 July stressed that from an administrative point of view the Allies had to gain possession of the Brittany peninsula.[37] M510 directed that once the First US Army reached the base of the Contentin at Avranches, VIII Corps – made up of three infantry divisions and one armoured – was to turn westwards into Brittany and advance towards Rennes and St Malo. Operations in Brittany would then come under the command of Third Army which would have the task of clearing the peninsula. Montgomery explained that plans were being produced for airborne operations in either St Malo or Quiberon Bay. He expressed a preference that the airborne troops should not be used for St Malo, leaving them available for his priority, Quiberon Bay.

11 July

A meeting took place at Southwick House on the morning of 11 July to discuss the Outline Plan for Hands Up, chaired by Richardson and attended by representatives of 21st Army Group branches.[38] Later the same day Richardson produced a set of detailed notes for De Guingand.[39]

Richardson felt that there was a danger of misconceptions regarding the object and scope of Hands Up. He noted that FUSAG had been preparing what he described as 'grandiose' plans including a corps of two infantry divisions and an armoured division. He argued that the maintenance and naval aspects of this plan were 'unsound' and that the Chief of Staff meeting should begin with a description of the operations up to the launching of Hands Up, and then a definition of the object of the operation. He argued forcefully that the old concept – based on a rapid decline in enemy resistance and a cheap way to occupy Brittany – must be abandoned. The Germans had resisted more strongly in Normandy than the Allies had suspected and this might increase if the deception of Operation Fortitude collapsed. 21st Army Group's first priority, he argued, should be to capture Quiberon Bay and Brest. He therefore argued for a strong thrust southwards from the Normandy bridgehead to reach the line of St Malo, Rennes and Laval. Richardson felt that it would not be possible to 'go cheap on Brittany' until that line had been reached, but that the chances of success might not be clear until Avranches had been reached.

Richardson suggested that the objective of Hands Up should be to '. . . secure Chastity as a harbour for "awkward convoys" by the date required by the navy'. 'Awkward convoys' were defined as tows for the Chastity project and smaller craft. Richardson felt that Quiberon would have to be captured by 15 August and suggested that it should have priority for all of 21st Army Group. However, he also stressed to De Guingand that before Hands Up could be considered at all the navy would have to say whether they would be willing to sail convoys to Quiberon Bay if Brest was still in enemy hands, particularly as the operation would require more than one convoy. He suggested that Brest might be captured a maximum of four weeks after Quiberon Bay. Richardson argued that the risk of U-boats from Brest and the likely deterioration of weather in the late summer and autumn meant that it would unwise to plan Hands Up as a standalone operation. Richardson also considered the possibility of linking up with the Hands Up force. He felt that the Allies might not know this likelihood of this being achieved for certain until they reached Rennes, as by that point that Germans would have had to have decided whether to evacuate Brittany or fortify the ports. He felt that once the Allies had reached Rennes they would be likely to reach Quiberon Bay, but that Hands Up could be launched as 'an insurance'. Richardson also argued that no resources should be withdrawn from Normandy for Hands Up so as not to prejudice progress on the main front. This would particularly be the case if the operation included seaborne landings as beach troops and other units would have to be withdrawn from Normandy for training, which would lead to an inflexible plan. He thought that the sea and air aspect was already complicated when taking into account weather and timing and would lead to postponements. As the whole object of Hands Up was to gain time, he argued, an inflexible plan and too many conditions for its launching meant that it would be of little use.

Richardson suggested that the operation should be completely airborne if possible and be supplemented by seaborne maintenance if necessary. Browning had also told him that the operation could be launched in the no-moon period. 21st Army Group's Q Staff had told Richardson that some form of seaborne maintenance would be essential, and that given recent experiences and transfer of aircraft to Anvil they were not optimistic about air supply. Richardson closed by stating that in his opinion a combined sea-air operation was not sound, but that it was for Browning to say whether an airborne-only operation could achieve the objective. As an afterthought Richardson also suggested that airborne forces could perhaps be used to help speed the advance from Rennes to Quiberon, by dropping a parachute brigade ahead of the advancing troops. He also felt that matters would be much simpler if a US airborne division could be withdrawn from Normandy for operations in Brittany.

On 11 July De Guingand wrote a document 'Hands Up – Conclusions and recommendations', which seems to have led to a flurry of meetings and planning activity over the following week or so. De Guingand stated that it was important that Quiberon Bay was captured with enough time to allow for the Chastity project to be in operation before the winter weather set in. He also suggested that the bad weather would start on 1 October, and that Quiberon Bay should therefore be in Allied hands by 1 September. He hoped that Third Army would be able to capture the objective by the required date without any outside help. He also thought that to operate against Brest and Quiberon Bay at the same time would require two corps of three divisions each, and that St Malo would be essential to support these operations. De Guingand assessed that 21st Army Group would have to be prepared to help Third Army's thrust towards Quiberon Bay with an airborne operation and he thought that this would help speed up the liberation of the whole Brittany peninsula. He felt that the Chastity project should not be launched until Third Army had advanced beyond Avranches and was in the Rennes area, and if the enemy had increased its resources available to defend Brittany. The Allied naval forces were not prepared to undertake a seaborne operation as part of Hands Up before Brest was captured as its use would be important in bad weather, the commitment of escorts would be too great and the shipping and craft requirements would have a serious effect upon the build-up in Normandy. The navy were also not prepared to sail 'awkward tows' required for Chastity until Brest was in Allied hands.

They would however accept the sailing of a special convoy for Hands Up on D+2. De Guingand thought – mistakenly, as is turned out – that there would be no air problems involved with Hands Up.

Despite the navy's objections De Guingand thought that preparations should be made to carry out Hands Up before Brest had been captured. The combined airborne and seaborne force would be commanded by Browning, who would in turn come under the command of Patton and Third Army on landing. De Guingand stated a target date of 'not before' 9 August and he felt that the airborne troops could be dropped in daylight if necessary. The operation would be planned by 21st Army Group, ANCXF and AEAF and at a later stage FUSAG would take over from 21st Army Group. Other points that needed 'special attention' during planning included information-gathering through the SAS, assistance from the Resistance, the need to treat Chastity as separate to Hands Up, the need to build two airstrips, deception, maps and casualty evacuation.

12 July

On 12 July a draft instruction for the airborne aspect of Hands Up was prepared by HQ Airborne Troops.[40] This document was not issued and was not planned to be issued, but was prepared as an indication of what the instructions might be. 1st Airborne Division's first task would be to capture the airfield at Vannes so that it could be put into operation as soon as possible for the flying-in of supplies and the operation of fighter aircraft. This would also include destroying flak on and around the airfield, control of the area around the airfield and keeping enemy mortars out of range. The division's second task would be to control the roads leading out of Vannes, especially the road between Theix and Auray to ensure communication along the beachhead. Urquhart would also make contact with the SAS and Maquis in the area, with the 504th Parachute Infantry Regiment around Surzur and St Armel and with the Polish Parachute Brigade at St Anne D'Auray and Kerdroguen. He was also ordered to observe the roads leading into the airhead and Vannes from the east and south east.

The Polish Parachute Brigade would form a firm defence in the Plouharnel area and destroy the coastal guns on the Quiberon Peninsula. The Brigade's secondary task would be to destroy other defences on the peninsula. Their third task would be to withdraw to the north-east once the 28th Infantry Division had landed and form a firm base at St Anne D'Auray and Kerdroguen, as well as controlling the road centre at Auray. The 28th Division would land on the beaches at Carnac and would be directed towards Belz to protect the western flank of the beachhead.

The 504th Parachute Infantry Regiment would secure the exits from the beaches between St Gildas and Port Navallo by holding the road centres at Surzur and St Armel. Their second task would be to patrol the roads running to the north, north-east and east. The pathfinders would land at 2359 the night before D-Day, and the parachute brigades would drop from 0100 onwards. The first glider lift, consisting of divisional troops, the airlanding brigade and glider elements of the parachute units, would start landing at 0700. The second glider lift would land on the airfield and selected LZs at 1400. The seaborne assault by the 28th Infantry Division was unlikely to take place until 24 hours after the first airborne landings. It was unlikely that the airfield would be ready to receive aircraft until at least 36 hours after its capture, but a first resupply would be dropped on the night of D-Day. Browning also proposed to form a corps reserve around Vannes airfield.

On 12 July SHAEF's Movement and Transport section wrote to Bedell Smith, the Chief of Transportation and Chief of Engineers at ETOUSA regarding Chastity.[41] It was now anticipated that Quiberon Bay would be captured on D+70 to 75, Brest on D+75 to 80, the north bank of the Loire on D+90 and the South bank on D+110. These dates were at least a month behind schedule and it was expected that the winter weather would break by 1 October. The programme for towing units of the Chastity project which had been prepared by the Chief of Transportation was now impracticable due to a shortage of ocean-going tugs. SHAEF were planning to reconstruct or build major ports at Cherbourg, Chastity and on the Loire, spacing them a month apart. Chastity would need to start before Cherbourg was ready, which would affect the allocation of engineer and transportation units. SHAEF therefore asked ETOUSA to reconsider the Chastity project.

On 12 July the Chief Engineer at 21st Army Group circulated an Engineer Appreciation for Hands Up.[42] He saw the principal engineer task as the preparation of airstrips, as these would be required for the landing of 52nd Division and an airlift of 1,200 tons of stores per day. This task would be complicated by the muddy clay and the lack of level sites. Vannes airfield had been heavily bombed – prior to the last two raids on the airfield there were 450 craters, including 88 on the runway itself. He therefore asked for bombing of the airfield to stop and for up-to-date aerial photos to be taken. He stressed that it would be essential to employ the US Army's Aviation Engineer Battalions. There were only two rivers in the area – the Pont du Lac and the

Bono – although the area was badly 'cut up' by estuaries. The bridges over these were long and if they were destroyed they could not be replaced easily. He also suggested including several sets of Bailey bridging with the stores and to have several more ready to be flown in in an emergency, and suggested taking outboard engines as these might be useful for crossing estuaries in locally-sourced boats. He also suggested using explosives to block enemy counter-movements by demolishing bridges over canals and rivers, particularly at La Roche Bernard and Henneb. The commander of 13 Army Group Royal Engineers, Colonel Mackay, was placed under Browning's command for the planning and execution of Hands Up. Other corps, such as those taking part in the campaign in Normandy, had their own organic engineering units, whereas HQ Airborne Troops was formed on a much more minimal establishment.

On 12 July Bull wrote to Bedell Smith regarding airborne operations in Brittany:

> With reference to possibilities of using airborne forces in Brittany – examination has been carried out, assuming the object is the early capture of Quiberon Bay, the use of which is essential before the worst of winter makes beach maintenance in the Neptune area impracticable. Owing to the submarine threat and the necessity for having a staging place for sheltering the constructional tows for the Quiberon Bay development project during their passage, the capture of BREST is an essential prerequisite to the development of Quiberon Bay . . . Our available airborne resources will only allow us to conduct one of these operations . . . If possible, we should clearly attempt to advance overland to Brest and Quiberon Bay simultaneously.[43]

Bull went on to explain that due to the threat of U-boats the Allied naval forces were not prepared to sail supply convoys into Quiberon Bay until after Brest had been captured. They were, however, prepared to 'fight through' one specially-escorted convoy to support the airborne forces. Bull thought that with the help of this convoy the airborne operation would be feasible if the opposition was light, but that it would be essential for the overland advance to 'be within reasonable striking distance, if an Anzio is to be avoided'. Bull concluded that an airborne operation in Brittany could help to unlock any delay to the overland advance. The spectre of Anzio suggests that the Allies were concerned about losing momentum in breaking out from beachheads.

13 July

A meeting took place at 21st Army Group Main HQ in the woods near Southwick Park on 13 July to discuss the troop requirements for Hands Up.[44] It was chaired by Brigadier Herbert, the head of the G(Staff Duties) branch, and attended by representatives from G(Plans), Ninth Air Force, FUSAG, COMZ, ETOUSA, HQ Airborne Troops, 13 Army Group Royal Engineers, D Survey branch, Q(Plans), G(Air), Q(M), Royal Artillery and Royal Signals. The object of the meeting was to decide the order of battle for planning purposes. Resources were limited and units would have to come from US forces or be withdrawn from 21st Army Group. The outline order of battle as of 13 July was 1st Airborne Division, the Polish Brigade, 52nd Division and either the 1st or 4th Special Service Brigade containing four Commandos. It was hoped that the seaborne landing planned for D+2 would be unopposed. There would be two convoys arriving on D+2 and D+15. The anti-aircraft protection of Vannes airfield would be provided by the light anti-aircraft resources from 1st and 52nd Divisions and the beaches would be protected by thirty-two heavy and thirty-two light anti-aircraft guns from the US Army.

As far as possible casualties would be evacuated by C-47 but a Casualty Clearing Station would hold wounded until air evacuation as possible. As these were normally a corps-level unit and HQ Airborne Troops was not established as an operational corps one would have to be found. This again emphasises that the Airborne Corps was not established for the task that it was being asked to do. Evacuation by LST would be unacceptable but LSIs could be used if medical personnel were provided. Hospital ships would not be available.

The airborne force was to be prepared to operate on its own for 14 days without maintenance, apart from air supply for the first four days. 1st Airborne Division's Anti-Tank Regiment would take eight 17-pounders, with the balance made up of 6-pounders. 52nd Division would have a much stronger complement of artillery than 1st Airborne, comprising a 25-pounder Field Regiment and two 3.7in regiments. The 52nd Division's Anti-Tank Regiment was still equipped with 6-pounders, but it also had much stronger divisional troops. The operation would require five Royal Army Service Corps companies that would have to be provided by the War Office and a Divisional Ordnance Field Park would be required for the Beach Maintenance Area, as well as a Royal Electrical and Mechanical Engineers Workshop. The meeting considered that the anti-aircraft protection of the beaches and the anchorages should be a US Army commitment and Ninth Air Force agreed to discuss providing units. A warning system, anti-aircraft operations room and searchlights would also be required and it was thought that the RAF would need to include 400 personnel among their ground units for flying control and servicing personnel. An artillery Forward Observation Officer would parachute in with 1st Airborne Division and a Royal Engineers Field Company would be required to act as corps troops, as well as an Electrical and Mechanical Section. HQ Airborne Troops required a significant increase in its signals provision, but there were no formed units available to meet this and 21st Army Group's signals staff were asked to work up proposals. HQ Airborne Troops were to submit proposals for Air Support Signals Units in conjunction with Ninth Air Force. HQ Airborne Troops also had no Civil Affairs or Psychological Warfare staff, which would need to be provided. A Beach Maintenance Area would need to be formed to handle British beach organisation and would come under the command of No. 1 Base Section. As a measure of how complicated preparing the order of battle for Hands Up was, the meeting ended with eleven actions for eight different headquarters.

Brigadier Oxborrow, the Brigadier General Staff (Air) at 21st Army Group, produced some notes in conjunction with 2nd Tactical Air Force on the close air support required for Hands Up, which were circulated on 13 July. 'Method A' was the normal system of support and would see formations such as brigades and division pass requests for air support up to a joint army and air force headquarters, with intervention by intermediate HQs to cancel requests. It was suggested that this would be most efficient as time delays were kept to a minimum. Disadvantages were that it involved considerable equipment and personnel, and communication by low-powered radio sets was unpredictable.

'Method B' was a miniature air support signals system, with a focus on the Force HQ which would then pass requests to the joint Army-Air HQ. For Hands Up it was suggested that this would be 1st Airborne Division. This method had the advantage of brigades being able to communicate with their divisional HQ fairly easily.

'Method C' would see units and formations pass air support requests through the normal command channels with air support links between the Force HQ and the Army-Air HQ. This system had the advantage of using existing signals, but there would be a greater delay in requests being received as they would need to be repeated through every link in the chain of command. This system would also be vulnerable if the Force HQ could not be established effectively.

Oxborrow recommended Method B if the necessary personnel and equipment could be provided, and if not Method C. A pencil note on the documents states that Method B was accepted. The BGS(Air) also

148

had much to say about aerial reconnaissance and argued that it should be treated as a high priority. Reconnaissance could be provided by units operating from Normandy with requests being made through the air support channels to the Army-Air HQ, and aircraft could report to the Hands Up force from the air using a simple code. Once landing strips had been prepared aircraft could also land in the Vannes area and pilots could pass on information verbally before returning to base. It was suggested that all fighter and fighter-bomber aircraft should be provided by the US forces as the operation was likely to be commanded by the US Third Army and their organic air support would come from XIX Tactical Air Command. It was also suggested that air support signals should be provided wholly from either the US Air Corps or the British Army as differences in procedures would otherwise cause problems. It was suggested that tentacles should be provided on the scale of four per division. 1st Airborne Division already had them as part of its establishment and 52nd Division was believed to have two. Additional tentacles would need to be provided at a maximum of eight air-transported tentacles and two control sets depending on the method employed. Special assault tentacles that had been provided for Second Army for the Normandy landings could be withdrawn and made available and that shortages of manpower could be made up from other air support signals units in Normandy. A direct link would be provided between the Force HQ and the fighters providing local defence. The BGS(Air) suggested that HQ Airborne Forces and the Amy-Air HQ would need to include experienced staff officers either from G3(Air) and G(Air) who were experienced with air support procedures. Again, the impression gained is of a corps that was seriously under-prepared.

The same day Brigadier Thursby-Pelham, the Deputy Signal Officer-in-Chief at 21st Army Group, wrote to Richardson regarding signals support for HQ Airborne Troops.[45] He stressed that for Browning to be able to control his forces he would need additional signals personnel and equipment, and that '. . . an early decision is required as Signal Units cannot be raised, trained and prepared for battle in a twinkling of an eye'. However, it is hard not to conclude that the headquarters hard clearly not been intended to go into action.

On the same day the Brigadier in Command of Build Up Control (West) wrote to 21st Army Group G(Plans) regarding the use of ships and landing craft to deliver the planned build-up in Normandy and how it would be impacted by Hands Up. BUCO were aware that SHAEF were submitting proposals to the Joint Chiefs of Staff to stabilise the planned build-up at a reduced rate from D+42 onwards.[46]

This reduction would free up twenty-five Motor Transport Coasters without affecting the build-up, along with LSTs, LCTs and LCI(L)s which could be provided. Stores Coasters were under the control of the Ministry of War Transport rather than BUCO but it was thought that a considerable number were being released from Overlord traffic and would be available.

14 July

The Ninth Air Force Outline Plan for Hands Up was written on 14 July and circulated the next day.[47] It assumed that Beneficiary would not be mounted, and that Lucky Strike would not be launched at the same time as Hands Up.

Also on 14 July Montgomery wrote to Bradley regarding 'subsidiary operations to further Overlord'.[48] He stated that it would not be necessary for FUSAG to carry out any further planning as a modified form of Hands Up would now be implemented by 21st Army Group in conjunction with ANXF and AEAF. When completed the plan would be handed over to FUSAG in case it was required. On the same day 21st Army Group G(Plans) asked SHAEF to provide a weather forecast for the Vannes area during the months of August and September.[49]

Brigadier MacKillop, the Deputy Quartermaster General for Movement and Transport at 21st Army Group, wrote to Richardson with his comments on the Outline Plans for Hands Up after discussions with ANCXF.[50] The navy's unwillingness to sail one fast convoy to Quiberon Bay before Brest had been captured meant removing the Coasters and LCTs from the convoy and finding additional Liberty ships to take their place. Ships in the anchorage would have to be unloaded by DUKWs, LCMs or LSTs, and LCMs could be carried on Liberty ships. The navy were also prepared to allow a second convoy to be loaded and made ready to sail in an emergency if Third Army did not join up with the Hands Up force. Otherwise they felt that a second convoy might not be economical. The navy were not prepared to include commando troops in the first convoy if they were to carry out a tactical landing as this would mean that the coast would not have been neutralised. ANXF were also keen to keep the size of convoys to a minimum and would not consider sailings for the Chastity project until Brest was captured.

21st Army Group's Outline Administrative Plan for Hands Up was completed and circulated on 14 July.[51] Although the object and scope of the operation has been well covered elsewhere it is noteworthy that the Administrative Plan stated that there would be 'no question of an assault by sea'. Com Z would be responsible for the technical direction of the Chastity project, delegated to Base Section No. 1. It was a condition of launching Hands Up that the maintenance of the troops landing over the beaches should not be prejudiced by preparations for Chastity. Responsibility for planning was divided between HQ Airborne Troops, Base Section No. 1 and Ninth US Air Force. The plan noted, tellingly, that branches and services of 21st Army Group would have to assist Browning and his staff. HQ Airborne Troops would be responsible for mounting the airborne forces involved, but the War Office would have to assist with marshalling and mounting 52nd Division. The build-up by air would be controlled by HQ Airborne Troops who would pass instructions for resupply to Troop Carrier Command Post at Eastcote. 21st Army Group would control the build up by sea. The general policy would be for the maximum number of administrative troops and vehicles to be provided from US sources. Base Section No. 1 would be responsible for unloading ships and landing craft in the beachhead and HQ Airborne Troops would collect their supplies from the beaches and deliver it to their forward units. 21st Army Group also planned for an Airborne Forward Delivery Airfield Group to be formed and flown in, for which HQ Airborne Troops had drawn up a war establishment. 21st Army Group proposed to request two convoys to Quiberon Bay from ANXF before Brest was captured, but this had not yet been agreed. HQ Airborne Troops were to submit their requirements for the first convoy by 17 July. A specially-prepared road transport convoy would be loaded with the maintenance requirements for British forces and would accompany Third Army on its advance south. The convoy would be able to carry a maximum of 600 tons and would be despatched from the 21st Army Group area in Normandy. It was unlikely that Hospital Ships could be provided so evacuation of casualties would be mainly by air. Base Section No. 1 were to investigate the condition of the beaches and determine equipment required to unload personnel, vehicles and stores. It was hoped that the beaches would be able to handle an estimated 3,000 tons per day. It would be the responsibility of airborne troops to clear mines from the beaches before the first convoy arrived, and all vehicles would need to be waterproofed.

The provisional order of battle for the AFDAG consisted of a Detail Issue Depot and an Ammunition Platoon from the Royal Army Service Corps, a Casualty Clearing Station, two Field Dressing Stations, two Field Surgical Units and two Field Transfusion Units; from the Pioneer Corps personnel for a stores dump, three Pioneer Companies and a Pioneer Platoon to carry out salvage of damaged equipment.

A list of British units to support the US Base Section troops was also assembled. It was suggested that a Beach Group Headquarters, of the type used in Normandy, would be a suitable headquarters and that it would need to consist of a DUKW Transport Company, a Defence Issues Detail, a Field Dressing Station, two Ordnance Beach Detachments and a Royal Navy Beach Party. Liaison parties would be required from each service to identify stores on the beaches.

The preliminary shipping plan produced as part of the Administrative Plan contained a more detailed allocation of ships to loads. In the first convoy four coasters would be allocated to British forces to bring in 8,000 tons of supplies and ammunition three coasters would bring in 1,000 tons of Petrol, Oil and Lubricants, Four Liberty ships would bring in 8,000 tons of supplies and ammunition along with 500 vehicles. Twelve LSTs would bring in 300 British and 300 US vehicles, including DUKWs. Six Liberty ships were allocated to the US forces to bring in 12,000 tons of stores and 720 vehicles, and 12 LCTs would arrive empty to assist with unloading onto shore. Six LCI(L)s would carry extra personnel. The second convoy on D+15 would see five Liberty ships bringing in 10,000 tons of supplies and 600 vehicles for the British and US forces, while 10 Liberty ships would bring in 20,000 tons and 1,200 vehicles solely for the Americans. These allocations were however based on the assumption that Brest would be captured by 15 September.

The division of planning tasks for Hands Up suggests just how complex the operation was to organise. A total of thirteen planning serials were identified, divided across five different Allied headquarters. The Allied planning staffs worked out the timescales for launching Hands Up by working backwards the time required to assemble, load and sail the sea convoys. Breakdowns of loads would be required for the first convoy by D-23, and for the second convoy by D-17. The first convoy would need to start loading on D-16, to be completed by D-6. It would sail on D-2 and arrive in Quiberon Bay on D+2. The second convoy would begin loading on D-3 ready to sail on D+10 for an estimated arrival in Quiberon Bay of D+15.

The Allies were clearly having to husband glider resources carefully and this influenced decisions over whether to launch airborne operations. On 1 August the Allies would have available 880 Horsas and Hamilcars of which it was estimated 500 Horsas and 28 Hamilcars would be required for Hands Up. If the operation took place on, say, 1 August the Allies would not have enough gliders to launch another operation until 15 September.

More Allied airborne formations would become available during August and September 1944 as new divisions arrived from the US and the divisions that had fought in Normandy were relieved. The 17th US Division would be available from 1 September while the 6th Airborne Division would be available again by 15 September. It was estimated that the two US airborne divisions that had fought in Normandy, the 82nd and 101st, would not be available again until 1 October. The Allied planners were also having to juggle the planning of several airborne operations at the same time – if the 1st Airborne Division and the Polish Brigade were used for Hands Up they would then not be available for Lucky Strike.

On 14 July Montgomery's highly trusted intelligence chief Brigadier Edgar 'Bill' Williams produced an assessment of the importance of Brittany to the Germans. He stressed that the principal strategic important of the peninsula lay in the naval ports of Brest, Lorient and St Nazaire which were central to German naval strategy, particularly the prosecution of the U-boat war. Williams also suggested that Brittany was important to the Germans in a negative sense as denying the use of the ports and airfields there would hamper the Allied build-up, particularly the ability to bring reinforcements directly from the US. The Germans had shown no signs of abandoning Brittany, and it had been used as what Williams described as a 'reservoir' for infantry reinforcements for Normandy. The Germans strength in Brittany was thought to be the equivalent of less than four divisions, plus a considerable number of fortress troops of low quality. Williams suggested that by the time the Allies reached Avranches even more German infantry would have been drawn to Normandy, in particular the 5th Parachute Division which was then around St Malo. Once the Allies reached Rennes they would threaten the German lines of communications across France and back to Germany, and at that point the Germans would have to decide whether to evacuate the peninsula or attempt to hold the fortified ports to the last.

Williams wrote that the most important consideration was the degree to which the fighting in Normandy drained German divisions from Brittany. He identified the 2nd Parachute Division as the only 'good' formation in the peninsula and that the Germans would have to decide whether to lose it in what he called a 'dog-in-the-manger' policy at Brest. Williams though that the Allies would find out once they reached St Malo and Rennes, but Williams thought that it was unlikely that the Germans would reinforce the peninsula. Williams also thought that the divisions in Brittany which had sent battlegroups to Normandy would have sent most of their transport with them and hence their mobility would be much reduced. They could be fought in series as the Germans would not be able to manoeuvre or reinforce

153

threatened sectors. The only formation left with any degree of mobility was the 2nd Parachute Division.

Williams suggested that the Germans had to decide whether the biggest threat to Brittany was either an Allied advance to St Malo or an airborne operation at Quiberon Bay. He thought that landings at Quiberon Bay would confuse the Germans as they would expect the Allies to advance to Lorient and St Nazaire and that they would therefore wait to see if the Allies did so. Williams thought that without mobile reserves the Germans would only be able to contain the landings. The future of Brittany, Williams concluded, was 'bound up with the future of 2 Para Div'. If it was moved to the front in Normandy it would weaken the German garrison in Brittany and give the Allies a straightforward task. If the division was withdrawn to Brest it might however draw out operations by denying the Allies the use of a key port as the autumn weather started to set in.

On 14 July Major General Miles Graham, Montgomery's Major General Administration, wrote to 21st Army Group's Staff Duties division regarding the Royal Artillery order of battle for Hands Up.[52] One Royal Artillery Forward Observation Unit would be added to 1st Airborne Division but it would not be possible to provide a Survey Battery. One Air Observation Post flight would be added to the division to be flown from the Normandy beachhead. Ground crew would be carried into the Hands Up area on the first convoy.

On 14 July Browning wrote to 21st Army Group G(Plans) about the airfield construction element of Hands Up. His letter included the recommendations of a planning syndicate of representatives from AEAF, Ninth Air Force Aviation Engineers, 38 Group, IX Troop Carrier Command and HQ Airborne Troops.[53] The object of the syndicate was to study where airstrips could be constructed to fly in 52nd Division as early as possible. The required strips would need to be 3,600ft by 150ft with a taxiway connecting each end of the runway and thirty-six to fifty hardstandings on the outside edge.

The syndicate had concluded that the operation would be seriously jeopardised if the 862nd Heavy Aviation Engineer Battalion was not included. The 878th Battalion would land at Vannes and get that airfield working by D+1 but would not be able to build a strip at Vannes and Presquil de Rhuys simultaneously. If the 862nd Battalion was included the force would have built two strips by D+4. Browning stressed the 'urgent necessity' of being given 862nd Battalion, which he understood had been earmarked to land in Normandy. Fighter cover for the operation would be provided from airfields in Normandy. The most convenient convoy size would be 36 aircraft an hour during daylight, which would allow for a daily turnaround of 576 aircraft. If Vannes airfield had not been mined or sabotaged it might be able to receive C-47s from 0700 on D+1 and if the Aviation Engineer Battalion was able to land nearby on the afternoon of D-Day. If the airfield had been damaged it would not be available until D+4 at the earliest. Weather would have a considerable effect on the construction of airstrips, in particular rain as the soil on the peninsula was made up of clay, which would be poor draining. The tracking required to build one airstrip would weight 750 tons, a prohibitive weight to bring in with the available shipping. Flying in by air would also be impossible as it would reduce their airlift available to 52nd Division. It would take 16 hours to lay the tracking for one strip.

The first draft of the naval plan for Hands Up was circulated for comment on 14 July.[54] The copy sent to 21st Army Group came with an introduction which leaves no doubt as to the anonymous author's thoughts on the operation: 'The attached first draft skeleton is circulated for early comment by staff officers concerned so that we may proceed in an agreed fashion should this horrid operation not die a natural death.' The only difference between the first draft of the naval plan and the later versions was that initially a seaborne assault was planned to take place at Anse de Succinio at first light on D-Day by the Special Service Brigade, landing from six Landing Craft Infantry (Small). The landing craft would approach in darkness guided by a submarine with nine destroyers as an escort. The early plan also stated that the stores convoy flagship would be the USS *Bayfield*.

15 July

On 15 July a meeting was held at 21st Army Group HQ to discuss the air aspects of Hands Up.[55] The agenda included airfield construction, systems for air command and control, the allotment of air forces, any air action required before D-Day, timings for the airborne assault, air action required to delay the movement of enemy reserves, the build-up by air, anti-aircraft defence of the beaches, and airfield and air reconnaissance. The air forces and Airborne Troops were asked to give a detailed plan for when airstrips could be completed and whether it would be possible to build strips closed to the sea and out of enemy artillery range. A decision was also required as to whether fighter squadrons could be based in the bridgehead and Airborne Troops was to give the air forces a comprehensive plan for what photographic reconnaissance they would require. On 15 July the Deputy Quartermaster-General for Movement and Transport at 21st Army Group, wrote to Graham, Montgomery's Major General Administration.[56] He stressed that although De Guingand had ordered that planning for Hands Up should proceed based on launching the operation on 9 August the earliest date that could be achieved would be 20 August to give time to withdraw units from Normandy for re-equipping and to plan, load and sail seaborne convoys. One of the major obstacles was the unwillingness of ANXF to provide escorts for large convoys sailing to Quiberon Bay before Brest had been captured, although a provisional convoy programme had been presented to ANXF for their approval. Between them Base Section No. 1 and Airborne Forces had requested 20,800 personnel and 4,801 vehicles for the convoy, but the main convoy would be limited to 14,000 personnel, 2,400 vehicles and 30,000 tons of stores. The main convoy was therefore 30 per cent deficient in lift for personnel and 50 per cent for vehicles. It was thought that as the role of the troops taking part was 'not a particularly mobile one', some of the bids for vehicles could be 'drastically reduced'. Graham was asked to consider whether the shipping ceiling should be accepted and if the suggested cuts were reasonable. It was proposed to cut the personnel on the main convoy from 20,800 to 13,000 and the vehicles from 4,801 to 2,400. Space for US anti-aircraft personnel would be cut by half, COMZ personnel from 12,000 to 8,000 and US Air Force personnel from 1,900 to 600. On the same day 21st Army Group also undertook to provide additional administrative units for the Special Service Brigade, including a Field Ambulance, a General Transport Platoon and Composite Section RASC.[57]

A Chief of Staff meeting on 15 July was chaired by De Guingand and attended by Browning, Ramsay's chief of staff Creasy, the Chief of Operations at AEAF and 'other staff officers'.[58] Creasy argued that the operation was 'not a sound one' from a naval perspective due to proximity of U-boat bases, the exposed nature of the anchorage and the vulnerability of the shallow waters to mining. ANXF were concerned that their commitment to Hands Up would be considerable and would be likely to increase. The possibility of operations at St Malo also made the availability of enough escort vessels unlikely. AEAF were also concerned about the number of fighters that would be needed to escort the naval convoys, provide fighter cover over the beaches and escort the troop-carrier columns. AEAF therefore wanted to have bases in the Rennes area before launching Hands Up. The representatives at the meeting relayed that Leigh-Mallory had decided that sufficient fighter squadrons could not be provided without prejudicing operations in Normandy, which he felt was unacceptable. De Guingand stated that three weeks would be required to mount the operation but that it was unlikely that it would be possible to forecast operational conditions so far ahead. The meeting concluded with an agreement that no action would be taken to prepare for Hands Up. An Outline Plan would be completed and filed for reference, but the possibility of using only 1st Airborne Division and the Polish Brigade in a tactical role to help Third Army capture Brest would be examined. This was clearly a turning point in the planning of airborne operations in Brittany.

On 15 July it was confirmed that the US anti-aircraft defences would be provided by the 50th Anti-Aircraft Brigade, comprised of the 114th Anti-Aircraft Group, the 124th Anti-Aircraft Gun Battalion, the 125th Anti-Aircraft Gun Battalion and the 551st Anti-Aircraft Automatic Weapons Battalion. The 2nd Airlanding Light Anti-Aircraft Battery would be placed under the command of 1st Airborne Division for Hands Up.[59]

16 July

On 16 July Bull wrote to Bedell Smith on the planning for Hands Up.[60] He described the meeting held at 21st Army Group the previous day where SHAEF were represented by himself and Brigadier Maclean, the head of the G3 planning section. Bull reported that the naval forces felt that Hands Up was unsound from their point of view and that Leigh-Mallory was not prepared to carry out the operation at the same time as Neptune, but felt that the airborne proposals were practicable.

After the meeting Bull spoke to De Guingand several times. He pointed out that Quiberon Bay was essential to the logistical effort and De Guingand undertook to make sure that planning continued. De Guingand also promised to discuss the operation with Montgomery after which the operation would either be approved or recommended to Eisenhower. Bull felt that time was pressing, especially from a naval perspective. He also felt that 'current planning seems to lack enthusiasm for the operation' and that the administrative implications of Hands Up needed to be given more weight, 'as a feeling of optimism on the part of others not responsible for administrative matters may have much to do with the alignment of difficulties now being presented'.

A pencil note on Bull's letter suggests that Bedell Smith subsequently spoke with Leigh-Mallory. It also recorded that Bedell Smith was to present the operation to Eisenhower later the same week. An intelligence assessment attached to Bull's letter to De Guingand sheds light on what German forces the Allies had identified in Brittany. The area around Lorient, Vannes and St Nazaire was garrisoned by the 275th Infantry Division, which was made up of two infantry regiments and divisional troops, totalling 11,500 men. There were also naval artillery and flak units in St Nazaire, Luftwaffe units in Nantes, two

Russian battalions whose location was unknown and a number of miscellaneous units. There were believed to be a total of 26,250 troops in the sector including 2,600 men on Belle Isle. There were thought to be 106,350 troops in Brittany in total.

On 16 July Richardson informed Base Section No. 1 that although that 15 July meeting had decided that planning for Hands Up would be completed, that no executive action would be taken to prepare for it, nor would any resources be committed.[61]

18 July

Lieutenant-Colonel Britten of 21st Army Group G (Plans) forwarded his comments on the Ninth Air Force plan on 18 July.[62] He stressed that due to the limited sea lift available there was 'no question' of 52nd Division being brought in by sea. He also stated that Belle Isle would not be captured during the initial stages of Hands Up as it was hoped that it could be neutralised by air and naval bombardment. Britten also stated that HQ Airborne Forces did not think that it was essential to bomb Vannes airfield and that they hoped to land two brigades under the flak defences under cover of darkness and then destroy the flak on the ground before daylight. HQ Airborne Troops also asked for searchlights for the defence of Vannes airfield. Britten queried whether it would be possible to provide medical facilities in the naval convoys, stating that HQ Airborne Troops would reject any proposals to evacuate wounded personnel by sea except for in hospital ships.

On 18 July Lieutenant-Colonel David Strangeways, the commander of 21st Army Group's R Force, wrote to Richardson regarding how his staff, who specialised in deception operations, might be able to assist with Hands Up.[63] Strangeways thought that use could be made of the planned airborne route to create a large-scale diversion in Normandy, but the actual diversion could not be planned until the route was better known and enemy dispositions were identified. Strangeways suggested that as the Germans were nervous about the Bordeaux area, the sailing of follow-up forces could be used to feign a threat there. He thought that the Germans would probably be aware of the destination of follow-up forces before they reached the area, so it might be possible to carry out diversions similar to those that took place on D-Day by suggesting that the convoys were heading to St Nazaire or Brest. A dummy parachute drop was being discussed with SHAEF, seaborne diversions with ANCXF and 'special means' with SHAEF. Strangeways also warned that if supply drops to the French Resistance in Brittany were increased the Germans were likely to react more strongly to any threat in the area.

19 July

On 19 July Lieutenant-Colonel Charles Mackenzie,[64] who at the time was GSO1 at HQ Airborne Troops, wrote to 52nd Division regarding the airstrips that they were likely to land on during Hands Up based on an earlier conversation at Moor Park.[65] Ninth Air Force Aviation Engineer Command had been consulted on the dimension and layout of airstrips. Each would be 3,600ft long and 150ft wide, and each end would be connected to a taxi runway with thirty-six to fifty hardstandings for aircraft to unload. Approximately 30 yards behind the hardstandings would be a track for motor transport which would be used for clearing stores dumped from the hardstandings. The exact layout would depend on the conditions on the ground. The hardstandings would be 75ft deep by 50ft wide and would be arranged for the maximum dispersal of aircraft, and if space allowed would be up to 150 yards apart. Potential sites for airstrips included alongside the existing airfield at Vannes and improvised sites south of Lezuis, south-east of St Armel, north of Trevanaste and north of Kercoquen.

On 19 July Major General Robert Crawford, the Assistant Chief of Staff in SHAEFs G4 staff, wrote to Bedell Smith about Brest.[66] The existing plans called for a major development of the port, primarily for receiving and staging troop reinforcements. After September the US planned to receive approximately five divisions per month and Brest was planned to receive up to 16,000 tons of supplies per day by October. The rail line to Rennes would have to be developed, which would take twice as long as repairing the line from Quiberon to Rennes. Given the likelihood of the Germans demolishing bridges reconstructing Brest was thought to be wasteful. Instead Crawford suggested that Nantes, St Nazaire, Quiberon Bay and Lorient should be reconsidered.

Crawford also wrote to Bedell Smith on the same day regarding the Chastity project. He explained that it would use the sheltered anchorage in Quiberon Bay as a major deep-water port, connected to the main US rail lines of communications and was designed primarily for handling supplies. It was estimated to handle 7,000 tons per day 30 days after it had been captured but if it was not captured before 1 September its development would be difficult due to the weather. Chastity would be difficult if Brest were not captured soon after, and Crawford stated that the whole project was now under question due to the late date of capture. However, he also argued that the development of Quiberon Bay would be logistically essential.

On 19 July Com Z signalled to the Deputy Major General Administration at 21st Army Group that the 1st Engineer Special

Brigade had been designated to take part in either Beneficiary or Hands Up.[67]

20 July

On 20 July Lieutenant-Colonel Bostwick forwarded the Ninth Air Force plan for Hands Up.[68] Although he requested comments, he also stressed that it was considered 'improbable that this Operation will be staged'. The Ninth Air Force plan suggests that FUSAG and Third Army had been studying the terrain and defences of Belle Isle and the Vannes and Quiberon Bay Region since May 1944.[69] The Ninth Air Force plan described Hands Up as '. . . the code name for the tactical operation to capture the beachhead around Quiberon Bay. The purpose of the operation is to enable a port to be built in the River Auray. The name of the administrative project covering the building of the port is Chastity.'

The target date was 9 August. All preparations were to be completed by then. D-Day and H-Hour would be advised later. The operation could be postponed or cancelled from day to day based on weather forecasts, and this would be communicated through AEAF to IX Troop Carrier Command at Eastcote before H-6 hours. A copy of the signal would be sent to Ninth Air Force Rear and Tactical HQs at Sunninghill and in France. Ninth Air Force would operate from bases in the UK and Normandy to transport airborne forces to the Quiberon Bay area. It would provide aerial bombardment of the German defences, fighter cover over the area and seaborne convoys, air warning and fighter control in the beachhead and prepare landing strips.

It was assumed that US forces would have reached the line St Malo-Rennes-Laval and that enemy opposition would be weak enough for Third Army to be confident about reaching Quiberon Bay within 14 days. Air attacks would be launched before D-Day to disrupt enemy road and rail networks and targets would be agreed between AEAF, 21st Army Group and SHAEF, including selected airfields. The naval forces would require the bombing of Lorient and St Nazaire on D-1 as well as the laying of mines. Bombing would target coastal batteries at Croisic Point, Plouharnel and Belle Isle. Naval bombardment would target the shore batteries at Kerdrean, Belle Isle and Plouharnel. Air spotting would take place from first light and naval gunfire observers would also be provided for the airborne forces.

The repair of Vannes airfield was to receive top priority and to preserve it all further bombing was to be cancelled. Two additional airstrips would be built alongside it as soon as possible by D+6 and it was hoped that part of the equipment required for this would be shipped in by sea. The 862nd Aviation Engineer Battalion would arrive by sea on D+2. Anti-aircraft protection of the beachhead would be provided by British airborne gunners at Vannes airfield and US forces on the beaches and airstrips. A total of 118 guns would be available. Requests for air support would be sent by tentacles with 1st Airborne Division to XIX Tactical Air Command who might in turn call on Ninth Air Force for support.

Weather forecasts would be provided to Browning by IX Troop Carrier Command and the Staff Weather Officer at Ninth Air Force would coordinate forecasts with other formations including FUSAG. The 21st Weather Region would provide an oceanographer to support the Chief Engineer who would advise on sea, surf and swell to support the movement of men over the beaches. The commander of XIX Tactical Command would provide a senior weather officer, an observer and two radio operators for the Fighter Direction Tender and a weather detachment for the anti-aircraft defences on the landing strips.

Ninth Air Force would provide a standing patrol of six night fighters over the Cherbourg peninsula. There would be six sorties to cover the troop-carrier planes, six sorties over the general area of Nantes to prevent interference from the south, and between eight and ten intruder sorties over enemy airfields in the area. Four Mosquitos would attack searchlights and flak defences in the Quiberon Bay area and Eighth Air Force would provide heavy bomber support. IX Troop Carrier Command would provide airlift for the airborne forces including dropping SAS Troops north of Quiberon and it would also provide medical evacuation and resupply missions. XIX Tactical Air Command would provide two flights of fighter aircraft over the beachhead during the day, a squadron of fighters to give continuous cover for the naval convoys, four groups of fighter-bombers on ground alert to attack pre-identified targets, fighter escorts for bombers and area cover for resupply missions. In the long term it would defend the beachhead and would need six airfields in the Rennes area, with additional airfields within 90 miles. IX Air Defence Command would provide night fighter cover for the beachhead and anti-aircraft defence. IX Air Force Service Command would provide beach parties to help identify air force supplies on the beaches, and personnel to operate air force supply dumps, while IX Engineer Command would build airstrips in the beachhead and would operate under Browning's command until relieved. IX Bomber Command would make available eleven groups of medium and light bombers to attack targets identified in the fire plan. The maximum number of administrative troops would be provided from US forces so that when the Third Army arrived the minimum number of British troops would need to be withdrawn. Routine missions by RAF Coastal Command in the Quiberon Bay area would be coordinated by AEAF to prevent interference with airborne missions.

All Ninth Air Force units in the area would be under the command of the senior air force officer who in turn would be under Browning's command. This would have been an intriguing prospect, given Browning's emnity with other American colleagues and his own RAF counterparts, not to mention his lack of experience commanding air forces. Fighters would initially be controlled by the IX Air Defence Command Fighter Control Centre on the Fighter Direction Tender until ground facilities were set up ashore. The Ninth Air Force Command Post was at the time in Grandcamp les Bains in Normandy while the Rear Headquarters was in Sunninghill in England.

The Ninth Air Force Intelligence Annex suggested that there were weaknesses in the German command that were becoming more obvious since the Normandy landings. The Luftwaffe had failed to react to the Normandy landings and it was predicted that they would not be able to oppose Hands Up either. In North West Europe the Germans had 270 single-engine fighters, 170 twin-engine fighters, 15 ground-attack aircraft, 180 long-range bombers and 50 reconnaissance aircraft. It was though that the Luftwaffe would only be capable of launching 500 sorties over a two-to-three-day period and as a result any air opposition to Hands Up was forecast to be minor. The Luftwaffe had thirty airfields or advanced landing grounds within 250 miles of Quiberon Bay with another fifty airfields that could potentially be used. The Luftwaffe were constantly occupying and abandoning airfields due to the changing situation on the ground.

Once Vannes airfield was in action it would be stocked with 7,500 gallons of aviation fuel in jerricans for any aircraft making an emergency landing. 'Gratuitous' RAC – Ration Accessory Convenience – would be issued to Ninth Air Force personnel in the marshalling areas as well as packets of tobacco, candy and 'toilet articles'. A minimum of three days' rations would be carried and 15 days' worth of rations would come in on the D+2 convoy, while airborne troops would carry two days' worth of maintenance. Fuel would be carried on the basis of 50 miles per vehicle.

The Ninth Air Force Plan also include more detail on medical arrangements. IX Troop Carrier Command would provide a Medical Dispensary Reception Station to land in gliders with 878th Battalion and further medical units would arrive on the seaborne convoy on D+2. COMZ were planning to establish a Field Hospital at Vannes from D+2 along with another at the airstrip itself. There would be an Evacuation Hospital at Surzur and another Field Hospital at Sarzeau, and until the hospitals were operational evacuation would be from unit aid stations to the Dispensary at Vannes. From D+2 an Ambulance Company would be available to transport casualties from aid stations to the airstrip. Air evacuation would start from D+4 and British casualties would be taken to RAF Blakehill Farm. Wounded would be evacuated by sea only if air transport was not possible and only in ships with medical facilities.

A specially loaded convoy of British motor transport with maintenance requirements would accompany Third Army on its advance south to Quiberon. British units operating the airfields would take with them 10 days' worth of supplies for C-47 aircraft and an emergency supply of tyres, casings, starters, generators, spark plugs, landing gears and tail wheel casings. The seaborne convoy would bring in tractors for the airstrips.

878th Battalion would land in 135 Waco gliders and six Hamilcars on the afternoon of D-Day on a landing area prepared by 1st Airborne Division engineers and immediately begin repairing the airfield at Vannes. As soon as this was complete 52nd Division would begin arriving. A recce party from 878th Battalion would accompany the first landings on D-Day. 862nd Battalion would arrive in the D+2 convoy over the beaches captured by the Polish Brigade and start work building an airstrip on the peninsula for transport aircraft by D+4 and another at Presquille de Rhuys for fighter aircraft. A recce party from 862nd Battalion would accompany the Polish Brigade.

The Air Defence Command Post would be established at St Pierre Eglise in the beachhead. Night fighters would be provided from 422 Squadron and 425 Squadron, both flying P-61 Black Widows. Anti-Aircraft defences would be provided by the 1st Anti-Aircraft Artillery Group comprising the 1st Anti-Aircraft Artillery Automatic Weapons Battalion, the 2nd Anti-Aircraft Artillery Gun Battalion, a searchlight detachment and a signal warning detachment.

In total the air defence contribution to Hands Up would consist of 2,653 men and 785 vehicles. Light and Medium Bomber support would be provided by the 97th, 98th and 99th Combat Bomb Wings. The 98th Wing were at the time of writing based in Southern England and within range of Quiberon Bay but would require a six-hour turnaround time between missions. The 97th and 99th Wings were not within the radius of action and would need to stage from 98th Wing airfields in Southern England. Bases in Normandy were discounted as they were not yet able to support bomber operations. Any bombing missions would also be hampered by the lack of coverage for the Oboe bomb-aiming system in the area.

On 20 July Richardson wrote to the Royal Artillery staff at 21st Army Group regarding the anti-aircraft defence of Hands Up.[70] 1st Airborne Division did not have its own anti-aircraft defence in the way that infantry divisions did, and the 6th Airborne Division's Light Anti-Aircraft Battery was still in Normandy. While the Light AA Regiment of 52nd Division would protect the airfield at Vannes it would not have enough guns to cover the airstrips as well. Richardson therefore requested that anti-aircraft units of Base Section No. 1 be made available for the Presquille de Rhuys peninsula.

21 July

On 21 July ANXF forwarded a draft of the Naval Outline Plan for Hands Up to 21st Army Group.[71] This document was only intended to expand upon the Joint Plan. The naval operation would be commanded by Rear Admiral Hall of the 11th Amphibious Task Force while anti-submarine groups and convoy protection would be provided by the Commander-in-Chief Plymouth. Before the operation mines would be dropped by air in the entrances to Brest, Lorient, St Nazaire, La Pallice and the Gironde estuary on D-2 and D-1. Three anti-submarine groups would operate to the south-west of the Brittany peninsula from the morning of D-1 to cover the convoys. During the assault phase the naval forces would land a commando brigade at Anse de Succinio to reinforce the 1st Polish Parachute Brigade. They would also carry out minesweeping in Quiberon Bay, provide bombardment support to cover the landing ships and minesweepers, bring in follow-up convoys from D+2 and protect the anchorage while the convoys were unloading.

The assault convoy would sail from Plymouth on either D-2 or D-1 and would consist of nine destroyers and six LSI(S). The minesweepers would sail from Plymouth at the same time, with one fleet minesweeping flotilla and one motor launch. Another convoy would sail from Plymouth on D-2 consisting of five anti-submarine escorts, two minesweeping flotillas, four motor launches, one Fighter Direction Tender, two small oilers and twelve LCT. Finally a stores convoy would sail on D-Day, passing Land's End in the morning and consisting of twelve anti-submarine escorts, six anti-submarine trawlers, fifteen Liberty ships, eighteen LST, six LCI(L) and twelve motor launches. It was thought that the LSI and LST would load and sail from the Plymouth and Falmouth areas, the Liberty ships from West Coast ports and South Wales and the naval forces from Plymouth.

The bombardment forces would sail to arrive at first light on D-Day. Group A would consist of the Battleship HMS *Rodney* with three destroyers, Group B the monitor HMS *Roberts* and two destroyers and Group C three cruisers. From D-2 a submarine would be stationed as a marker approximately 195 degrees and 4.5 miles off the Les Grands Cardnaux lighthouse. The Fleet Minesweeping Flotilla would then stream sweeps at about H-3.5, sweeping and marking channels inshore for approximately seven miles. The assault convoy would then arrive in position by the submarine marker at H-3 and follow the swept channels inshore before lowering their landing craft seven miles from the beach.

H-Hour was to be at nautical twilight. The first waves would land in LCA lowered from the LSIs preceded by four Landing Craft Personnel (Large) towing minesweeping gear. Close support would be provided by four destroyer escorts who would also lay a smokescreen if needed. However, it was hoped that the Polish paratroopers would already have captured the beaches and the landings would be unopposed. Shore batteries would be bombarded from half an hour before sunrise onwards. HMS *Roberts* and one cruiser would attack the battery at Kerdrean, one cruiser would bombard Point de Taillefer on Belle Isle, and HMS *Rodney* and another cruiser would bombard Plouharnel. They would be assisted by three pairs of spotting aircraft. The shore batteries and radar stations at Le Croisic and Le Palais on Belle Isle would be bombed by night bombers immediately after the airborne landings and then again during the day by heavy bombers.

The 'miscellaneous convoy' would arrive at around 0800 on D-Day after which the arriving minesweepers would the sweep the eastern part of Quiberon Bay while the remaining ships anchored in the lee of Haedik Island. Motor Launches and LCP(L) would patrol closer inshore. The Headquarters Ship – the LSI HMS *Royal Ulsterman* – would re-enter the convoy and work with the Fighter Direction Tender to control the defence of the anchorage. The *Royal Ulsterman* would be relieved by the USS *Ancon*, a Headquarters Ship, when she arrived on D+2. The Fighter Direction Tender would control the day and night fighters protecting the area, until a Ground Controlled Interception set could be landed with the follow up convoy. Minesweepers and merchant ships would also fly barrage balloons. Coastal Command would also provide convoy escorts, patrol the entrance to the anchorage and carry out offensive anti-submarine patrols off the U-boat bases. From D-Day onwards anti-submarine patrols would be carried out in the entrance to the bay by destroyers, escorts, trawlers and Motor Launches. The stores convoy would arrive at the entrance of the bay one hour after civil twilight on D+2 and would enter and anchor in the eastern part of the bay. Unloading the stores convoy was estimated to take about 10 days. LSTs would unload and then be available to assist LCTs unloading vehicles from Liberty ships. Stores would be carried ashore by LCTs, LCMs carried on Liberty ships and by DUKWs.

On 21 July Bull wrote to the Chief of the Plans Section enclosing two papers produced by SHAEF G4 on Quiberon Bay and Brest.[72] Bull argued that the capture of Quiberon Bay remained essential to supporting the US build-up and that the development of the port later than September was being examined. Brest would have to be captured either before or at the same time as Quiberon Bay due to naval considerations and Bull thought that it would be possible to develop Brest to handle additional tonnage and personnel to make up for deficiencies elsewhere. Using Brest instead of Quiberon Bay would lead to a reduction the build-up due to its smaller capacity, and this would lead to a considerable delay in operations to the east due to the necessity for rail construction. De Guingand had told Bull that the naval and air objections to Hands Up appeared to make it impossible. He also felt that in view of the present progress of the battle in Normandy Hands Up would have to be cancelled, to which Bull agreed. Not for the first time, even when opinion seemed firmly set against an airborne operation, planning continued.

On 21 July SHAEF's Movement and Transport Section signalled the Logistics Plans Section.[73] ETOUSA had been asked to carry out a study of the Chastity project in consultation with ANXF. The original plan for the capture of the Brittany ports envisaged Quiberon Bay being reached on D+40 and Brest on D+50, a timescale which would have seen Quiberon Bay receiving 7,000 tons of supplies a day by September and Lorient handling 2,000 tons. Brest would only be used to supply troops in the immediate area but would receive 5,300 tons a day. The situation on the ground by late July was however clearly quite different and these timescales were long out of date. The Allies' experience at Cherbourg suggested that the Germans were likely to mine the docks and this led to a decision to concentrate on clearing only the major ports. SHAEF and ETOUSA therefore suggested looking elsewhere for port capacity including at St Malo and Brest. However the Allied supply situation was already becoming critical and the drastic possibility of delaying the Seine crossing until 1945 was even suggested. The Allies were also considering the possibility of continuing to unload supplies over the Normandy beaches into October and November. The logistical planners had assessed that the Allies would require 54,434 tons per day by 4 October but at the time of writing in late July it was estimated that the daily total would already be 5,334 tons short. This was also reliant on the ports that were in Allied hands taking more than their average capacity on good-weather days. All assessments still relied on the Allies using the surviving Mulberry Harbour off Arromanches and the smaller Normandy ports into January 1945, which was clearly not ideal.

Montgomery published his directive M512 on 21 July. It stressed the importance of securing the Brittany ports.[74] US VIII Corps would turn into the Brittany peninsula and Third Army Headquarters would be close behind ready to take command of operations once activated. Interestingly M512 did not mention airborne operations. The provisional plan for Hands Up was issued on the same day as Montgomery's directive along with a lengthy and detailed intelligence dossier and defence overprints. The first provisional plan circulated by HQ Airborne Troops differed from those developed for previous operations, in that it asked more questions of subordinate formations and commanders than it answered. Addressees were requested to submit their comments to HQ Airborne Troops by 1 August.

Rear Admiral Hall, the naval force commander, was asked for numerous clarifications including the beaches to be used, lanes to be cleared of mines, the state of tide at which the seaborne assault should take place, whether unloading could take place on beaches 24 hours per day and whether naval bombardment could neutralise enemy coastal batteries at the neck of the Quiberon Peninsula. Ninth Air Force were asked to investigate the feasibility of carrying out twelve photographic sorties per day and the viability of operating fighters from Vannes airfield or from improvised airstrips, and whether the coastal batteries on the Quiberon Peninsula could be silenced by air bombardment. Hollinghurst was asked if it would be feasible to operate transport aircraft from Vannes airfield. 52nd Division, who would be airlifted into Vannes airfield soon after its capture, were ordered to bring their Reconnaissance Regiment ashore on the seaborne convoy that would arrive on D+2 as a high priority.

That the first plan for Hands Up asked for more information from formations and commanders than it provided was an unusual departure from the usual pattern of airborne planning. Ordinarily strategic objectives were dictated by higher headquarters, HQ Airborne Troops stipulated the operational framework and its subordinate formations then developed their own tactical plans. The first plan for Hands Up suggests that HQ Airborne Troops did not at that point have a firm grasp on the context of planning the operation and was looking for lower headquarters to fill in the gaps, without saying as much. It is hard to escape the conclusion that Hands Up was muddled.

The objective was to assist and expedite the cutting off of the Brittany peninsula and the capture of Quiberon Bay by Third Army. No date had yet been envisaged as the likelihood of mounting Hands Up depended on the progress of the overland forces. 1st Airborne Division would land and capture Vannes airfield, neutralise flak and dominate the area. They were also to contact the Maquis and the French SAS Battalion who were operating to the north. As an exploitation task the division was also ordered to patrol towards Auray with a view to reconnoitring the port area. The Polish Parachute Brigade would land around Surzur and St Armel to protect the exists from the beaches on the Presquelle de Rhys. They would also form a firm base around Theix as part of the perimeter. A Special Service Brigade of Commandos would be under command for the operation and would form the seaborne element of the operation. The brigade would land on the beach at Landrezac and clear Presquelle de Rhys as far west as Navallo. They would then clear lanes on the beaches for a follow-up convoy expected on D+2. After this had been done the brigade would form a firm base around La Trinite and Surzur and patrol towards Muzillac. 52nd Division would be flown in to Vannes airfield soon after its capture. The division would protect the right flank of the lodgement area by forming a firm base around Trefflean and Elven.

In common with most British Army operational planning – something that has often been misunderstood and misinterpreted – the units involved in Hands Up were given exploitation tasks that they might be asked to complete after achieving their main objectives. In the case of Hands Up, either 1st Airborne or 52nd Division would be ordered to capture Auray as soon as the north and right flanks of the perimeter were secure.

The first plan for Hands Up also contained a time schedule. The first parachute landings would take place at 0010 on D-Day followed by the Special Service Brigade landing at first light. The first glider lift would land at 0700, followed by the second glider lift at 1400. On D+1 the Airborne Forward Delivery Airfield Group would arrive, followed on D+2 by a seaborne convoy carrying the seaborne tail of the airborne formations, 52nd Division and the US Army's No. 1 Base Section. Unlike in previous operations, where HQ Airborne Troops stipulated drop zones, the plan for Hands Up asked the airborne formations to request their own and HQ Airborne Troops would then call a co-ordinating meeting with the air forces to discuss. One controversial aspect of airborne operations planned between D-Day and Arnhem has been the presence of Browning's Airborne Corps Headquarters and in the way it used valuable glider assets. For Hands Up, it was planned that HQ Airborne Troops – as it was called at the time of the operation – would use twenty Horsa gliders. The Corps allocation of gliders would continue to grow incrementally with each operation.

The intelligence dossier created for Hands Up was the most detailed and extensive produced for any of the airborne operations planned during 1944. Unlike those created for other operations it even had its own front cover complete with Pegasus illustration. The strategic picture of the German forces in Brittany was taken from Williams' earlier summary. The dossier contained considerable location information including details of bridges, roads, railways, beaches and landing stages in the area as well as local politics, police structures, newspapers and the postal service. There were considerable coastal defences in the Quiberon Bay area with four 150mm guns at Ponte de Gavres, four 105mm guns at Plouhinec, four heavy 380mm guns at Plouharnel and four 150mm guns on Belle Isle. There were also two heavy railway guns at Kerdrean. A map included with the dossier showed that the coastal guns, along with anti-aircraft guns and field guns further inland, had interlocking ranges for mutual support.

The Quiberon area itself was manned by the 275th Division. The coastal defences consisted of concrete pillboxes roughly every mile with each manned by a reinforced platoon, mainly of Russian troops. There were reported to be 400 naval troops in Vannes, and Belle Isle was garrisoned by two naval artillery battalions. Vannes airfield was manned by Luftwaffe troops and there was a flak school just north of the airfield.

The French Resistance was active in Brittany, as were Allied special forces. Both the Free French and communist resistance had units in the area, with an estimated total strength of 9,000 in the Morbihan department alone. The 4th French Parachute Battalion, an SAS unit, were also operating in the area in uniform. Around 350 French paratroopers were working in small groups to liaise with and train the Resistance and both would be available to carry out resistance or small coup-de-main tasks.

Vannes itself had seen significant hardship only recently. Although the town normally had a population of 20,500 people it was believed that a large part of the population had been deported for forced labour and to clear the coastal zone of civilians.

Planning for Hands Up does not seem to have advanced far below corps level. The operation is only mentioned once in the 1st Airborne Division war diary, in the form of a map trace of drop zones.[75] But the broader context of capturing the Brittany ports dictated training. 1st Airborne Division's Exercise Bones, which took place in the Grimsby area between 23 and 25 July, was aimed at studying the capture of a defended port town. As Operation Beneficiary had been put aside by this stage it was likely that Bones had Quiberon Bay in mind rather than St Malo.[76]

22 July

On 22 July the second draft of the Ninth Air Force plan was sent to Montgomery, explaining that 21st Army Group's comments had been taken on board.[77] HQ Airborne Troops had responded to the Ninth Air Force plan on 20 July, to which Bostwick at Ninth Air Force replied on 22 July.[78] Browning had stated categorically that there was no possibility of 52nd Division being brought in by sea and that it had to be flown in. Browning had also queried why US Air Support signals were to be used, to which Bostwick replied that the air support would be provided by US forces and that he had asked for two tentacles for 1st Airborne Division and one for Corps HQ. Browning also wished for the airfield and airstrips to be used straight away but would not give a date for when this might be. He also requested that the Americans extend their area of anti-aircraft cover from the beaches to include the airfields on the peninsula, as the British airborne forces had only enough guns to protect Vannes airfield. Requests for air supply were to be sent from HQ Airborne Troops to TCCP at Eastcote, 'after consultation with Ninth Air Force'. Browning argued with the distinction between ground troops and airborne troops in some sections of the Ninth Air Force plan, possibly wishing to ensure that he commanded as many troops as possible, and refused to submit his air supply demands through CATOR.

On 22 July Ramsay wrote to Eisenhower, Montgomery, Leigh-Mallory and Bradley regarding Beneficiary and Hands Up. Ramsay stated that due to 'recent divisions' neither operation would be staged as originally envisaged. Instead St Malo and Quiberon Bay would be opened and operated only after the US forces had reached them overland. The opening of both ports would therefore be an administrative task rather than a military operation.[79] This seems to have been the final death knell for any realistic prospect of Hands Up taking place.

Planning continued however. The Joint Planning Staff Outline Plan for Hands Up was published on 22 July.[80] A particular concern was identifying a period of four consecutive days where the cloud base would be above 3,000ft. There were predicted to be only two or three such periods in an average year but there was a 50 per cent chance of there being none in any given year. Looking at August and September overall it was thought that the best operational weather for Hands Up would be found in the second half of August and the first half of September. Analysis of weather patterns in the Bay of Biscay found that the wind speed increased markedly in late September and early October, with periods of Force 5, 6 and 7 winds doubling compared to early August. In the fortnight between 1 and 16 October for example it was predicted that there could be an average of six days of strong winds and a maximum of 10 days. Whilst the cloud and visibility might be suitable for the operation, it improved from late August onwards and into the first fortnight of September. Conditions were likely to deteriorate into the second half of September, particularly regarding south-westerly winds, which would obviously be a problem in Quiberon Bay.

On 22 July the Commander of US Naval Forces in Europe, Admiral Harold Stark, wrote to Rear Admiral Hall asking him to involve representatives from US Naval Forces Europe in planning for Chastity. However planning for Chastity had not been devolved to Hall as his force had not been released from Operation Neptune.[81]

23 July

On 23 July 38 Group produced a loose minute detailing a suggested method for delivering 52nd Division by air.[82] 52nd Division would be landed on Vannes airfield and other airstrips as they became available. Once they had landed the division would protect the right flank of the beachhead in Tresflean and Elven. Detachments would patrol on the line of the Rau De Kervily and carry out reconnaissance to the north, north-east, east and south.

The airborne route would take advantage of navigation aids, especially Gee, and efforts were made to use natural landmarks and to avoid enemy flak. The columns would cross the coast at St Albans Head, then make landfall at Cap Frenel before reaching the Vannes area. The rate at which the division could be landed would be limited by the size of the airstrips. IX Troop Carrier Command thought that thirty-six aircraft could be handled by day and twenty-seven an hour at night. All aircraft would fly in groups of these numbers to ease handling and to help the fighters to provide better cover. The formations would take 25 minutes to take off and 18 minutes to land.

As soon as sufficient airstrips had been completed long-range day fighters would be positioned in the beachhead to escort transport aircraft from Cap de la Hague to Vannes and back. After escorting the transport aircraft to Vannes the fighters would then circle the airfield before escorting the returning group to Cap de la Hague. Night fighter cover would be arranged formations flying at night.

52nd Division was significantly stronger than an airborne division with three infantry brigades and battalions at a much higher establishment than parachute or airlanding units, a tank squadron and a reconnaissance regiment, three field regiments of artillery, an anti-tank regiment and a light anti-aircraft regiment. It is hard not to conclude that the division would have made a valuable addition to any operation were it possible to get it into battle.

It would take six days and 2,000 aircraft sorties to deliver the 52nd Division. D+1 would see the 5th Battalion of the Highland Light Infantry landed along with the Tactical Divisional headquarters, two sections of the divisional defence platoon and one battery of the Light Anti-Aircraft Battery with their 40mm guns. The D+1 lift would take an estimated 150 aircraft sorties. D+2 and D+3 would see the arrival of the 156th Brigade Group including a Field Regiment of artillery, along with the 1st Mountain Regiment Royal Artillery. This lift would take 700 aircraft sorties. The 153rd Brigade Group would arrive between D+3 and D+5, along with the 3rd Mountain Regiment Royal Artillery and the rest of divisional headquarters. This lift would take 600 sorties. The rest of the division would arrive on D+5 and D+6 including the 157th Brigade Group minus the 5th Highland Light Infantry with an estimated 500 aircraft sorties.

Additional sorties would be required to land the RAF Flying Control and airfield ground crews, the 6th Airlanding Light Battery, ground crews for the fighter and tactical reconnaissance squadrons and the AFDAG. These sorties would need to be factored into the programme for landing 52nd Division. The provisional plan for delivering the HQ Airborne Troops 'corps troops' sheds light on just how improvised it was as a formation. Its order of battle for Hands Up included HQ SAS Troops, 6th Airlanding Light Battery, 618th Field Company Royal Engineers, 878th Battalion, HQ Glider Pilots and 1 and 2 Wings of the Glider Pilot Regiment. It also had the AFDAG under command along with a Royal Engineers Field Park Company and Stores Dump, several Royal Army Service Corps units including a Supply Dump Platoon, a Defence Issues Detail, a POL Dump Platoon, an ammunition platoon and a light transport company. It would also require an Ordnance Dump and a REME Workshop. One of the most serious deficiencies was in medical services where it would need a Casualty Clearing Station, two Field Dressing Stations, two Field Transfusion Units and a

Medical Stores Dump. There was also a requirement for three Provost Sections, two Pioneer Companies and a Pioneer Platoon. Many of these units had yet to be allocated to Airborne Troops and it was not clear where they would come from.

The Provisional Air Movement Table produced by 38 Group indicated where units were to take off from and where they were to land. The first parachute lift would see the pathfinders of the 21st Independent Parachute Company take off from Keevil and Fairford and land on Drop Zones N and V. 1st Parachute Brigade would then land on Drop Zone N. Brigade HQ would take off from Barkston Heath along with the 1st Parachute Battalion, 16th Parachute Field Ambulance, 1st Parachute Squadron Royal Engineers and a detachment from divisional headquarters. The 2nd Parachute Battalion would take off from Saltby while the 3rd Parachute Battalion would leave from Folkingham along with the 1st Airborne Reconnaissance Squadron. The 4th Parachute Brigade meanwhile would land on Drop Zone V. Brigade HQ would take off from Spanhoe along with the 10th Parachute Battalion, the 4th Parachute Squadron Royal Engineers and a party from divisional headquarters. The 11th and 156th Parachute Battalions would leave from Cottesmore along with the 133rd Parachute Field Ambulance.[83]

The first glider lift would land on Landing Zone A later on D-Day. Divisional Headquarters would take off from Brize Norton along with the gliderborne elements of 1st Parachute Brigade while the Airlanding Brigade HQ would leave from Blakehill Farm along with part of one of the airlanding battalions and 181st Airlanding Field Ambulance. The other airlanding battalions would take off from Broadwell and Down Ampney while the balance of the other battalion would leave from Brize Norton and Down Harwell. The Light Regiment Royal Artillery would take off from Harwell, the 2nd Anti-Tank Battery from Fairford along with the 9th Parachute Field Company Royal Engineers and the gliderborne elements of 4th Parachute Brigade. The reconnaissance squadron jeeps would leave from Tarrant Rushton along with two gliders carrying bulldozers to be used for constructing airstrips. HQ Airborne Troops advance headquarters would leave from Tarrant Rushton in 20 gliders.

The second glider lift would see the balance of the second glider lift being landed with gliders taking off from Greenham Common, Membury, Ramsbury and Tarrant Rushton. The 17-pounder anti-tank battery would arrive in ten gliders. It was hoped that some gliders would be able to land on Vannes airfield by D+1.

24 July

On 24 July – the day that Operation Cobra started – Brigadier General Maclean of SHAEF G3 Plans Section wrote to Bull.[84] The SHAEF planners agreed with speeding-up operations in Brittany as they felt that future operations in France depended on capturing the peninsula early. It was not thought that the combined capacity of Quiberon Bay and Brest would be enough and that delays in capturing Brittany would lead to equal delays in the advance to the Seine in Normandy. The impending winter weather added urgency as decisive action towards the east from Normandy would be harder. Maclean suggested that the immediate objective should be not to capture Quiberon Bay or Brest alone, but the whole peninsula as soon as possible. He suggested that resistance was likely to be heavy at Avranches but once the Allies had 'turned the corner' they would have a free run into Brittany with the main delays being in capturing ports, which were likely to be fortified. He ruled out amphibious assaults as the coast was unsuitable but did not exclude the possibility of airborne landings followed by seaborne reinforcements. He felt that the use of airborne forces would be very limited with only one and one-third airborne divisions available until mid-September.

Maclean argued that all available airborne forces and aircraft would be required for the latter if Cobra was successful, and that 'Airborne forces must not be frittered away on minor enterprises which will only pay small dividends'. He did however suggest that airborne forces could assist with passing round Avranches. He argued that they would not be strong enough to capture ports on their own and would therefore only be useful for harassing enemy lines of communications. He also felt that dropping airborne forces to link up with the Maquis would 'do little good' and would raise expectations prematurely. For naval reasons Maclean argued that any combined airborne and seaborne operations would have to be confined to the north coast of the peninsula. Maclean argued that if Cobra failed that airborne forces should instead be used to 'get round' Avranches and that FUSAG had already been ordered to plan this operation.

The Base Section No. 1 and Com Z plan for Hands Up was published on 24 July. The mission of Base Section No. 1 would be to coordinate the mounting of all US forces with equipment and supplies for 14 days, unload all ships in Quiberon Bay, operate beaches and deliver supplies to truckheads and reconnoitre for the Chastity project. The plan stated that a minimum of 30 days would be required prior to D-Day to requisition and load supplies and to train an Engineer Special Brigade, as prior to the operation all troops in the Engineer Special Brigade would be trained in beach operations. The operation would not be launched unless it was certain that Third Army would be able to join up with the airborne forces within 14 days. Liberty ships would start loading on D-16 followed by coasters on D-12 and landing craft on D-10. All loading would need to be completed by D-6 and the convoy would sail on D-2. Beaches 188 and 189 would be secured and cleared by the airborne forces and underwater obstacles and mines would be cleared jointly by naval personnel and the Engineer Special Brigade. Base Section No. 1 would have 15,992 troops ashore by D+2 among a total of 30,126 of all units in the beachhead. 52nd Division would be complete by D+7.

Beach dumps would be established in the rear of the beaches from which all US forces would draw their supplies. Two truckheads would be established in the vicinity of Thiers and Surzur and a general storage area would be set up in the vicinity of Vannes. British airborne forces would draw their supplies from the truckheads after submitting daily requisitions to Base Section No. 1, but all units would land with a reserve of 14 days of supplies. After the D+2 convoy no other convoys could be expected until Brest was captured, which was predicted for D+24. Medical units would hold casualties until a link-up was achieved around D+14. Casualties would then be evacuated from the airfields where a holding medical unit would be set up. Burial grounds would be divided into plots to accommodate dead by nationality. Fifteen officers and twenty men from Base Section No. 1 would act as a Civil Affairs detachment. Base Section Engineers would set up a regional employment office around Vannes on D+3 and would only be used to construct beach exits and roads.

Beaches 188 and 189 were on the Sarzeau peninsula and four to six exits would be built from each beach. The beach troops would be established within a mile of the beaches including signals, engineers, medical, quartermaster, ordnance, ammunition and chemical while the Base Section Command Post would be at Sarzeau. A Field Hospital would be established to the west of Sarzeau with another south of Vannes and an Evacuation Hospital at Surzur. There would be a truckhead south-west of Surzur and another north-west of Thiex on the road to Vannes. 1st Airborne Division would be positioned north of Vannes airfield and 52nd Division would occupy Elven. The Sarzeau peninsula would be cleared by the British Special Service Brigade and the Polish Parachute Brigade. The Special Service Brigade would take up positions at Surzur and the Polish Brigade would occupy Thiex.

175

The Intelligence Annex attached to the Base Section No. 1 Plan was exhaustive. It gave information on the ethnic background of the local people, their languages and religion. Intelligence suggested that neither the Germans nor the Vichy French had gained much support from the Bretons and there were thought to be less than 1,000 collaborators in the region. Less than five per cent of the local police were thought to be German sympathisers. The Germans were expected to try and use spies against the Allied landings and to attempt to spread dissatisfaction and defeatism among civilians and Allied troops.

The intelligence summary concluded that the Germans had already prepared to demolish important facilities and had already evacuated some equipment from the Quiberon Bay area. They had carried out effective demolitions and evacuations in the Normandy fighting with limited time, and it was assumed that the same would happen in Brittany. The Germans were known to have laid mines and had increased mining activity in recent weeks. There were believed to be a small number of German surface vessels in the Biscay ports and the Germans had human torpedoes within range of Quiberon Bay. The Germans were also expected to leave behind agents and saboteurs after their withdrawal, probably making use of collaborators. They were also thought to have evacuated skilled labour including port operatives.

Base Section No. 1 Engineers would be responsible for constructing beach exits and a road network from the beaches to the beach dumps that would supply the assault troops in the Quiberon Bay area. These would be completed by D+7. Any beach obstacles would have been cleared earlier by the airborne engineers. The beaches themselves would be operated by an Engineer Special Brigade and would have a capacity of 3,000 tons per day. HQ Airborne Troops and Ninth Air Force would provide detachments at all supply points and storage areas to help identify and supervise the handling of their own supplies. Where practical supplies would be delivered forwards by transport personnel but units could also pick them up themselves in an emergency. An Engineer dump would be established as close to the beach as possible and an engineer maintenance shop would also be set up nearby to service the Special Brigade. Apart from beach exits and roads the only other planned construction would be two tented hospitals. Materials for these would be brought in on the first convoy. To speed up the treatment of casualties the hospitals would begin accepting patients before being completed. Materials would also be shipped in to build a 200ft by 200ft prisoner of war cage, to be built by the prisoners themselves. A hydrographic survey would be made

176

of the River Auray to inform more details plans for the development of the Chastity project. This would be undertaken as soon as possible by the 1053rd Port Construction and Repair Group.

The Base Section's Quartermaster plan sheds light on the complexity of supporting a joint amphibious and airborne operation. The Base Section's Quartermaster units would operate the truckheads at Thiex and Surzur which would move supplies from the beaches forward to the assault troops. They would also identify areas for further quartermaster installations once the Quiberon Bay area was developed as a port. Although supplies would initially be stored in beach dumps depots would be established in the Vannes area as soon as possible. US forces would be catered for by 10-in-1 rations if possible, and if not then the 'best available' emergency rations. The Quartermaster troops would number 1,129 men and 88 vehicles and would be commanded by the HQ of the 578th Quartermaster Battalion. Three Service Companies – the 3184th, 988th and 954th – would serve as beach dump labour troops. The 193rd Gasoline Supply Company would operate the beach fuel dumps and the 573rd Railhead Company would operate the truckheads. The headquarters and one platoon of the 621st Depot Supply Company would supervise the beach dumps, and the headquarters and two platoons of the 611th Graves Registration Company would register graves.

The Base Section's Ordnance Plan would require 345 men and 90 vehicles. These would include the 651st Ammunition Company, the 3507th Medium Automotive Maintenance Company and the 37th and 39th Ordnance Bomb Disposal Squads. They would also be augmented by a small British ammunition detachment. The 3507th Company would establish a workshop in the vicinity of Sarzeau and the ammunition dump would be set up alongside the road running from the beach north-east to Sarzeau. All vehicles coming by sea would be waterproofed and would have to be de-waterproofed after landing by units. This was a time-consuming process that involved unsealing much of the vehicle and checking it for water. The Engineer Shore Brigade would also have its own ordnance units – the 572nd Ammunition Company, an Ordnance Maintenance Detachment and two British detachments covering maintenance and ammunition.

The Base Section's transportation units would control road traffic from the beach dumps to the truck heads in conjunction with the Provost Marshal of the Base Section, who would also assign military police to patrol the roads. Transport units included the Headquarters of a Quartermaster Truck Battalion, a Quartermaster Truck Company and a detachment of a Traffic Regulating Group. The Base Section

Transportation officer would arrange for supplies to moved forward to the truckheads at Thiex and Surzur. All motor transport ashore would be pooled and used as necessary, including staff vehicles and the four Quartermaster Truck Companies assigned to the Engineer Shore Brigade. A Motor Transport Pool would be established west of Sarzeau and the dispatching of vehicles would be handled from there.

Whatever can be said about Hands Up, the planning was extensive and clearly did not lack detail, with much of the complex planning taking place even after it seemed unlikely that the operation would take place.

27 July

A preliminary conference on the air side of Hands Up was held at Eastcote on the afternoon of 27 July.[85] It was chaired by Hollinghurst and attended by officers from IX Troop Carrier Command, 38 Group, AEAF, Ninth Air Force, the Glider Pilot Regiment and HQ Airborne Troops. Almost immediately the meeting agreed that no further planning could be carried out until the airborne forces completed their landing tables. Mackenzie was asked to ensure that this was done. Hollinghurst stated that the purpose of the conference was to discuss the air build up from D+1 onwards, particularly the fly-in of 52nd Division. The division would be billeted in the Aldershot area and taken to transit camps in the Newbury and Swindon areas just prior to emplaning. IX Troop Carrier Command would lift elements of the Division from Aldermaston, Membury, Greenham Common, Ranston, Welford and Chilbolton while 46 Group would take off from Broadwell, Down Ampney and Blakehill Farm.

Many points regarding the air side of Hands Up were undecided, including the number of airstrips that would be available, their size, condition and facilities. Hollinghurst asked 46 Group and IX Troop Carrier Command to investigate these points and to work out an establishment for airfield control with HQ Airborne Troops. HQ Airborne Troops were also asked to ensure that one of the infantry battalions in 52nd Division was trained to help unload aircraft and special facilities were allocated to help with this. Hollinghurst also asked Ninth Air Force to prepare detailed proposals for air cover for the airborne columns and for a standing fighter patrol over Vannes airfield. Mackenzie stated that he thought that Browning would 'require' tactical reconnaissance aircraft to operate from Vannes airfield. Hollinghurst was taken aback by this, and said that it was the first that he had heard of it.

29 July

On 29 July Richardson circulated the Joint Planning Staff's Outline Plan for Hands Up to others at 21st Army Group HQ. The plan had been approved by Ramsay and Montgomery but approval from Leigh-Mallory was pending.[86]

31 July

On 31 July Commander J.R.A. Seymour of ANXF sent a message from SHAEF Forward Headquarters to SHAEF G4's Movement and Transport Branch.[87] He argued that in order to capture Quiberon Bay then Brest would have to be captured first, otherwise enemy naval action would require a four-day passage from the UK with no possibility of shelter from the weather. However, if Brest were captured it could be used as a staging port and would reduce the passage to two days. He also suggested that once captured Quiberon Bay could be developed through the winter. Seymour was not in favour of the beaches on the Cancale peninsula which he thought were very flat and muddy.

2 August

On 2 August the Deputy Adjutant-General of 21st Army Group wrote to the Operations 'A' staff regarding Hands Up:[88] 'The complexity of Operation Hands Up from a reinforcing and medical point of view requires no stressing. I would be grateful, therefore, if you could give me the earliest possible information as to the likelihood of it taking place.' A pencil note on the message simply states 'Phoned answer "never" 10/8/44'.

7 August

On 7 August Group Captain Cleave of the AEAF Air Plans Staff wrote to Richardson at 21st Army Group to suggest that given the sudden developments in the Battle of Normandy and in Brittany, Leigh-Mallory felt that Hands Up had been overtaken by events and could be shelved.[89] This was the final coup de grace for Hands Up.

Conclusion

Hands Up was a concept for an operation that was not planned for in any detail by 1st Airborne Division, but was discussed and planned at a high level of detail by higher headquarters. Hands Up is not mentioned in brigade or battalion war diaries and it is unlikely that most of the airborne personnel would have known much about it.

Hands Up raises several interesting points. It was perhaps the high point of intelligence that was available for airborne operations, at a level that was not always the case for other operations before of afterwards. This suggests how useful the French Resistance and special forces activity in Brittany was, along with the interrogation of prisoners of war who had been diverted from Brittany. Allied intelligence of the picture in Brittany suggested that Hands Up would be a walkover and that Germans would not resist. But, reflecting the dilemma faced by airborne planners, would this make it decisive?

It is also intriguing that in contrast to Wild Oats and Market Garden the air forces did not object to the high presence of flak in the area, including at Vannes airfield. The airborne operation was also planned to take place at night, with a parachute drop at 0010.

It is a paradox that the most detailed airborne planning of the campaign was for one of the least well known operations. Hands Up is also perhaps the most pertinent example of the mistake of seeing airborne operations as just airborne. In reality all of the operations that we have considered would have been much more complex, and would never have taken place in a vacuum – they were always aimed at contributing to a wider strategy.

Hands Up was also the last of what might be grouped as the 'Brittany port' operations. Despite extensive planning, none were launched. They may well have been very costly for the lightly-equipped airborne forces. Although Third Army cleared much of Brittany relatively quickly, several of the fortress ports held out for much longer. St Malo fell on 2 September, and Brest on 20 September, long after the Allied armies had advanced towards Germany and the Low Countries. St Nazaire and Lorient held on until after VE-Day, and U-boats would therefore have been an ongoing threat to any shipping using the Brittany ports.

CONCLUSION

As the Allies cleared much of Brittany and looked to inflict a significant defeat on the Germans in Normandy, despite significant planning no airborne operations had been mounted since D-Day. Despite investing significant time and resources in developing a formidable airborne force, the Allies did not use it in its intended role until the middle of September 1944.

It is clear from studying these operations that there was no universal experience in terms of how Allied airborne personnel were affected by the planning and cancellations. As a divisional commander Roy Urquhart was involved in everything, or at least everything that his superior Browning would allow. In his memoir shortly after the war he summarised the period as 'operational plans tumbled one over the other' and that he was 'frustrated and disappointed'.[1] Interviewed some years later he was more candid: 'It was exasperating. It was maddening . . . every operation entailed troops moving from their original billets to an assembly area, and loading the aircraft and gliders, and briefing.'[2] Urquhart also described how this period impacted on the ability of him and his staff to plan subsequent operations:

> It all had to be done very quickly on existing information without any research or any background stuff at all ... it was very much an ad-hoc business, and our staff work became particularly rushed. We thought that we were very highly trained . . . everyone thought, 'will it come off this time?', and were not really surprised when it was cancelled.

One of Urquhart's brigadiers, John Hackett, recalled the period in a similar vein, and also reflected on the process of emplaning and then disembarking as operations were cancelled.

> We trained very hard and we planned for something like 12 operations which didn't come off and for three of them we were already in the

181

aeroplane ready to take off, last letters written and everything tidied up. A chap comes round and hammers on the outside of the aircraft, 'alright, dismount, its all off' and everybody going on three days leave.[3]

By contrast, the average soldier in 1st Airborne Division would have known little about some of the cancelled operations, as planning did not progress far enough for personnel to move to airfields or to be briefed. Most of them would have found out about the full extent after the war. Jeffrey Noble was a Private serving with the 156th Parachute Battalion: 'We were kept by as standby reserves and were briefed for up to 17, I believe, other operations were planned, either in France or Belgium and so on, for the forces in Europe.'[4]

Indeed, the number of cancelled operations quoted by veterans varies wildly. This is in no way to say that any of them are incorrect – most of them would have had no way of knowing in 1944 – but an observation that the history of such a high-profile campaign, and the popular culture impact of a film such as *A Bridge Too Far*, can both have a powerful effect on perceptions.

The airborne operations planned for Normandy and Brittany fall into two broad phases. Firstly, Tuxedo, Wastage and Wild Oats were focussed on either reinforcing the initial beachhead or supporting its enlargement. They were discarded when the Allies gained a secure foothold, and when the front solidified and German resistance stiffened. Secondly, Beneficiary, Swordhilt and Hands Up were aimed at securing deep-water ports in Brittany.

A common dilemma between all of these operations was the need to balance risk and benefit, and working with what were at times very narrow windows of opportunity. Operations were already becoming more and more complex, with an increasing number of commanders, headquarters and planners involved. Risks were already starting to increase, including the distance that airborne forces would be dropped from the relieving ground forces and the time that they would be expected to operate alone before being relieved.

Browning was continuing to develop his position, but this was also increasingly becoming a problem. There is no evidence that his previously administrative headquarters had been authorised as a deployable corps, but nevertheless the size of his tactical headquarters had already been increasing, requiring aircraft that could otherwise be used by other airborne units.

After the end of the Battle of Normandy the Allies were heading for the Low Countries and the German border. They still had a powerful airborne reserve held in readiness and had formed an Army-level headquarters to command it. More operations would be planned and cancelled before the airborne army finally took off for Operation Market Garden. But the seeds of what would unfold in the autumn had already been sown.

APPENDICES

APPENDIX 1 – TAC HQ AIRBORNE FORCES ESTABLISHMENT, JUNE 1944

Serial	Designation	Officers	NCOs	Privates	To be found by	Remarks
1	General Officer Commanding	1			Lt-Gen F.A.M. Browning	Already in France
2	Batman		1			Already in France
3	Drivers			2		One for Caravan, one for Jeep
4	Aide-de-Camp	1			Major H. Cator	Already in France
5	Batman			1		At present sick in UK
6	Driver			1		
7	GSO2 (Operations)	1			Major N.J.L. Field	
8	Batman/Driver			1		To be found from 6 Div residue
9	GSO3 (Intelligence)	1			Capt C. McArthur	
10	Batman/Driver			1		To be found from 6 Div residue

(Continued)

Serial	Designation	Officers	NCOs	Privates	To be found by	Remarks
11	Rep 9 Troop Carrier Command	1			Lt-Col A.B. Harris	Already in France
12	Batman/Driver			1		To be found from 6 Div residue
13	Rep Airborne Section FUSAG	1			Lt-Col J.G. Cornett	
14	Batman/Driver			1		To be found from 6 Div residue
15	Corps Commander's Escort		1			Already in France
16	Clerks		1	1	G Branch	Pte Blackman already in France, Sjt Anker also to go
17	Drivers			3	6 Div Residue	One for each staff and sigs
18	General Duties		1	1	Sjt from Officers Mess, Pte from 'G' Orderlies	Sjt Blunden Tpr Brown
19	Signals	1	6	10	One Cipher operator by sigs 21 Army Gp Remainder by sigs Airtps	
20	Total	7	9	24		
21	Total all ranks		40			
22	Total yet to go to France	4	8	20		

Serial	Designation	Officers	NCOs	Privates	To be found by	Remarks
23	Signals Officer	1			CSO HQ Airtps	Capt Hart
24	Batman			1	6 Div Residue	
25	Driver			1	6 Div Residue	
26	Cipher Operators		4		3 by CSO Airtps – 1 by Sigs 21 A Gp	
27	Despatch Riders			2	CSO Airtps	
28	i/c Wireless crew OWL		1		CSO Airtps	Crew of 12 High Power set in 3 tonner
29	Signalmen OWL			2	CSO Airtps	
30	Signalmen ES			1	CSO Airtps	
31	Driver			1	CSO Airtps	
32	i/c Wireless Crew OWL			1	CSO Airtps	Crew of reserve 12 High Power set in 3 tonner
33	Signalmen OWL			2	CSO Airtps	
34	Signalmen ES			1	CSO Airtps	
34	Driver			1	6 Div Residue	Driver of sig stores 3 tonner

Source: TNA WO 171/369

APPENDIX 2 – 1ST AIRBORNE DIVISION AIR MOVEMENT TABLE FOR WILD OATS PARACHUTE AIRCRAFT

Airborne Unit	Air Unit	Chalk numbers	Airfield	LZ or DZ
21 Independent Company	38 Gp	1-12	Brize Norton	Y
4 Para Bde Recce	PPS	13-16	Fairford and North Witham	Y
3 Para Bn	313 Gp	31-66	Folkingham	X
Det 16 Field Ambulance	313 Gp	67	Folkingham	X
Recce Squadron	313 Gp	68-75	Folkingham	X
156 Para Bn	316 Gp	76-109	Cottesmore	Y
Det 133 Field Ambulance	316 Gp	110-111	Cottesmore	Y
Det 133 Field Ambulance	316 Gp	112-114	Cottesmore	Y
11 Para Bn	316 Gp	114-147	Cottesmore	Y
2 Para Bn	314 Gp	148-183	Saltby	X
Det 16 Field Ambulance	314 Gp	184	Saltby	X
1 Para Sqn RE	314 Gp	185-190	Saltby	X
Platoon RASC	314 Gp	191-192	Saltby	X
10 Para Bn	315 Gp	193-226	Spanhoe	Y
Det 133 Field Ambulance	315 Gp	227-228	Spanhoe	Y
HQ 4 Para Bde	315 Gp	229-237	Spanhoe	Y
4 Para Sqn RE	315 Gp	238-246	Spanhoe	Y
Platoon RASC	315 Gp	247-248	Spanhoe	Y

Airborne Unit	Air Unit	Chalk numbers	Airfield	LZ or DZ
Det Div HQ	315 Gp	249-251	Spanhoe	Y
1 Para Bn	61 Gp	252-287	Barkston Heath	X
HQ 1 Para Bde	61 Gp	288-296	Barkston Heath	X
16 Field Ambulance	61 Gp	297-300	Barkston Heath	X
HQ 1 Para Sqn RE	61 Gp	301-303	Barkston Heath	X
Det Div HQ	61 Gp	304-305	Barkston Heath	X

Glider aircraft

Airborne Unit	Air Unit	Chalk Nos	No of gliders	Airfield	DZ or LZ
7 KOSB less two companies		359-398	49	Membury	B
1 Border less two companies		399-447	49	Welford	A
HQ 1 Airlanding Brigade		448-456	9	Greenham Common	A
1 company 1 Border		457-462	6	Greenham Common	A
1 company 2 S Staffs		463-468	6	Greenham Common	A
1 company 7 KOSB		469-474	6	Greenham Common	A
181 Field Ambulance		475-478	4	Greenham Common	A
9 Field Company RE		479-494	16	Greenham Common	A
Admin		495-500	6	Greenham Common	A
2 S Staffs less two companies		501-549	49	Ramsbury	C
1 company 1 Border	46 Gp	600-605	6	Broadwell	A
1 Battery 1 Airlanding Light Regiment RA	46 Gp	606-632	27	Broadwell	A
Admin	46 Gp	633-637	5	Broadwell	A

(Continued)

PROPOSED AIRBORNE ASSAULTS DURING OPERATION OVERLORD

Airborne Unit	Air Unit	Chalk Nos	No of gliders	Airfield	DZ or LZ
1 Para Bde HQ	46 Gp	638-649	12	Blakehill Farm	C
4 Para Bde HQ	46 Gp	650-661	12	Blakehill Farm	C
1 Battery 1 Airlanding Light Regiment RA	46 Gp	662-694	33	Down Ampney	A
Admin	46 Gp	695-699	5	Down Ampney	A
1 company 7 KOSB	38 Gp	700-705	6	Brize Norton	C
Div HQ	38 Gp	706-728	23	Brize Norton	C
1 Airlanding Light Regiment RA less 2 Batteries	38 Gp	729-767	39	Harwell	A
1 Anti-Tank Battery	38 Gp	768-770	3	Tarrant Rushton	
2 Anti-Tank Battery	38 Gp	771-773	3	Tarrant Rushton	
HQ 1 Airlanding Brigade	38 Gp	774-775	2	Tarrant Rushton	
Recce Squadron	38 Gp	776-795	20	Tarrant Rushton	B
1 company S Staffs	38 Gp	796-801	6	Fairford	B
2 Ant-Tank Battery	38 Gp	802-829	28	Fairford	
1 Anti-Tank Battery	38 Gp	830-857	28	Keevil	C

Source: TNA AIR 37/774

APPENDIX 3 – US ARMY TROOP LIST FOR OPERATION BENEFICIARY

28th Infantry Division	Personnel	Vehicles
109th Infantry Regiment	3,207	358
110th Infantry Regiment	3,207	358
112th Infantry Regiment	3,207	358
HQ & HQ Battery 28th Div Artillery	127	31
107th Field Artillery Battalion	501	134
108th Field Artillery Battalion	516	145
109th Field Artillery Battalion	501	134
229th Field Artillery Battalion	501	134
103rd Engineer Construction Battalion	635	126
103rd Medical Battalion	444	92
HQ 28th Infantry Division	169	
HQ Support Troops	25	
HQ Company	102	65
Military Police Platoon	71	27
Band	58	
28th Quartermaster Company	186	109
28th Signal Company	239	73
728th Ordnance Company	141	45
28th Reconnaissance Regiment	149	48
Total	**13,936**	**2,227**

(Continued)

Attached	Personnel	Vehicles
Field Artillery Group (3 Bns 105mm Self Propelled)	1,933	466
Field Artillery Observation Battery	151	39
Tank Battalion (Composite)	718	231
Tank Battalion (DD)	740	134
Tank Battalion (DD)	740	134
Tank Destroyer Battalion (Self Propelled)	642	187
Engineer Construction Battalion	635	126
Engineer Construction Battalion	635	126
9 Naval Fire Support Control Parties	81	36
Ammunition Supply Point #5	8	6
Ammunition Supply Point	8	6
Prisoner of War Interrogation Team #71	6	3
Prisoner of War Interrogation Team #74	6	3
OB Unit	3	1
MII Team #438	6	3
Photographic Interpretation Team	6	3
Counter Intelligence Corps Det #14 (Prov)	16	12
8th Det 165th Signals Photo Company	7	2
Platoon, Quartermaster Company	23	4
Company, Quartermaster Battalion (Truck)	110	104
Total	**7,152**	**1,770**

Source: TNA WO 205/845

APPENDIX 4 – HQ AIRBORNE TROOPS PLANNING PROGRAMME 1–15 JULY 1944

Date	Time	Place	Event	To attend
Sat 1 July	0930	Moor Park	Conf – Composition Tac HQ Airtps	G plans, Int, AQ, CSO,
	AM-PM	Moor Park	G Plans Staff Study – Beneficiary	services as detailed
Sun 2 July	AM	Moor Park	G Plans Staff Study – Lucky Strike	
	PM	Moor Park	P Plans prepare draft outline – Beneficiary	
Mon 3 July	AM	Moor Park	BGS considers notes on Lucky Strike	
	AM	FUSAG	FUSAG starts considering Hands Up	
	AM		Draft outline Beneficiary to FUSAG	
	PM	Moor Park	Brig Williams – to discuss Lucky Strike with BGS	
Tue 4 July	AM	Moor Park	G Plans – prepare final draft Lucky Strike Airborne appreciation	
	1900		Appreciation to reach 21 AG	

(Continued)

Date	Time	Place	Event	To attend
Weds 5 Jul	1000	COHQ	Conf on beach recce – Beneficiary	GSO2 Int
	1200	Moor Park	Planning teams 1 Div and 504 RCT arrive	
	1400	Moor Park	Tie up details Beneficiary with XX Corps	
	1600	Moor Park	Issue intelligence information and start studying Hands Up	G Plans, G int, 1 Div and 504 RCT planning teams
Thurs 6 July	1000	Moor Park	Complete planning Op Beneficiary	
	1400	Moor Park	Comds Conf Op Hands Up	
Sun 9 Jul	1400	Moor Park	Air co-ordinating conference Hands Up	
Sat 15 Jul	PM		All plans for Hands Up to be complete	

Source: TNA AIR 37/329

196

NOTES

Part I – Planning Before D-Day

'Penny Packets: Early Airborne Planning for D-Day
1. John C. Warren, *Airborne Operations in World War II, European Theatre* (1956), p.10.
2. TNA DEFE 2/529: Rattle Part 1, 1943.
3. Brigadier Claud Oxborrow was serving on the staff of GHQ Home Forces in 1943. He later became Brigadier General Staff (Air) at 21st Army Group during the North West Europe campaign.
4. Warren, *Airborne Operations*, p.10.
5. Ibid., p.11.
6. Roger Cirillo, *The Market Garden Campaign: Allied operational command in northwest Europe* (Cranfield University PhD thesis, 2001), p.62.
7. Ibid., p.63.
8. Warren, *Airborne Operations*, p.15.
9. IWM Documents.10866: The Private Papers of Air Chief Marshal Sir Leslie Hollinghurst.
10. Ibid.
11. IWM Documents.9487: The Private Papers of Brigadier AG Walch OBE.
12. Warren, *Airborne Operations*, p.16.
13. TNA WO 32/10927: Policy and Functions of First Allied Airborne Army.
14. William F. Buckingham, *Arnhem 1944* (Tempus, 2004), p.16. Browning had previously commanded 1st Airborne Division but as of D-Day had seen no active service during the Second World War.

'High Hopes': Airborne Planning from January to June 1944
1. Warren, *Airborne Operations*, p.16.
2. IWM Hollinghurst papers.
3. Warren, *Airborne Operations*, p.17.
4. IWM Hollinghurst papers.
5. Ibid.
6. TNA WO 285/1: Papers of General Sir Miles Dempsey: Planning 2nd Army attack on Normandy, Feb-Mar 1944.
7. Carlo D'Este, *Decision in Normandy: the Unwritten Story of Montgomery and the Allied Campaign* (Harper Collins, 1983).
8. IWM Hollinghurst papers.
9. Ibid.
10. Buckingham, *Arnhem 1944*, p.26.
11. IWM Oral History.21034: Robert Elliot Urquhart.

12 Buckingham, *Arnhem 1944*, p.33.
13 IWM Oral History 21034: Robert Elliot Urquhart.

'Suitable Agency': the Formation of the First Allied Airborne Army

1 TNA WO 219/2930: Organisation of combined airborne H.Q. and airborne corps in the European theatre of operations, Dec 1943.
2 IWM Walch papers.
3 Ibid.
4 Cirillo, *Operation Market Garden*, p.179.
5 TNA WO 219/2930.
6 TNA WO 171/368: HQ Airborne Troops Main War Diary, Jan-May 1944.
7 IWM Documents.4835: Private Papers of Lieutenant-General GC Bucknall CB MC DL.
8 TNA WO 219/2930.
9 Several major Allied headquarters were based in or around Southwick House, including Allied Naval Expeditionary Force, 21st Army Group and Eisenhower's forward command post.
10 TNA WO 205/78: Operation Overlord: organisation of airborne forces, Mar-Oct 1944.
11 Warren, *Airborne Operations*, p.91.
12 Cirillo, *Operation Market Garden*, p.194.
13 Ibid., pp.183–4.
14 IWM Documents.1838: Montgomery Ancillary Collection: General Sir Frank Simpson.
15 TNA WO 219/2860: Formation of 1 Allied Airborne Army, May 1944-May 1945.
16 TNA WO 219/2860.
17 Ibid.
18 General James M. Gavin, *On to Berlin* (New York: Bantam, 1978), p.83.
19 The US Army Group was routinely referred to as First United States Army Group, or FUSAG, as part of the Allies deception operations before D-Day.
20 TNA WO 219/2860.
21 Ibid.
22 Ibid.
23 Ibid.
24 Ibid.
25 TNA WO 171/369: HQ Airborne Troops Main War Diary, Jan-July 1944.
26 Warren, *Airborne Operations*, p.90.
27 TNA WO 219/2860.
28 Ibid.
29 Ibid.
30 Ibid.
31 TNA WO 219/106: Organisation: First Allied Airborne Army, Jun-Dec 1944.
32 TNA WO 219/2860.
33 Ibid.
34 TNA AIR 37/776: Air Commander-in-Chief, AEAF: 1st Allied Airborne Army formation and employment, 1944.
35 TNA WO 219/106.
36 Ibid.
37 TNA WO 205/197: 21st Army Group G Operations: Airborne Plans, Jul-Aug 1944.

38 Lewis Brereton, *The Brereton Diaries: The War in the Air in the Pacific, Middle East and Europe, 3 October 1941 – 8 May 1945* (New York: William Morrow & Co, 1946), p.308.
39 Ibid., p.309.
40 TNA WO 219/2860.
41 Cirillo, *Operation Market Garden*, p.27.
42 TNA WO 219/2860.
43 TNA WO 219/106.
44 TNA AIR 37/1057: SHAEF (Main and Rear): AEAF: historical record June-Aug 1944; WO 219/2860.
45 TNA WO 219/106.
46 TNA WO 219/2930.
47 Ibid.
48 Ibid.
49 Brereton, *Diaries*, p.317.
50 TNA WO 219/106.

Part II – Normandy

Operations Wastage and Tuxedo

1   IWM Oral History 10641: Jeffrey Noble, 156 Para Bn.
2   James Sims, *Arnhem Spearhead* (Imperial War Museum, 1978), p.25.
3   TNA WO 285/1.
4   TNA WO 171/392: 1st Airborne Division G Staff War Diary, Jan-Aug 1944.
5   Ibid.
6   TNA WO 171/368.
7   TNA WO 171/594: HQ 4 Parachute Brigade War Diary, Jan-Sept 1944.
8   TNA AIR 37/1057.
9   TNA WO 205/5B: 21st Army Group Communications between Commander in Chief and Chief of Staff, Jun 1944-Mar 1945.
10 IWM Oral History 21034: Roy Urquhart.
11 IWM Oral History 21583: Francis Moore, 1 AL AT Bty RA.

Operation Wild Oats

1   TNA AIR 37/413: 38 Group Operation 'Overlord': 1st Airborne Division, 1944.
2   TNA WO 171/392.
3   TNA WO 171/369.
4   TNA WO 205/196: 21st Army Group G Plans Airborne operations: plans, May-Jun 1944.
5   IWM Bucknall papers.
6   TNA WO 285/9: General Sir Miles Dempsey personal war diary, Jun-Sept 1944.
7   IWM Simpson papers.
8   TNA WO 285/9.
9   TNA WO 171/258: 1 Corps G Staff War Diary, Jan-Jul 1944.
10 TNA WO 285/9.
11 IWM Bucknall papers.
12 Ibid.
13 TNA WO 171/258.
14 Ibid.
15 IWM Bucknall papers.

16 TNA WO 171/258.
17 TNA WO 171/592: 1st Parachute Brigade War Diary, Jan-Dec 1944.
18 TNA WO 171/594.
19 TNA WO 171/592.
20 Ibid.
21 IWM Bucknall papers.
22 TNA WO 171/527: 51st Highland Division G Staff War Diary, Jan-Jun 1944.
23 TNA WO 171/592.
24 IWM Bucknall papers.
25 General Sir Charles Richardson, *Flashback: A Soldier's Story* (London: William Kimber & Co, 1985), p.179.
26 IWM Simpson papers.
27 William F. Buckingham, *Paras: The Birth of British Airborne Forces from Churchill's Raiders to 1st Parachute Brigade* (The History Press, 2005); and Buckingham, *Arnhem 1944*.
28 IWM Simpson papers.
29 Cirillo, *Operation Market Garden*, p.99.
30 IWM Bucknall papers.
31 Ibid.
32 Buckingham, *Arnhem 1944*, p.64.
33 Major General R.E. Urquhart, *Arnhem* (London: Cassell, 1958), p.28
34 Major General John Frost, *A Drop too Many* (London: Buchan and Enright, 1982), p.197.
35 IWM Oral History 20136: John Waddy, 156 Para Bn.
36 IWM Oral History 15534: William Carter, 1 Para Bn.
37 IWM Oral History 29996: Mike Brown, Glider Pilot Regiment.
38 IWM Oral History 29549: John McGeough, Glider Pilot Regiment.

Part III: Brittany

Operation Beneficiary

1   TNA WO 205/5B.
2   TNA AIR 37/413.
3   TNA WO 285/2: General Sir Miles Dempsey Papers, letters and directives from General Montgomery C in C 21st Army Group, Mar 1944-Apr 1945.
4   TNA AIR 37/1057.
5   TNA WO 171/392.
6   TNA WO 171/369.
7   TNA WO 171/392.
8   TNA WO 219/2504: Operations Lucky Strike, Hands Up and Beneficiary: planning for a drive towards the River Seine after capture of ports in Brittany, Jun-Jul 1944.
9   TNA AIR 37/329: 38 Group, Operation Hands Up, 1944.
10 TNA WO 219/2504.
11 TNA WO 219/649: Operation Beneficiary: Joint land, sea and air forces plans, Jul 1944.
12 TNA WO 171/369.
13 TNA WO 205/845: 21st Army Group, Operation Beneficiary, Jul 1944.
14 Tentacles were liaison teams with two-way radios who accompanied ground forces to provide communications with the air forces.
15 TNA WO 205/845.

16 TNA WO 219/648: Operation Beneficiary: Joint land, sea and air forces plans, Jul 1944.
17 TNA WO 205/845.
18 Ibid.
19 Ibid.
20 TNA WO 285/2.
21 TNA WO 219/2504.
22 Ibid.
23 IWM Simpson Papers.
24 USCARL Colonel X.H. Price: Beach Obstacles and Defenses at St Malo, Dinard, Mont St Michel, and Cabourg, France, 2 October 1944.
25 Urquhart, *Arnhem*, p.28.

Operation Swordhilt

1   TNA WO 205/676: Operation Swordhilt: formation of planning group: outline of build up, maps and directive, Jul 1944.
2   Ibid.
3   Ibid.
4   Ibid.
5   Ibid.
6   Ibid.
7   Ibid. Around this time FUSAG became known as 12th US Army Group.
8   Ibid.
9   TNA WO 285/2.
10 TNA WO 205/676.

Operation Hands Up

1   TNA WO 219/2505: SHAEF G3 Plans, Operations Chastity and Hands Up: securing of Quiberon Bay and Atlantic ports, Apr-Sept 1944.
2   Ibid.
3   Ibid.
4   Ibid. It is not clear whether this was to Bradley, who at the time was commanding First Army. Although General Patton was notionally the commander of FUSAG, this was a deception as part of Operation Fortitude.
5   Ibid.
6   Ibid.
7   Ibid.
8   TNA WO 205/5B.
9   Ibid.
10 TNA AIR 37/1057.
11 TNA WO 219/2505.
12 Ibid.
13 Ibid.
14 Ibid.
15 Ibid.
16 TNA WO 205/665: 21st Army Group G Plans, Operation Hands Up: outline plans, order of battle, naval and aircraft availability, Jun-Jul 1944.
17 TNA WO 219/2505.
18 TNA WO 205/665.
19 TNA WO 205/862: 21st Army Group Operational Reports, Operation Hands Up, Jun-Jul 1944.

20 TNA AIR 37/1057.
21 TNA WO 219/2504.
22 TNA WO 205/665.
23 TNA WO 219/2505.
24 TNA WO 205/665.
25 TNA AIR 37/329.
26 TNA WO 205/665
27 Ibid.
28 Ibid.
29 TNA WO 219/2504.
30 TNA WO 205/665.
31 IWM Hollinghurst Papers.
32 TNA WO 219/2505.
33 TNA WO 205/665.
34 Ibid.
35 Ibid.
36 TNA WO 171/369.
37 TNA WO 285/2.
38 TNA WO 205/665.
39 Ibid.
40 Ibid.
41 TNA WO 219/2505.
42 TNA WO 205/665.
43 TNA WO 219/2504.
44 TNA WO 205/665.
45 Ibid.
46 Ibid.
47 TNA WO 205/666: 21st Army Group G Plans, Operation Hands Up: 9 Air Force
    outline plans, Jul 1944.
48 TNA WO 219/2505.
49 TNA WO 205/665.
50 Ibid.
51 Ibid.
52 Ibid.
53 Ibid.
54 Ibid.
55 Ibid.
56 Ibid.
57 Ibid.
58 Ibid.
59 TNA WO 219/2505.
60 Ibid.
61 TNA WO 205/665.
62 TNA WO 205/666.
63 TNA WO 205/665.
64 Lieutenant Colonel Charles Mackenzie later joined 1st Airborne Division as GSO1.
65 TNA AIR 37/329.
66 TNA WO 219/2505.
67 TNA WO 205/862.
68 TNA WO 205/666.
69 Ibid.
70 TNA WO 205/665.

71 Ibid.
72 TNA WO 219/2505.
73 Ibid.
74 TNA WO 285/2.
75 TNA WO 171/392.
76 TNA WO 171/592.
77 TNA WO 205/666.
78 Ibid.
79 TNA WO 205/665.
80 TNA WO 205/862.
81 TNA WO 219/2505.
82 TNA AIR 37/329.
83 Ibid.
84 TNA WO 219/2505.
85 TNA AIR 37/329.
86 TNA WO 205/665.
87 TNA WO 219/2505.
88 TNA WO 205/862.
89 TNA WO 205/665.

Conclusion

1 Urquhart, *Arnhem*, p.28.
2 IWM Oral History 21034: Roy Urquhart.
3 IWM Oral History 12022: John Hackett.
4 IWM Oral History 10641: Jeffrey Noble.

BIBLIOGRAPHY

Archive Sources

Imperial War Museum (IWM)
Documents:
0866: The Private Papers of Air Chief Marshal Sir Leslie Hollinghurst.
1838: Montgomery Ancillary Collection: General Sir Frank Simpson.
4835: The Private Papers of Lieutenant General G.C. Bucknall CB MC DL.
9487: The Private Papers of Brigadier A.G. Walch OBE.
15783: The Private Papers of Major General R.E. Urquhart CB DSO.
19517: Montgomery Ancillary Collection: Major General R.F.K. Belchem.

Oral History:
12022: Brigadier John Hackett, 4th Parachute Brigade.
10641: Jeffrey Noble, 156th Parachute Battalion.
15534: William Carter, 1st Parachute Battalion.
20136: Major John Waddy, 156th Parachute Battalion.
21034: Major General R.E. Urquhart, GOC 1st Airborne Division.
21583: Francis Moore, 1st Airlanding Anti-Tank Battery Royal Artillery.
29549: John McGeough, Glider Pilot Regiment.
29996: Mike Brown, Glider Pilot Regiment.

The National Archives, UK (TNA)
AIR 37/329: 38 Group, Operation Hands-up, 1944.
AIR 37/413: 38 Group, Operation 'Overlord': 1st Airborne Division, 1944.
AIR 37/776: Air Commander-in-Chief, AEAF: 1st Allied Airborne Army formation
    and employment, 1944.
AIR 37/1057: SHAEF (Main and Rear): AEAF: historical record June-Aug 1944.
DEFE 2/529: Rattle Part 1, 1943.
HS 6/239: Special Operations Executive Support for military and naval operations:
    Overlord and Linnet, 1944.
WO 32/10927: Policy and Functions of First Allied Airborne Army.
WO 171/258: 1 Corps G Staff War Diary, Jan-Jul 1944.
WO 171/368: HQ Airborne Troops Main War Diary, Jan-May 1944.
WO 171/369: HQ Airborne Troops Main War Diary, Jan-July 1944.

WO 171/392: 1st Airborne Division G Staff War Diary, Jan-Aug 1944.

WO 171/527: 51st Highland Division G Staff War Diary, Jan-Jun 1944.

WO 171/592: 1st Parachute Brigade War Diary, Jan-Dec 1944.

WO 171/594: 4th Parachute Brigade War Diary, Jan-Sept 1944.

WO 205/5B: 21st Army Group Communications between Commander in Chief and Chief of Staff, Jun 1944-Mar 1945.

WO 205/8: 21st Army Group, Operational plans submitted to the Chief of Staff, Jun 1944-Feb 1945.

WO 205/78: Operation Overlord: organisation of airborne forces, Mar-Oct 1944.

WO 205/142: 21st Army Group G Ops, Crossing of Water Obstacles, Oct 1943-Sept 1944.

WO 205/194: 21st Army Group G Ops, Airborne operations plans, Sept 1944-Apr 1945.

WO 205/195: 21st Army Group G Ops, Airborne operations plans, May 1944.

WO 205/197: 21st Army Group G Operations: Airborne Plans, Jul-Aug 1944.

WO 205/665: 21st Army Group G Plans, Operation Hands Up: outline plans, order of battle, naval and aircraft availability, Jun-Jul 1944.

WO 205/666: 21st Army Group G Plans, Operation Hands Up: 9 Air Force outline plans, Jul 1944.

WO 205/676: Operation Swordhilt: formation of planning group: outline of build up, maps and directive, Jul 1944.

WO 205/845: 21st Army Group, Operation Beneficiary, Jul 1944.

WO 205/862: 21st Army Group Operational Reports, Operation Hands Up, Jun-Jul 1944.

WO 219/106: Organisation: First Allied Airborne Army, Jun-Dec 1944.

WO 219/260: SHAEF Operations Overlord and Neptune: post-operational planning, Sept 1944.

WO 219/552: SHAEF AG, 1 Allied Airborne Army: organisation and order of battle. Establishment of Combined Airborne Headquarters, Aug-Dec 1944.

WO 219/648: Operation Beneficiary: Joint land, sea and air forces plans, Jul 1944.

WO 219/649: Operation Beneficiary: Joint land, sea and air forces plans, Jul 1944.

WO 219/2504: Operations Lucky Strike, Hands Up and Beneficiary: planning for a drive towards the River Seine after capture of ports in Brittany, Jun-Jul 1944.

WO 219/2505: SHAEF G3 Plans, Operations Chastity and Hands Up: securing of Quiberon Bay and Atlantic ports, Apr-Sept 1944.

WO 219/2860: Formation of 1 Allied Airborne Army, May 1944-May 1945.

WO 219/2930: Organisation of combined airborne H.Q. and airborne corps in the European theatre of operations, Dec 1943.

WO 219/4975: SHAEF First Allied Airborne Army, Organisation and functions of the H.Q, Aug 1944-Jul 1945.

WO 219/4980: SHAEF First Allied Airborne Army, Operation Boxer, Aug 1944.

WO 285/1: General Sir Miles Dempsey, Planning 2nd Army attack on Normandy, Feb-Mar 1944.

WO 285/2: General Sir Miles Dempsey Papers, Letters and directives from General Montgomery C in C 21st Army Group, Mar 1944-Apr 1945.

WO 285/9: General Sir Miles Dempsey personal war diary, Jun-Sept 1944.

US Army Combined Arms Research Library

Price, Colonel X.H., 'Beach Obstacles and Defenses at St Malo, Dinard, Mont St Michel, and Cabourg', France, 2 October 1944.

Kogard, Oberst Rudolf, Brest, 343rd Infantry Division (May–18 Sep 44).

Unpublished Sources

Cirillo, Roger, *The Market Garden Campaign: Allied operational command in northwest Europe* (Cranfield University PhD thesis, 2001).

Published Sources

Belchem, Major General David, *All in the Day's March* (London: Collins, 1978).

——————————————, *Victory in Normandy* (London: Chatto & Windus, 1981).

Bennett, David, *Magnificent Disaster: The Failure of Market Garden, The Arnhem Operation September 1944* (Newqbury: Casemate, 2008).

Blumenson, Martin, *Breakout and Pursuit* (Washington: US Army Centre of Military History, 1993).

Brereton, Lewis, *The Brereton Diaries: The War in the Air in the Pacific, Middle East and Europe, 3 October 1941 – 8 May 1945* (New York: William Morrow & Co, 1946).

Brooke, Field Marshal Lord Alan, *War Diaries 1939-1945* (London: Phoenix Press, 2002).

Buckingham, William F., *Arnhem 1944* (Stroud: Tempus, 2004).

——————————————, *Paras: The Birth of British Airborne Forces from Churchill's Raiders to 1st Parachute Brigade* (Stroud: Tempus, 2005).

Buckley, John, *Monty's Men: The British Army and the Liberation of Europe* (Yale University Press, 2014).

Clark, Lloyd, *Arnhem: Jumping the Rhine 1944 and 1945* (London: Headline, 2008).

Daglish, Ian, *Over the Battlefield: Operation Goodwood* (Barnsley: Pen and Sword, 2005).

——————————, *Over the Battlefield: Operation Epsom* (Barnsley: Pen and Sword, 2007).

Delaforce, Patrick, *The Black Bull: From Normandy to the Baltic with the 11th Armoured Division* (Stroud: Sutton, 1993).

Delaforce, Patrick, *Churchill's Desert Rats in North West Europe* (Barnsley: Pen and Sword, 2010).

D'Este, Carlo, *Decision in Normandy: the Unwritten Story of Montgomery and the Allied Campaign* (Harper Collins, 1983).

Doherty, Richard, *None Bolder: The History of the 51st Highland Division in the Second World War* (Stroud: Spellmount, 2006).

Ellis, Major L.F., *Victory in the West: Vol I, The Battle of Normandy* (London: HMSO, 1962).

Eisenhower, Dwight D., *Crusade in Europe* (London: Heinemann, 1948).

Forty, George, *Villers-Bocage: Battlezone Normandy* (Stroud: Sutton, 2004).

Fraser, David, *And we shall shock them: The British Army in the Second World War* (London: Hodder and Stoughton, 1983).

French, David, *Raising Churchill's Army* (Oxford: University Press, 2002).

Frost, Major General John, *A Drop too Many* (London: Buchan and Enright, 1982).

Fullick, Roy, *Shan Hackett: The pursuit of exactitude* (Barnsley: Pen and Sword, 2003).

Gavin, General James M., *On to Berlin* (New York: Bantam, 1978).

Greenacre, John, *Churchill's Spearhead: the Development of Britain's Airborne Forces during World War II* (Barnsley: Pen and Sword, 2010).

Hamilton, Nigel, *Monty: the Making of a General 1887-1942* (London: Hamish Hamilton, 1981).

_____, *Monty: Master of the Battlefield 1942-1944* (London: Hamish Hamilton, 1983).

Harrison, Gordon A., *Cross-Channel Attack* (Washington: US Army Centre of Military History, 1993).

Hibbert, Christopher, *Arnhem* (Phoenix: London, 2003).

HMSO, *By Air To Battle: The Official Account Of The British Airborne Divisions* (London: HMSO, 1945).

Holland, James, *Normandy '44: D-Day and the Battle for France* (London: Bantam, 2019).

Horne, Alistair and Montgomery, David, *Lonely Leader: Monty 1944-1945* (London: Macmilan, 1994).

Horrocks, Sir Brian, *A Full Life* (London: Collins, 1960).

_____, *Corps Commander* (London: Sidgwick and Jackson, 1977).

Keegan, John (ed), *Churchill's Generals* (London: Warner, 1991).

_____, *Six Armies in Normandy* (Random House, 1992).

Kent, Ron, *First in! Parachute Pathfinder Company* (London: Batsford, 1979).

Kershaw, Robert, *D-Day: Piercing the Atlantic Wall* (Hersham: Ian Allan, 1993).

Kessell, Lipmann, *Surgeon at Arms* (Barnsley: Pen and Sword, 2011).

Kite, Ben, *Stout Hearts: the British and Canadians in Normandy 1944* (Solihull: Hellion, 2014).

Lamb, Richard, *Montgomery in Europe 1943-45: Success or Failure?* (London: Buchan and Enright, 1983).

Magry, Karel, *Operation Market-Garden Then and Now Vols 1 and 2* (After the Battle, 2002).

McKee, Alexander, *Caen: Anvil of Victory* (London: Papermac, 1985).

Mead, Richard, *General 'Boy': The Life of Lieutenant General Sir Frederick Browning* (Barnsley: Pen and Sword, 2010).

_____, *The Men Behind Monty* (Barnsley: Pen and Sword, 2015).

Middlebrook, Martin, *Arnhem 1944: The Airborne Battle* (London: Penguin, 1994).

Montgomery, Bernard, *The Memoirs of Field Marshal Montgomery* (London: Collins, 1958).

Neillands, Robin, *The Battle of Normandy 1944* (London: Cassell, 2002).

Newton-Dunn, Bill, *Big Wing: The biography of Air Chief Marshal Sir Trafford Leigh-Mallory* (Shrewsbury: Airlife, 1992).

Otway, Lieutenant-Colonel Terence, *Airborne Forces of the Second World War* (London: HMSO, 1951).

Peters, Mike and Buist, Luuk, *Glider Pilots at Arnhem* (Barnsley: Pen and Sword, 2009).

Pogue, Forrest C., *George C. Marshall: Organizer of Victory* (New York: Viking, 1973).

_____, *The Supreme Command* (Washington: US Army Centre of Military History, 1989).

Powell, Geoffrey, *The Devil's Birthday: The Bridges to Arnhem 1944* (London: Buchan and Enright, 1984).

_____, *Men at Arnhem* (Barnsley: Pen and Sword, 2003).

Richardson, General Sir Charles, *Flashback: A Soldier's Story* (London: William Kimber & Co, 1985).

Ritchie, Sebastian, *Arnhem: Myth and Reality* (Ramsbury: Hale, 2011).

Rostron, Peter, *The Military Life & Times of General Sir Miles Dempsey GBE KCB DSO MC* (Barnsley: Pen and Sword, 2010).

Ruppenthal, Roland G., *Logistical Support of the Armies, Vol I: May 1941-September 1944* (Washington: US Army Centre of Military History, 1995).

Ryan, Cornelius, *A Bridge too Far* (Wordsworth Editions, 1999).

Sims, James, *Arnhem Spearhead* (London: Imperial War Museum, 1978).

Stacey, Colonel C.P., *The Victory Campaign: The Operations in North West Europe 1944-1945* (Ottawa: Queens Printer and Controller of Stationery, 1960).

Terraine, John, *The Right of the Line* (Ware: Wordsworth, 1997).

Urquhart, Major General R.E., *Arnhem* (London: Cassell, 1958).

Warner, Philip, *Horrocks: The General who Led from the Front* (Barnsley: Pen and Sword, 2005).

Warren, John C., *Airborne Operations in World War II, European Theater* (USAF Historical Division, 1956).

Webster, David Kenyon, *Parachute Infantry* (London: Random House, 2014)

Wilmot, Chester, *The Struggle for Europe* (Ware: Wordsworth, 1997).

INDEX

Note – operations that are the subject of chapters are only indexed where they appear outside of those chapters